Perceptions of Libraries
and Information Resources

A Report to the OCLC Membership

Perceptions of Libraries and Information Resources

A Report to the OCLC Membership

Principal contributors

Cathy De Rosa, M.B.A., Vice President, Marketing and Library Services

Joanne Cantrell, Marketing Analyst

Diane Cellentani, M.B.A., Market Research Consultant to OCLC

Janet Hawk, M.B.A., Manager, Market Research & Analysis

Lillie Jenkins, Ph.D., M.S.I.S., Market Research Support Specialist

Alane Wilson, M.L.I.S., Senior Library Market Consultant

Graphics, layout and editing

Brad Gauder, Senior Marketing Writer

Andy Havens, Manager, Creative Services

Rick Limes, Art Director

OCLC Online Computer Library Center, Inc.
Dublin, Ohio USA

Cataloged in WorldCat® on November 17, 2005
OCLC Control Number: 62293968

ISBN: 1-55653-364-0
10 09 08 07 06 05   1 2 3 4 5 6

Table of Contents

Introduction

In 2003, OCLC published *The 2003 OCLC Environmental Scan: Pattern Recognition* as a report to the OCLC membership to identify and describe issues and trends that are impacting and will impact OCLC and, in particular, libraries. The goal of the report was first to inform OCLC's key decision makers to guide them in strategic planning and later to serve as a reference document for librarians as they work on strategic planning for their institutions and communities. Over 7,500 copies of the *Scan* are in circulation and more than 15,000 librarians have engaged in discussions with colleagues and OCLC management on findings and future opportunities.

In the introduction to the *Scan* (page ix), we wrote: "It has become increasingly difficult to characterize and describe the purpose of using libraries [...] The relationships among the information professional, the user and the content have changed and continue to change." Another way of stating this is that trends indicate a dissonance between the environment and content that libraries provide and the environment and content that information consumers want and use. Three major trends were identified in the *Scan* that provide evidence of that dissonance. Self-service, satisfaction and seamlessness seem to exemplify the expectations of the information consumer in the huge "infosphere" in which libraries operate. The characteristics that support self-service, satisfaction and seamlessness, such as ease of use, convenience and availability, appeared to many information professionals, including the authors of the *Scan*, to be as important to the information consumer as information quality and trustworthiness.

The *Scan* provides references to studies, articles and reports that support the identification and analysis of these overarching trends. But, few of these resources emanated from the part of the infosphere that OCLC and libraries inhabit and there are no major recent empirical studies that look specifically and broadly at the role libraries and librarians play in the infosphere, from the point-of-view of the information consumer. How are libraries perceived by today's information consumer? Do libraries still matter? On what level? Will library use likely increase or decrease in the future?

As a consequence, early in 2005, OCLC Market Research staff, with input from many other OCLC staff and hundreds of librarians who have contributed to discussions and workshops, conceived of a project designed to better understand these trends as they relate to libraries and the information consumer. To that end, OCLC commissioned Harris Interactive Inc., a company that for 45 years has provided custom research to a broad range of clients including nonprofit organizations and governmental agencies, to administer the resulting survey on behalf of OCLC. We were clear as to the goals of the survey. We wanted to know more about people's information-seeking behaviors, how familiar people are with the variety of e-resources libraries provide for their users and how libraries fit into the lives of the respondents. One of the most important goals of the project as a whole was to collect information that would help us build a better understanding of the "Library" brand.

The topics explored in the survey include the perceptions and preferences of information consumers; users' relationship with and use of libraries, including usage of and familiarity with electronic information resources; awareness of libraries and resources offered; the "Library" brand and its ubiquity and universality; trust of libraries and their resources; and people's perceptions of the library's purpose/mission.

We wanted to survey a broad set of information consumers. Our goal was to gather survey data across a wide range of age groups and geographic regions. We also wanted to understand more about college students as information consumers, both inside and outside the United States. Given budget constraints and geographic reach goals, this survey was administered electronically and in English. All respondents therefore use the Internet, are at least somewhat familiar with using electronic Web resources and took the survey in English. Respondents could have taken this survey in a library that provides Internet access, as some respondents indicated they access the Internet via the library.

We understand that the results, therefore, represent the online population, a subset of library users. Please read the survey results with this in mind. We did. We are also mindful that the survey respondents do represent a significant, and potentially growing, percent of library and potential library users. As outlined more fully in the Methodology section of the report, the survey was weighted demographically and fairly represents the online population of all countries surveyed except India, due to low sample size. Recent surveys report that over 60 percent of the Australia, Canada, Singapore, United Kingdom and United States populations have Internet access and

My mom loves the library and is there all the time **but I never think of it.** *I think they should look into ways to bridge the generation gap.*

33-year-old from the United States

Source: *Perceptions of Libraries and Information Resources*, OCLC, 2005, question 1240, "If you could provide one piece of advice to your library, what would it be?"

the growth in Internet access over the last five years is staggering. Most countries surveyed have seen an increase in Internet access of 50 to 100 percent. Information consumers are using the Internet more—both at the library and elsewhere.

The findings presented in this report do not surprise, they confirm. During the hundreds of *Scan* discussions and meetings held over the past 24 months, several recurring themes surfaced. "Users are not aware of the electronic resources libraries make freely available." Our survey findings bear this out. "Users are as comfortable using Web information sources as library sources." Our study shows this perception also to be true, across countries, across U.S. age groups, across library card holders and non-card holders. "The library brand is dated." Again, our survey findings do not surprise, they confirm.

We collected over 20,000 open-ended responses from information consumers. This bank of data represented a valuable source of unedited views about users' perceptions, thoughts and attitudes about libraries and electronic resources. The respondents provided over 3,000 statements of advice for libraries. They cover everything from content, to community, to coffee and conversation. We have worked hard to incorporate as many of these views and ideas as possible and to provide a balanced view of their comments. Appendix B provides a sample of approximately 2,000 respondent comments.

Trends toward increased information self-service and seamlessness are clearly evident in the survey results. Libraries' mindshare in this new self-service e-resource environment is also clear: behind newer entrants. Libraries' continued importance as a trusted information provider is evident and, overall, users have positive, if outdated, views of the "Library." Our collective challenge is, therefore, to take this information—both the positive and the challenging—and evaluate where to invest more, invest less, invent new and invert old, communicate more and market better.

Cathy De Rosa
Vice President, Marketing & Library Services

Methodology

OCLC Market Research staff defined a research project to look at library resource use, perceptions and impressions of libraries, and people's preferences for using information discovery tools. OCLC commissioned a blind survey of information users from Harris Interactive Inc. Harris drew a sample of potential respondents from the Harris Poll Online panel consisting of millions of individuals worldwide. The respondents were interviewed between May 20 and June 2, 2005. Target respondents ranged from young people age 14 to people age 65 and older.

The online survey was open to English-speaking male and female residents of Australia, Canada, India, Singapore, the United Kingdom (U.K.) and the United States (U.S.). Responses from Australian, Singaporean and Indian residents are combined and are referred to throughout the report as the geographic region of Australia/Singapore/India.

The majority of youth surveyed reside in the U.S. Respondents outside the U.S. were generally age 18 and over. The U.S. respondents' data were segmented by age to provide another perspective. The sample sizes for the other geographic regions were not large enough to report by age segment.

As the poll was conducted online, all respondents are at least familiar with online resources and have access to the Internet. The survey was conducted in English, and 3,348 respondents completed the survey.

The collected data have an overall statistical margin of error of +/- 1.69 percent at the 95 percent confidence level for the online population in the countries surveyed. The online population may or may not represent the general population of each country surveyed. Based on statistics from www.internetworldstats.com, the following table shows the percentage of residents in the countries surveyed who have Internet access. The table also shows the penetration of Internet access in 2000, as an indication of its growth in the last five years.

Internet Access and Population—*by Country*[1]

Country	Population	Internet users	Penetration of Internet access in 2005	Penetration of Internet access in 2000[2]
Australia	20,507,264	13,991,612	68.2%	34.5%
Canada	32,050,369	20,450,000[3]	63.8%[3]	42.1%
India	1,094,870,677	39,200,000	3.6%	0.54%
Singapore	3,547,809	2,421,800	68.3%	32.4%
United Kingdom	59,889,407	36,059,096	60.2%	26.4%
United States	296,208,476	203,466,989	68.7%	44.1%

1. Table content is based on data at http://www.internetworldstats.com, accessed November 15, 2005.
2. World Bank, World Development Indicators, http://devdata.worldbank.org/data-query/, accessed November 15, 2005.
3. http://www.internetworldstats.com/stats2.htm, accessed November 15, 2005; data is from December 2003.

All survey data were weighted demographically, except for data from Indian respondents due to the relatively small number of respondents. In general, question wording and issues related to conducting surveys may introduce some error or bias into opinion poll findings.

Percentages in data tables may not total 100 percent due to rounding or because respondents frequently were asked to select all responses that may apply or respondents were not required to answer the question.

Eighty-three questions were asked of the 3,348 respondents. The survey included a series of branching questions such that responding either *yes* or *no* to a question led to a series of follow-up questions. The survey also asked open-ended questions to ensure that respondents had the opportunity to provide input in their own words. Several of the following parts include samples of the verbatim comments. The comments are included as written by the survey respondents, including misspellings and grammatical errors.

It is not possible to provide all the data or the over 20,000 verbatim responses collected from the survey in this report; however, results are presented for all major topics explored in the survey, and 10 percent of the verbatim comments are provided in Appendix B as these will be rich sources of information about what is on the minds of respondents with regard to their libraries.

Once the survey was complete, the OCLC Market Research team analyzed and summarized survey results in order to produce this report. In addition to presenting the analyses of the survey data, team members did correlation analyses on several of the interrelated questions to elicit additional value from the results and these are included in the report.

Throughout the report, the phrase "information consumer" is used, as it was in *The 2003 OCLC Environmental Scan,* to refer to people who seek, ingest and sometimes purchase information.

The survey results show that information consumers are familiar with libraries. Nearly all survey respondents have visited a library in the past. Survey respondents were asked to indicate the type of libraries they have visited. Ninety-six percent of respondents have visited a public library.

Respondents were asked to identify the library that they use primarily (e.g., public, college/university, community college, school, corporate, other) and were asked to answer all library-related questions with that library in mind.

"College students" is used in the report to refer to postsecondary students, both graduate and undergraduate, responding to the survey; these students reside in all geographic regions surveyed.

The term "library card holder" is used in the report to refer to those respondents throughout all geographic regions surveyed who indicated that they are registered users of a library.

Total Respondents to the OCLC Survey— *by Geographic Region*

Geographic Region	Number of Respondents
Australia/Singapore/India	535
Canada	491
United Kingdom	468
United States	1,854

Source: *Perceptions of Libraries and Information Resources*, OCLC, 2005.

Total U.S. Respondents—*by Age of Respondent*

U.S. Ages	Number of Respondents
Age 14-17	621
Age 18-24	403
Age 25-64	449
Age 65 and older	381

Source: *Perceptions of Libraries and Information Resources*, OCLC, 2005.

Total College Students—*by Age of Respondent*

The survey included 396 college students, both undergraduate and graduate, from all geographic regions included in the study. This table shows the breakdown of college students by age group.

College Student Ages	Percentage of College Students per Age Range
Age 14-17	3%
Age 18-24	65%
Age 25-64	31%
Age 65 and older	0%

Source: *Perceptions of Libraries and Information Resources*, OCLC, 2005.

Total Library Card Holders—*by Geographic Region*

The survey asked respondents to indicate if they are registered users of a library. This table shows the percentage of registered users by geographic region.

Geographic Region	Percentage of Library Card Holders
Australia/Singapore/India	71%
Canada	71%
United Kingdom	59%
United States	75%

Source: *Perceptions of Libraries and Information Resources*, OCLC, 2005, question 805.

Report Structure

This report is structured to provide readers with a sequenced view of how the information consumer finds, uses, evaluates and favors information resources, including physical and online libraries. The findings are presented in five parts, not in the order in which the survey tool presented them, but in such a way as to categorize the actions, attitudes and brand values of respondents.

Part 1, **Libraries and Information Sources—Use, Familiarity and Favorability,** reviews respondents' familiarity and use of libraries and information, as well as the information sources that are most frequently selected and used by survey respondents. We explore respondents' favorability toward information resources. For purposes of this report, we categorized questions into three groupings— information sources, electronic resources and information brands—that are used in subsequent parts of the report.

We asked questions about five places, physical and virtual, that respondents use to search for information and content. These we refer to as **information sources** and they are:

- Search engines
- Libraries
- Bookstores
- Online libraries
- Online bookstores

We asked questions about the kinds of electronic resources respondents are familiar with and use to get information. These we refer to as **electronic resources** and they are:

- Search engines*
- Online bookstores*
- Electronic magazines/journals
- Electronic books (digital)
- Topic-specific Web sites
- Instant messaging
- E-mail information subscriptions
- Online librarian question services
- Library Web sites
- Online news
- Blogs
- Online databases
- E-mail
- RSS feeds
- Ask-an-expert services
- Audiobooks (downloadable/digital)

* Search engines and online bookstores are included as both information sources and electronic resources.

We asked questions about respondents' perceptions of, attitudes toward and familiarity with well-known information sources and resources associated with them. These we refer to as **information brands**. The branded sources are:

information brands

- About.com
- AllTheWeb.com
- AltaVista.com
- AOL Search
- Ask an expert (e.g., Homework Helper)**
- Ask Jeeves.com
- Clusty.com
- Dogpile.com
- Excite.com
- Gigablast.com
- Google.com

- HotBot.com
- iWon.com
- Library Web sites**
- LookSmart.com
- Lycos.com
- MSN Search
- Netscape Search
- Online librarian question services (Ask a librarian)**
- Teoma.com
- Yahoo.com

**Ask an expert, library Web sites and online librarian question services are not brand names, they are electronic resources. They are included as choices in order to contrast respondents' perceptions and attitudes about information brands with their perceptions and attitudes about libraries.

Part 2, Using the Library—In Person and Online, reports on what we discovered about how information consumers are using libraries and how newer information sources, electronic resources and information brands are impacting and influencing the behaviors of respondents.

Part 3, The Library Brand, explores the "Library" brand, looking closely at traditional brand determinants such as positive and negative attributes, trust, price and lifestyle fit. We report the findings about top-of-mind perceptions of libraries among respondents, as well as perceptions about the purpose, or brand potential, of libraries.

Part 4, Respondents' Advice to Libraries, provides unedited views and advice about libraries' services, resources and facilities. Respondents were generous with their advice—over 3,000 responses were submitted—and many were clearly knowledgeable about libraries and their services, as evidenced by their choice of words. Appendix B includes a sample of 10 percent of the verbatim responses.

Part 5, Libraries—A "Universal" Brand?, looks at the consistency and uniformity of responses across all geographic regions surveyed. The consistency of stated perceptions, attitudes and practices suggests the "Library" brand is both local and universal.

The **Conclusion** summarizes the findings outlined in the report.

Appendices provide additional supporting data tables and sample verbatim responses.

About OCLC gives an overview of OCLC, including the vision and key products, partnerships and research projects.

Related OCLC Research and Reports

In 2002, OCLC commissioned Harris Interactive Inc. to conduct a study of U.S. college students age 18–24 and their usage of the Internet and its resources. The resulting report, *OCLC White Paper on the Information Habits of College Students,* concentrated on the Web-based information habits of college students, particularly their use of campus library Web sites. This study found that college and university students looked to campus libraries and library Web sites for their information needs and that they valued access to accurate, up-to-date information with easily identifiable authors. They were aware of the shortcomings of information available from the Web and of their needs for assistance in finding information in electronic or paper formats. To access the results of this study, visit the OCLC Web site at: **www.oclc.org/research/announcements/2002-06-24.htm**

Five-Year Information Format Trends, released in early 2003, provides a snapshot look at how trends and innovation in information formats (e.g., Web pages, electronic books, MP3 audio) create new challenges and opportunities for librarians, who must integrate new formats with existing formats and build new information management processes while balancing resource allocation. To access the report, visit the OCLC Web site at: **www.oclc.org/reports/2003format.htm**

The 2003 OCLC Environmental Scan: Pattern Recognition report was published in January 2004 for OCLC's worldwide membership to examine the significant issues and trends impacting OCLC, libraries, museums, archives and other allied organizations, both now and in the future. The *Scan* provides a high-level view of the information landscape, intended both to inform and stimulate discussion about future strategic directions. To access the *Scan,* visit the OCLC Web site at: **www.oclc.org/reports/2003escan.htm**

2004 Information Format Trends: Content, Not Containers returned to the subject of information format management introduced in the *Five-Year Information Format Trends* report of 2003. The report examined the "unbundling of content" from traditional containers (books, journals, CDs) and distribution methods (postal mail, resource sharing). As the boundaries blurred among content, technology and the information consumer, the report showed how format was beginning to matter less than the information within the container. To access the report, visit the OCLC Web site at: **www.oclc.org/reports/2004format.htm**

Part 1: Libraries and Information Sources—Use, Familiarity and Favorability

96%

have visited a public library.

Survey results indicate a high level of both use of and familiarity with a wide variety of information resources. Ninety-six percent of respondents across all geographic regions and demographics have visited a public library. Seventy-four percent of respondents have used e-mail, and 72 percent have used an Internet search engine. Thirty percent of all information consumers surveyed have used a library Web site.

Seventy-two percent of respondents hold a library card. Over 80 percent of U.S. youth and young adults, respondents 14 to 24 years old, hold a library card—more than any other U.S. age demographic. Thirty-three percent of respondents visit a public library at least once a month; 73 percent visit at least once a year.

Respondents' familiarity with electronic information resources varies widely. Respondents are very familiar with e-mail, search engines and online news, but are not familiar with Ask an Expert resources or RSS feeds. Twenty percent of respondents are not aware of online libraries, and 30 percent have never heard of online databases.

51%

have used instant messaging.

While most electronic information resources, from e-mail to online databases to audiobooks, are used by a portion of all information consumers surveyed, frequency of use is clearly dominated by three resources: e-mail, search engines and instant messaging. Almost all respondents begin their searches for information with a search engine.

Respondents generally choose electronic resources in the same ways they choose other types of information resources. Sixty-one percent identify *friends* as their top choice in identifying new electronic resources to use. Less than 15 percent of respondents indicate that they discover new electronic resources from *librarians* or *teachers*.

30%

have never heard of online databases.

Favorability of information sources is similar to the data related to familiarity, with search engines again dominating as the favored choice for all respondents. Eighty percent of respondents said the search engine would be their first choice the next time they need a source for information.

Nearly one-third of respondents say their library use has decreased in the past three to five years. Respondents expect their library use to remain fairly constant over the next three to five years.

1.1 Library Use

Ninety-six percent of respondents have visited a public library in person.

Seventy-two percent of the total respondents are registered users of a library (e.g., have a library card).

Public Library Usage—by Region of Respondent

	Total Respondents	Australia Singapore India	Canada	United Kingdom	United States
Visited a public library in person	96%	97%	97%	97%	96%

Source: *Perceptions of Libraries and Information Resources,* OCLC, 2005, question 815.

The number of respondents who reported visiting a public library Web site was lower and varied considerably by geographic region. Twenty-seven percent of total respondents indicated that they had visited a public online library. This varied by geographic region, from 42 percent of Canadian respondents to 9 percent of respondents from the U.K.

Public Library Web Site Usage—by Region of Respondent

	Total Respondents	Australia Singapore India	Canada	United Kingdom	United States
Visited an online library (Web site)	27%	31%	42%	9%	27%

Source: *Perceptions of Libraries and Information Resources,* OCLC, 2005, question 815.

Seventy-two percent of respondents indicated that they are registered users of a library. The response was consistent across all geographic regions except from the U.K., where 59 percent of respondents hold a library card. College students are more likely to have a library card than any other segment surveyed; 90 percent indicated that they are registered users. U.S. 14- to 24-year-olds are more likely to be registered users than those 25 and older, with over 80 percent indicating they have a library card.

Percent of Library Card Holders—by Region of Respondent

Total Respondents	Australia Singapore India	Canada	United Kingdom	United States
72%	71%	71%	59%	75%

Source: *Perceptions of Libraries and Information Resources,* OCLC, 2005, question 805.

Amount of books/music available

Use of computers if needed

57-year-old from the United Kingdom

Source: *Perceptions of Libraries and Information Resources,* OCLC, 2005, question 812a, "Please list two positive associations with the library."

Percent of Library Card Holders—
by College Students across all Regions

College Students
90%

Source: *Perceptions of Libraries and Information Resources,* OCLC, 2005, question 805.

*Percent of Library Card Holders—*by Age of U.S. Respondent

Total U.S. Respondents	U.S. 14-17	U.S. 18-24	U.S. 25-64	U.S. 65+
75%	83%	82%	74%	71%

Source: *Perceptions of Libraries and Information Resources,* OCLC, 2005, question 805.

Frequency of Library Use

Use of the public library (at least monthly) in the United States is consistent across all age groups. College students use the public library more frequently than the total respondents and frequently use more than one type of library (i.e., public and academic).

The frequency with which respondents use a library varies by age and region. Sixty-five percent of college students use their **college/university** library at least monthly, with 14 percent using it daily. Forty percent of college students also use their **public** library at least monthly.

I seldom have to buy books anymore— almost anything I want is at the Library!

Being able to reserve books online is the greatest!!

42-year-old from Canada

Source: *Perceptions of Libraries and Information Resources,* OCLC, 2005, question 807, "What is the first thing you think of when you think of a library?"

*Frequency of Public Library Use—*by Region of Respondent

How frequently do you go to the following libraries?
[Only "public library" responses included below.]

	Total Respondents	Australia Singapore India	Canada	United Kingdom	United States
Daily	1%	1%	1%	1%	1%
Weekly	13%	21%	15%	9%	12%
Monthly	19%	21%	19%	18%	18%
Several times/year	24%	25%	24%	24%	24%
At least once/year	16%	12%	17%	12%	18%
Not even once/year	27%	21%	23%	36%	27%

Source: *Perceptions of Libraries and Information Resources,* OCLC, 2005, question 820.

*Frequency of Public Library Use—*by Age of U.S. Respondent

How frequently do you go to the following libraries?
[Only "public library" responses included below.]

	Total U.S. Respondents	U.S. 14-17	U.S. 18-24	U.S. 25-64	U.S. 65+
Daily	1%	3%	4%	1%	1%
Weekly	12%	12%	12%	12%	14%
Monthly	18%	19%	14%	18%	18%
Several times/year	24%	28%	22%	23%	26%
At least once/year	18%	28%	20%	17%	15%
Not even once/year	27%	10%	29%	29%	26%

Source: *Perceptions of Libraries and Information Resources,* OCLC, 2005, question 820.

Frequency of Library Use—
by College Students across all Regions

How frequently do you go to each of the following libraries?

	College/University Library	Public Library
Daily	14%	1%
Weekly	34%	18%
Monthly	17%	21%
Several times/year	21%	25%
At least once/year	10%	14%
Not even once/year	6%	20%

Source: *Perceptions of Libraries and Information Resources,* OCLC, 2005, question 820.

Past and Future Library Use

Nearly one-third of respondents say their library use has decreased in the past three to five years. Respondents expect their library use to remain fairly constant.

The survey asked respondents if their usage increased or decreased in the last three to five years. Forty-four percent of total respondents report their library usage has remained the same and 31 percent state that their usage decreased during that time period. The reported past library usage is very similar across all geographic regions surveyed.

College students were more likely to indicate that their library usage has increased, at 44 percent. U.S. respondents 65 and older were the U.S. age group most likely to indicate a decrease in library usage, at 34 percent.

*Past Library Use—*by Region of Respondent

How much has your personal library use changed over the last three to five years?

Past Usage	Total Respondents	Australia Singapore India	Canada	United Kingdom	United States
Increased	25%	27%	29%	24%	24%
About the same	44%	41%	46%	44%	45%
Decreased	31%	32%	26%	32%	31%

Source: *Perceptions of Libraries and Information Resources,* OCLC, 2005, question 1220.

Past Library Use—
by College Students across all Regions

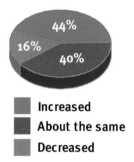

■ Increased
■ About the same
■ Decreased

Source: *Perceptions of Libraries and Information Resources,* OCLC, 2005, question 1220.

Past Library Use—by Age of U.S. Respondent

How much has your personal library use changed over the last three to five years?

Past Usage	Total U.S. Respondents	U.S. 14-17	U.S. 18-24	U.S. 25-64	U.S. 65+
Increased	24%	35%	33%	21%	22%
About the same	45%	39%	44%	46%	44%
Decreased	31%	25%	23%	33%	34%

Source: *Perceptions of Libraries and Information Resources*, OCLC, 2005, question 1220.

Past Library Use—by Library Card Holders and Non-Card Holders across all Regions

How much has your personal library use changed over the last three to five years?

Past Usage	Total Respondents	Library Card Holders	Non-Card Holders
Increased	25%	30%	12%
About the same	44%	43%	48%
Decreased	31%	27%	39%

Source: *Perceptions of Libraries and Information Resources*, OCLC, 2005, question 1220.

I haven't carried a library card since I was in high school so I really don't have a negative **and do not know anything about this library online,** *but would be most interested in trying it.*

59-year-old from the United States

Source: *Perceptions of Libraries and Information Resources*, OCLC, 2005, question 812b, "Please list two negative associations with the library."

Respondents also were asked to project the level of their anticipated future library usage. Sixty-two percent of all respondents anticipate their usage in the next three to five years will remain the same. The anticipated future library use is very similar across all geographic regions surveyed.

U.S. 14- to 24-year-olds were more likely to anticipate increased library use in the next three to five years than other U.S. age demographics. Forty-one percent of U.S. 14- to 17-year-olds and 31 percent of U.S. 18- to 24-year-olds anticipate increasing their use of the library.

Throughout the geographic regions, 38 percent of college students surveyed anticipate increased library usage.

*Anticipated Future Library Use—*by Region of Respondent

How do you anticipate your personal usage of the library
to change over the next three to five years?

Future Usage	Total Respondents	Australia Singapore India	Canada	United Kingdom	United States
Will increase	20%	20%	21%	14%	22%
Will stay the same	62%	59%	67%	61%	61%
Will decrease	18%	20%	12%	24%	18%

Source: *Perceptions of Libraries and Information Resources*, OCLC, 2005, question 1225.

*Anticipated Future Library Use—*by Age of U.S. Respondent

How do you anticipate your personal usage of the library
to change over the next three to five years?

Future Usage	Total U.S. Respondents	U.S. 14-17	U.S. 18-24	U.S. 25-64	U.S. 65+
Will increase	22%	41%	31%	20%	15%
Will stay the same	61%	47%	47%	63%	68%
Will decrease	18%	12%	22%	17%	17%

Source: *Perceptions of Libraries and Information Resources*, OCLC, 2005, question 1225.

*Anticipated Future Library Use—*by Library Card Holders and Non-Card Holders across all Regions

How do you anticipate your personal usage of the library
to change over the next three to five years?

Future Usage	Total Respondents	Library Card Holders	Non-Card Holders
Will increase	20%	24%	11%
Will stay the same	62%	61%	62%
Will decrease	18%	15%	27%

Source: *Perceptions of Libraries and Information Resources*, OCLC, 2005, question 1225.

Anticipated Future Library Use—
by College Students across all Regions

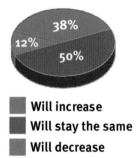

■ **Will increase**
■ **Will stay the same**
■ **Will decrease**

Source: *Perceptions of Libraries and Information Resources*, OCLC, 2005, question 1225.

1.2 Familiarity with and Usage of Multiple Information Sources

Respondents are familiar with search engines.
Over half of respondents are not familiar with online libraries.

The survey asked respondents to rate their familiarity with the following five information sources: search engines, libraries, bookstores, online libraries and online bookstores.

More than 60 percent of all respondents, regardless of geographic region, are *extremely familiar, very familiar* or *somewhat familiar* with search engines. Just 1 percent of all respondents surveyed have *never heard of* search engines.

In the 12 years that search engines have been in existence, they have achieved a familiarity rating that is slightly higher than that of physical libraries and considerably higher than that of online libraries.

Respondents have similar levels of familiarity with libraries and bookstores: over 25 percent of all respondents are *extremely familiar* with both. Respondents have less familiarity with the online versions of the library and bookstore. Twenty percent have *never heard of* online libraries. Across geographic regions surveyed, college students were the most likely to state that they are *extremely familiar* with online libraries, at 20 percent. Thirteen percent of U.S. 18- to 24-year-olds indicated that they are *extremely familiar* with online libraries.

Tables detailing usage of information sources by region, U.S. age and college students are included in Appendix A.

Make access to the online search engines much easier.
Much of the information I look for does not have enough of a description to really decide whether it is good information, especially if I have to do an interlibrary loan.

Mostly the descriptions are too vague.
I do research for History, and I find it hard to find 'primary' resources—I usually have to go online for these.

46-year-old from Canada

Source: *Perceptions of Libraries and Information Resources*, OCLC, 2005, question 1240, "If you could provide one piece of advice to your library, what would it be?"

Familiarity Ratings for Information Sources—
by Total Respondents

Please rate how familiar you are with the following sources/places where you can obtain information.

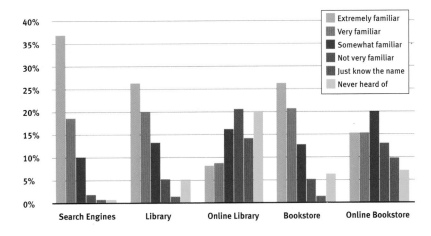

Source: *Perceptions of Libraries and Information Resources*, OCLC, 2005, question 1305.

Familiarity Ratings for Information Sources— by Region of Respondent

Please rate how familiar you are with the following sources/places where you can obtain information.

	Total Respondents	Australia Singapore India	Canada	United Kingdom	United States
Search engines					
Extremely familiar	36%	38%	37%	35%	35%
Very familiar	18%	19%	23%	19%	16%
Somewhat familiar	10%	8%	8%	10%	12%
Not very familiar	2%	1%	1%	2%	2%
Just know the name	1%	0%	1%	1%	2%
Never heard of	1%	0%	1%	1%	1%
Physical library					
Extremely familiar	26%	27%	30%	18%	27%
Very familiar	20%	21%	24%	17%	20%
Somewhat familiar	13%	13%	12%	17%	13%
Not very familiar	5%	3%	4%	7%	6%
Just know the name	1%	1%	2%	3%	1%
Never heard of	5%	4%	4%	12%	4%
Physical bookstore					
Extremely familiar	26%	24%	29%	21%	27%
Very familiar	21%	24%	23%	17%	20%
Somewhat familiar	13%	16%	14%	12%	12%
Not very familiar	5%	2%	2%	8%	5%
Just know the name	1%	1%	2%	3%	1%
Never heard of	6%	4%	4%	13%	6%
Online library					
Extremely familiar	8%	8%	9%	3%	9%
Very familiar	9%	12%	14%	4%	8%
Somewhat familiar	16%	20%	21%	12%	15%
Not very familiar	21%	20%	22%	23%	20%
Just know the name	14%	11%	12%	17%	15%
Never heard of	20%	15%	11%	34%	21%
Online bookstore					
Extremely familiar	15%	12%	15%	15%	16%
Very familiar	15%	16%	15%	12%	16%
Somewhat familiar	20%	25%	22%	21%	17%
Not very familiar	13%	15%	16%	12%	12%
Just know the name	10%	9%	9%	11%	10%
Never heard of	7%	6%	4%	12%	7%

Source: *Perceptions of Libraries and Information Resources*, OCLC, 2005, question 1305.

Familiarity Ratings for Information Sources—
by Age of U.S. Respondent

Please rate how familiar you are with the following sources/places
where you can obtain information.

*Get a website
so that I can see
what materials
are available in
the library.*

**51-year-old from the
United States**

Source: *Perceptions of Libraries
and Information Resources*, OCLC,
2005, question 1240, "If you could
provide one piece of advice to your
library, what would it be?"

	Total U.S. Respondents	U.S. 14-17	U.S. 18-24	U.S. 25-64	U.S. 65+
Search engines					
Extremely familiar	35%	34%	40%	38%	22%
Very familiar	16%	12%	18%	15%	20%
Somewhat familiar	12%	6%	8%	12%	18%
Not very familiar	2%	1%	1%	2%	6%
Just know the name	2%	1%	1%	1%	4%
Never heard of	1%	6%	2%	1%	1%
Physical library					
Extremely familiar	27%	25%	26%	30%	20%
Very familiar	20%	16%	18%	21%	21%
Somewhat familiar	13%	11%	23%	12%	11%
Not very familiar	6%	3%	2%	6%	9%
Just know the name	1%	2%	0%	0%	3%
Never heard of	4%	7%	2%	4%	8%
Physical bookstore					
Extremely familiar	27%	22%	30%	29%	21%
Very familiar	20%	12%	17%	22%	19%
Somewhat familiar	12%	14%	12%	12%	12%
Not very familiar	5%	5%	8%	4%	11%
Just know the name	1%	4%	0%	1%	1%
Never heard of	6%	8%	6%	5%	9%
Online library					
Extremely familiar	9%	8%	13%	8%	6%
Very familiar	8%	7%	7%	9%	7%
Somewhat familiar	15%	24%	23%	14%	11%
Not very familiar	20%	17%	15%	20%	26%
Just know the name	15%	11%	17%	15%	16%
Never heard of	21%	18%	13%	22%	26%
Online bookstore					
Extremely familiar	16%	12%	18%	18%	10%
Very familiar	16%	13%	18%	17%	11%
Somewhat familiar	17%	22%	21%	16%	17%
Not very familiar	12%	16%	9%	11%	20%
Just know the name	10%	11%	10%	9%	15%
Never heard of	7%	8%	3%	7%	13%

Source: *Perceptions of Libraries and Information Resources*, OCLC, 2005, question 1305.

Familiarity Ratings for Information Sources—
by College Students across all Regions

Please rate how familiar you are with the following sources/places where you can obtain information.

	Total Respondents	College Students
Search engines		
Extremely familiar	36%	45%
Very familiar	18%	17%
Somewhat familiar	10%	10%
Not very familiar	2%	0%
Just know the name	1%	1%
Never heard of	1%	0%
Physical library		
Extremely familiar	26%	34%
Very familiar	20%	21%
Somewhat familiar	13%	16%
Not very familiar	5%	1%
Just know the name	1%	1%
Never heard of	5%	0%
Physical bookstore		
Extremely familiar	26%	36%
Very familiar	21%	20%
Somewhat familiar	13%	13%
Not very familiar	5%	4%
Just know the name	1%	1%
Never heard of	6%	2%
Online library		
Extremely familiar	8%	20%
Very familiar	9%	15%
Somewhat familiar	16%	23%
Not very familiar	21%	12%
Just know the name	14%	9%
Never heard of	20%	4%
Online bookstore		
Extremely familiar	15%	25%
Very familiar	15%	17%
Somewhat familiar	20%	23%
Not very familiar	13%	7%
Just know the name	10%	4%
Never heard of	7%	1%

Source: *Perceptions of Libraries and Information Resources,* OCLC, 2005, question 1305.

My Library is half an hour's car ride away.

It is small and therefor[e] more limited [than] the main libraries. ALSO once I get past the age when driving is a possibility— local transport is not available to take me there.

59-year-old from Australia

Source: *Perceptions of Libraries and Information Resources,* OCLC, 2005, question 812b, "Please list two negative associations with the library."

Awareness and Usage of Electronic Resources

The majority of respondents have used e-mail, search engines and instant messaging.

Respondents were asked to indicate their level of awareness and usage of 16 electronic resources.

- Search engines
- Library Web sites
- Online bookstores
- Online news
- Electronic magazines/journals
- Audiobooks (downloadable/digital)
- Electronic books (digital)
- Online databases

- Topic-specific Web sites
- E-mail
- Instant messaging/online chat
- E-mail information subscriptions
- Ask an expert
- Online librarian question services
- RSS feeds
- Blogs

Respondents show a wide familiarity with and usage of these electronic resources. The use of e-mail and search engines are the highest among all resources across all segments surveyed, but all electronic resources are used by at least 5 percent of respondents.

College students are the most familiar with all the electronic resources and show a substantially higher use of electronic magazines/journals, online databases and electronic books.

Library Web site usage is also highest among college students, at 61 percent. Both the U.S. 14- to-17-year-old and 18- to 24-year-old segments indicate high use of the library Web site, at 44 percent each, but usage by other U.S. age groups is low.

Forty-seven percent of the total respondents have used an online bookstore. U.S. 14- to 17-year-olds and U.S. respondents 65 and older report the lowest usage among the U.S. age groups, at 41 percent. College students report the highest usage among all segments surveyed, at 62 percent. Although respondents from Australia/ Singapore/India are aware of online bookstores, with 61 percent at least somewhat familiar, their usage at 36 percent is the lowest among the geographic regions surveyed.

We have included tables detailing usage of all 16 electronic resources and familiarity of the top four electronic resources by region, U.S. age and college students. Tables detailing familiarity with all 16 electronic resources by region and U.S. age are included in Appendix A.

Usage of Electronic Resources—
by Total Respondents

Please indicate if you have used the following
electronic information sources, even if you have used them only once.

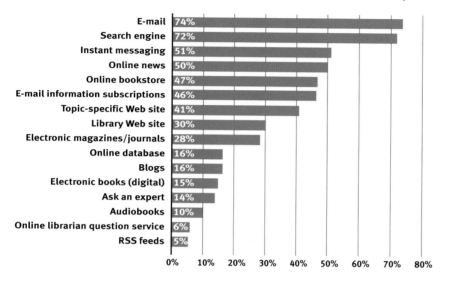

E-mail	74%
Search engine	72%
Instant messaging	51%
Online news	50%
Online bookstore	47%
E-mail information subscriptions	46%
Topic-specific Web site	41%
Library Web site	30%
Electronic magazines/journals	28%
Online database	16%
Blogs	16%
Electronic books (digital)	15%
Ask an expert	14%
Audiobooks	10%
Online librarian question service	6%
RSS feeds	5%

Source: *Perceptions of Libraries and Information Resources*, OCLC, 2005, question 505.

*1- A wealth of
information
2- The availabilty
of computers at
the library*

**62-year-old from the
United States**

Source: *Perceptions of Libraries
and Information Resources*, OCLC,
2005, question 812a, "Please list
two positive associations with the
library."

Usage of Electronic Resources—
by Region of Respondent

Please indicate if you have used the following
electronic information sources, even if you have used them only once.

	Total Respondents	Australia Singapore India	Canada	United Kingdom	United States
E-mail	74%	74%	74%	70%	74%
Search engine	72%	74%	73%	70%	71%
Instant messaging/online chat	51%	50%	58%	37%	53%
Online news	50%	51%	56%	39%	51%
Online bookstore	47%	36%	42%	48%	52%
E-mail information subscriptions	46%	47%	48%	36%	47%
Topic-specific Web sites	41%	33%	36%	17%	50%
Library Web site	30%	30%	37%	17%	31%
Electronic magazines/journals	28%	36%	36%	23%	25%
Blogs	16%	15%	15%	7%	19%
Online database	16%	21%	17%	9%	16%
Electronic books (digital)	15%	22%	17%	14%	13%
Ask an expert	14%	12%	13%	13%	15%
Audiobooks (downloadable/digital)	10%	18%	7%	10%	9%
Online librarian question service	6%	10%	6%	4%	5%
RSS feeds	5%	7%	6%	4%	5%

Source: *Perceptions of Libraries and Information Resources*, OCLC, 2005, question 505.

Usage of Electronic Resources—
by Age of U.S. Respondent

Please indicate if you have used the following
electronic information sources, even if you have used them only once.

	Total U.S. Respondents	U.S. 14-17	U.S. 18-24	U.S. 25-64	U.S. 65+
E-mail	74%	81%	82%	73%	69%
Search engine	71%	81%	78%	71%	59%
Instant messaging/online chat	53%	75%	69%	52%	34%
Online news	51%	57%	59%	51%	41%
Online bookstore	52%	41%	57%	54%	41%
E-mail information subscriptions	47%	57%	48%	48%	37%
Topic-specific Web sites	50%	40%	48%	54%	39%
Library Web site	31%	44%	44%	29%	23%
Electronic magazines/journals	25%	35%	34%	24%	17%
Blogs	19%	39%	24%	18%	11%
Online database	16%	18%	24%	17%	9%
Electronic books (digital)	13%	18%	17%	13%	7%
Ask an expert	15%	22%	12%	16%	8%
Audiobooks (downloadable/digital)	9%	14%	9%	9%	6%
Online librarian question service	5%	10%	7%	4%	5%
RSS feeds	5%	7%	8%	4%	2%

Source: *Perceptions of Libraries and Information Resources*, OCLC, 2005, question 505.

Dewey system can be hard to navigate. Also **the internet has now put all the librarys of the world [at] your fingertips**

71-year-old from the United States

Source: *Perceptions of Libraries and Information Resources*, OCLC, 2005, question 812b, "Please list two negative associations with the library."

Usage of Electronic Resources—
by College Students across all Regions

Please indicate if you have used the following
electronic information sources, even if you have used them only once.

	Total Respondents	College Students
E-mail	74%	83%
Search engine	72%	82%
Instant messaging/online chat	51%	69%
Online news	50%	64%
Online bookstore	47%	62%
E-mail information subscriptions	46%	51%
Topic-specific Web sites	41%	50%
Library Web site	30%	61%
Electronic magazines/journals	28%	58%
Blogs	16%	29%
Online database	16%	34%
Electronic books (digital)	15%	31%
Ask-an-expert	14%	21%
Audiobooks (downloadable/digital)	10%	16%
Online librarian question service	6%	8%
RSS feeds	5%	7%

Source: *Perceptions of Libraries and Information Resources*, OCLC, 2005, question 505.

Familiarity of the Top Four Electronic Resources— by Region of Respondent

Please indicate how familiar you are with each of the following electronic information sources.

Note: This table includes the top four electronic resources based on survey responses.

Detailed data for all 16 electronic resources are included in Appendix A. Respondents were not required to respond, so the totals for each resource do not equal 100 percent.

	Total Respondents	Australia Singapore India	Canada	United Kingdom	United States
E-mail					
Extremely familiar	48%	51%	53%	45%	47%
Very familiar	10%	8%	9%	12%	10%
Somewhat familiar	3%	1%	2%	3%	3%
Not very familiar	1%	0%	0%	0%	1%
Just know the name	0%	0%	1%	0%	0%
Never heard of	0%	0%	1%	1%	0%
Search engine					
Extremely familiar	42%	46%	46%	41%	40%
Very familiar	13%	10%	12%	12%	14%
Somewhat familiar	6%	4%	5%	7%	7%
Not very familiar	1%	0%	1%	1%	2%
Just know the name	1%	0%	1%	1%	1%
Never heard of	1%	0%	1%	1%	1%
Instant messaging/online chat					
Extremely familiar	26%	26%	33%	21%	25%
Very familiar	13%	13%	15%	11%	13%
Somewhat familiar	15%	16%	11%	16%	15%
Not very familiar	10%	9%	7%	12%	10%
Just know the name	9%	6%	9%	14%	8%
Never heard of	2%	3%	1%	5%	2%
Online bookstore					
Extremely familiar	21%	17%	20%	22%	23%
Very familiar	19%	19%	19%	15%	20%
Somewhat familiar	17%	25%	21%	15%	14%
Not very familiar	8%	8%	10%	8%	7%
Just know the name	9%	8%	10%	11%	8%
Never heard of	3%	5%	6%	4%	2%

Source: *Perceptions of Libraries and Information Resources,* OCLC, 2005, question 505.

It is tedious to go to library, it is easy to trace the information on internet.

54-year-old from India

Source: *Perceptions of Libraries and Information Resources,* OCLC, 2005, question 810, "What do you feel is the main purpose of the library?"

Familiarity of the Top Four Electronic Resources—
by Age of U.S. Respondent

Please indicate how familiar you are with each of the following electronic information sources.

Note: This table includes the top four electronic resources based on survey responses.

Detailed data for all 16 electronic resources are included in Appendix A. Respondents were not required to respond, so the totals for each resource do not equal 100 percent.

Free audio books free DVDs

68-year-old from the United States

Source: *Perceptions of Libraries and Information Resources,* OCLC, 2005, question 812a, "Please list two positive associations with the library."

	Total U.S. Respondents	U.S. 14-17	U.S. 18-24	U.S. 25-64	U.S. 65+
E-mail					
Extremely familiar	47%	41%	49%	49%	42%
Very familiar	10%	5%	6%	10%	16%
Somewhat familiar	3%	4%	2%	3%	2%
Not very familiar	1%	0%	1%	1%	0%
Just know the name	0%	0%	0%	0%	0%
Never heard of	0%	4%	0%	0%	0%
Search engine					
Extremely familiar	40%	37%	51%	41%	27%
Very familiar	14%	6%	7%	14%	20%
Somewhat familiar	7%	3%	3%	7%	14%
Not very familiar	2%	1%	1%	2%	4%
Just know the name	1%	1%	1%	0%	2%
Never heard of	1%	5%	0%	0%	2%
Instant messaging/online chat					
Extremely familiar	25%	34%	40%	24%	13%
Very familiar	13%	7%	14%	14%	10%
Somewhat familiar	15%	7%	8%	16%	23%
Not very familiar	10%	1%	3%	12%	13%
Just know the name	8%	2%	0%	7%	21%
Never heard of	2%	6%	2%	1%	3%
Online bookstore					
Extremely familiar	23%	22%	33%	23%	15%
Very familiar	20%	17%	18%	22%	18%
Somewhat familiar	14%	18%	13%	13%	17%
Not very familiar	7%	7%	3%	8%	8%
Just know the name	8%	7%	7%	6%	17%
Never heard of	2%	9%	2%	1%	6%

Source: *Perceptions of Libraries and Information Resources,* OCLC, 2005, question 505.

Familiarity of the Top Four Electronic Resources— by College Students across all Regions

Please indicate how familiar you are with each of the following electronic information sources.

Note: This table includes the top four electronic resources based on survey responses.

Detailed data for all 16 electronic resources are included in Appendix A. Respondents were not required to respond, so the totals for each resource do not equal 100 percent.

	Total Respondents	College Students
E-mail		
Extremely familiar	48%	56%
Very familiar	10%	6%
Somewhat familiar	3%	1%
Not very familiar	1%	0%
Just know the name	0%	0%
Never heard of	0%	0%
Search engine		
Extremely familiar	42%	53%
Very familiar	13%	9%
Somewhat familiar	6%	1%
Not very familiar	1%	0%
Just know the name	1%	0%
Never heard of	1%	0%
Instant messaging/online chat		
Extremely familiar	26%	42%
Very familiar	13%	14%
Somewhat familiar	15%	8%
Not very familiar	10%	2%
Just know the name	9%	1%
Never heard of	2%	3%
Online bookstore		
Extremely familiar	21%	29%
Very familiar	19%	22%
Somewhat familiar	17%	14%
Not very familiar	8%	3%
Just know the name	9%	3%
Never heard of	3%	2%

Source: *Perceptions of Libraries and Information Resources*, OCLC, 2005, question 505.

Starting an Information Search

Respondents use search engines to begin information searches.

The survey asked respondents to indicate, from a list of the same 16 electronic resources, the electronic resource they typically use to **begin** an information search. The survey findings indicate that 84 percent of information searches begin with a search engine. Library Web sites were selected by just 1 percent of respondents as the source used to begin an information search. Very little variability in preference exists across geographic regions or U.S. age groups. Two percent of college students start their search at a library Web site.

Where Electronic Information Searches Begin—
by College Students across all Regions

■ Search Engine: 89%

▨ Library Web site: 2%

▨ Online database: 2%

■ E-mail: 1%

□ Topic-specific Web sites: 1%

■ E-mail information subscriptions: 1%

▨ Online news: 1%

▨ Online bookstore: 1%

Instant messaging/ Online chat: 0%

Where Electronic Information Searches Begin—
by Total Respondents

Where do you typically begin your search for information on a particular topic?

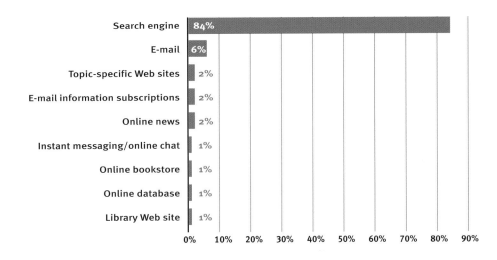

Tables detailing where electronic information searches begin by region, U.S. age, college students and library card holders are included in Appendix A.

Search Engine Used Most Recently

The majority of respondents used Google.com for their most recent information search.

Respondents who indicated that they use search engines were asked to identify the search engine used in their most recent search. Respondents were asked to select from a list of 21 brand-specific search engines. Google was used most frequently by 62 percent of all respondents. Yahoo! ranked second at 18 percent, followed by MSN Search at 7 percent and Ask Jeeves at 3 percent. Google was the dominant choice across all geographic regions and U.S. age groups.

23-year-old from the United States

Source: *Perceptions of Libraries and Information Resources*, OCLC, 2005, question 812a, "Please list two positive associations with the library."

Search Engine Used Most Recently— by Total Respondents

Earlier you stated you typically begin your search for information using search engines. Which search engine did you use for your most recent search?

Base: Respondents who begin their search using a search engine, question 520.

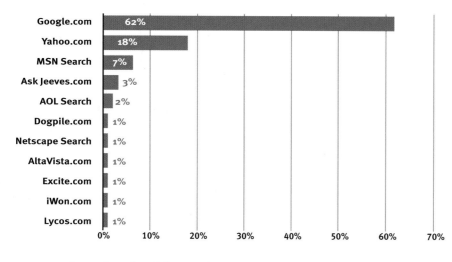

Source: *Perceptions of Libraries and Information Resources*, OCLC, 2005, question 645.

Search Engine Used Most Recently (Top Five)— by Region of Respondent

Earlier you stated you typically begin your search for information using search engines. Which search engine did you use for your most recent search?

Base: Respondents who begin their search using a search engine, question 520.

	Total Respondents	Australia Singapore India	Canada	United Kingdom	United States
Google.com	62%	64%	71%	66%	59%
Yahoo.com	18%	19%	13%	13%	21%
MSN Search	7%	6%	7%	6%	7%
Ask Jeeves.com	3%	1%	1%	6%	3%
AOL Search	2%	0%	0%	3%	3%

Source: *Perceptions of Libraries and Information Resources*, OCLC, 2005, question 645.

Search Engine Used Most Recently (Top Five)—
by Age of U.S. Respondent

Earlier you stated you typically begin your search for information using search engines. Which search engine did you use for your most recent search?

Base: Respondents who begin their search using a search engine, question 520.

	Total U.S. Respondents	U.S. 14-17	U.S. 18-24	U.S. 25-64	U.S. 65+
Google.com	59%	63%	69%	57%	55%
Yahoo.com	21%	22%	24%	20%	20%
MSN Search	7%	4%	3%	9%	5%
Ask Jeeves.com	3%	5%	2%	2%	3%
AOL Search	3%	2%	1%	3%	6%

Source: *Perceptions of Libraries and Information Resources*, OCLC, 2005, question 645.

Make a way to search through all of the databases

with one search engine,

instead of having to search each database individually.

21-year-old from the United States

Source: *Perceptions of Libraries and Information Resources*, OCLC, 2005, question 1240, "If you could provide one piece of advice to your library, what would it be?"

1.3 How Respondents Learn about New Information Resources

Other than search engines, most respondents learn about new electronic information resources from friends. Eight percent of respondents indicate they use librarians.

When search engines are excluded as a referral tool, most respondents indicate they learn about new electronic information sources by word of mouth from friends, relatives or colleagues. Sixty-one percent of all respondents learn about electronic information sources from *friends*, followed closely by *links from electronic information sources or Web sites*. The top four mentions include:

- Friend: 61 percent
- Links from electronic information sources or Web sites: 59 percent
- News media: 52 percent
- Promotions/advertising: 39 percent

Fifteen percent of respondents learn about new electronic information sources by *referencing the library Web site*. *Reference from a library Web site* rated the highest among college students (36 percent). Twenty percent of library card holders surveyed rely on *references from a library Web site* to identify new electronic information sources, while only 3 percent of non-card holders rely on library Web sites.

The *librarian* was ranked lowest, at 8 percent, as a source of information about electronic resources for the total respondents. Usage of the *librarian* among college students throughout the geographic regions surveyed was the highest among all segments surveyed, at 33 percent.

Tables detailing where respondents learn about information sources by region, U.S. age, college students and library card holders are included in Appendix A.

Learning about Electronic Information Sources—
by Total Respondents

Other than search engines, how do you learn about
electronic information sources? (Select all that apply.)

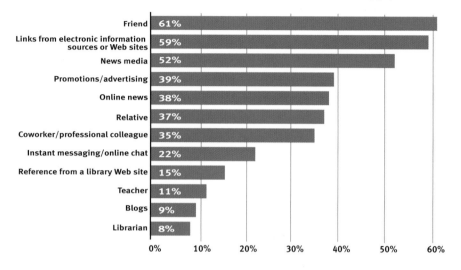

Source: *Perceptions of Libraries and Information Resources*, OCLC, 2005, question 605.

Learning about Electronic Information Sources—
by College Students across all Regions

Other than search engines, how do you learn
about electronic information sources? (Select all that apply)

	Total Respondents	College Students
Friend	61%	67%
Links from electronic information sources or Web sites	59%	61%
News media	52%	44%
Promotions/advertising	39%	26%
Online news	38%	42%
Relative	37%	26%
Coworker/professional colleague	35%	37%
Instant messaging/online chat	22%	26%
Reference from a library Web site	15%	36%
Teacher	11%	50%
Blogs	9%	13%
Librarian	8%	33%

Source: *Perceptions of Libraries and Information Resources*, OCLC, 2005, question 605.

*Not always
open when
you want.*

*Harder to search for
what you want, than
using a search
engine on line.*

60-year-old from Canada

Source: *Perceptions of Libraries and
Information Resources*, OCLC, 2005,
question 812b, "Please list two negative associations with the library."

1.4 Impressions of Information Sources

The majority of respondents view search engines
very favorably as a source for information.
Libraries and bookstores are viewed favorably.

Search engines have the highest favorability ratings of the five information sources evaluated. The search engine is viewed as *very favorable* or *favorable* by 88 percent of all respondents. The library is viewed as *very favorable* or *favorable* by 79 percent. Fifty-seven percent of the U.S. respondents 65 and older gave a *very favorable* rating for the library—significantly higher than any other U.S. age segment.

Both the online bookstore and online library received neutral ratings, with 35 and 46 percent respectively of respondents expressing *neither favorable nor unfavorable* ratings.

Favorable Ratings for Information Sources—
by Total Respondents

Based on your overall impressions, please indicate how you would rate each source/place with respect to the information available. Even if you haven't used one or more of the sources/places, rate each one based on what you have seen, read or heard about them.

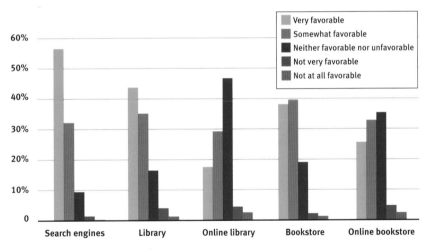

Source: *Perceptions of Libraries and Information Resources*, OCLC, 2005, question 1315.

Nearly half or more of the U.S., Canadian and Australian/Singaporean/Indian respondents have at least a favorable (either *very favorable* or *favorable)* opinion of the online library. Sixty-six percent of the college students stated that they have at least a favorable view of the online library. Conversely, 22 percent of the U.S. respondents age 14 to 17 reported an unfavorable *(not very favorable* or *not at all favorable)* view of the online library, the highest of any age segment. Fifty-two percent of library card holders have at least a favorable view of the online library, as compared to 33 percent of non-card holders.

Favorable Ratings for Information Sources— by Region of Respondent

Based on your overall impressions, please indicate how you would rate each source/place with respect to the information available. Even if you haven't used one or more of the sources/places, rate each one based on what you have seen, read or heard about them.

	Total Respondents	Australia Singapore India	Canada	United Kingdom	United States
Search engines					
Very favorable	56%	62%	55%	56%	55%
Somewhat favorable	32%	32%	34%	34%	31%
Neither favorable nor unfavorable	9%	5%	9%	8%	11%
Not very favorable	1%	0%	1%	1%	2%
Not at all favorable	0%	0%	1%	1%	0%
Physical library					
Very favorable	44%	44%	43%	30%	47%
Somewhat favorable	35%	40%	38%	34%	33%
Neither favorable nor unfavorable	16%	12%	16%	27%	15%
Not very favorable	4%	3%	3%	6%	4%
Not at all favorable	1%	1%	0%	4%	1%
Physical bookstore					
Very favorable	38%	35%	39%	32%	40%
Somewhat favorable	39%	45%	41%	37%	38%
Neither favorable nor unfavorable	19%	16%	18%	27%	18%
Not very favorable	2%	3%	1%	3%	2%
Not at all favorable	1%	1%	2%	2%	1%
Online library					
Very favorable	17%	21%	16%	9%	19%
Somewhat favorable	29%	37%	36%	21%	27%
Neither favorable nor unfavorable	46%	36%	42%	61%	47%
Not very favorable	4%	4%	3%	4%	5%
Not at all favorable	3%	2%	3%	5%	2%
Online bookstore					
Very favorable	25%	23%	20%	20%	29%
Somewhat favorable	33%	35%	36%	33%	31%
Neither favorable nor unfavorable	35%	35%	36%	39%	34%
Not very favorable	5%	5%	4%	4%	5%
Not at all favorable	2%	2%	4%	3%	2%

Source: *Perceptions of Libraries and Information Resources,* OCLC, 2005, question 1315.

I despise searching the library for books and other sources.

It takes a long time

and rarely can you find sources needed. This difficult process is the first thing I think of when I think of using the library.

18-year-old from Canada

Source: *Perceptions of Libraries and Information Resources,* OCLC, 2005, question 807, "What is the first thing you think of when you think of a library?"

Favorable Ratings for Information Sources—
by Age of U.S. Respondent

Based on your overall impressions, please indicate how you would rate each source/place with respect to the information available. Even if you haven't used one or more of the sources/places, rate each one based on what you have seen, read or heard about them.

Happiness...

I love the library!

All that knowledge in one place.

27-year-old from the United States

Source: *Perceptions of Libraries and Information Resources*, OCLC, 2005, question 807, "What is the first thing you think of when you think of a library?"

	Total U.S. Respondents	U.S. 14-17	U.S. 18-24	U.S. 25-64	U.S. 65+
Search engines					
Very favorable	55%	53%	49%	57%	51%
Somewhat favorable	31%	25%	33%	32%	32%
Neither favorable nor unfavorable	11%	16%	17%	9%	14%
Not very favorable	2%	0%	1%	2%	3%
Not at all favorable	0%	6%	0%	0%	0%
Physical library					
Very favorable	47%	37%	37%	47%	57%
Somewhat favorable	33%	30%	40%	34%	25%
Neither favorable nor unfavorable	15%	22%	18%	14%	15%
Not very favorable	4%	4%	5%	4%	2%
Not at all favorable	1%	7%	1%	0%	0%
Physical bookstore					
Very favorable	40%	32%	37%	42%	39%
Somewhat favorable	38%	34%	40%	39%	37%
Neither favorable nor unfavorable	18%	25%	18%	17%	19%
Not very favorable	2%	3%	3%	2%	3%
Not at all favorable	1%	7%	3%	1%	2%
Online library					
Very favorable	19%	14%	15%	21%	18%
Somewhat favorable	27%	19%	35%	28%	18%
Neither favorable nor unfavorable	47%	45%	35%	47%	57%
Not very favorable	5%	12%	10%	4%	4%
Not at all favorable	2%	10%	5%	0%	3%
Online bookstore					
Very favorable	29%	16%	22%	33%	21%
Somewhat favorable	31%	23%	36%	31%	30%
Neither favorable nor unfavorable	34%	36%	29%	32%	43%
Not very favorable	5%	14%	9%	4%	4%
Not at all favorable	2%	11%	3%	0%	2%

Source: *Perceptions of Libraries and Information Resources*, OCLC, 2005, question 1315.

Favorable Ratings for Information Sources—
by College Students across all Regions

Based on your overall impressions, please indicate how you would rate each source/place with respect to the information available. Even if you haven't used one or more of the sources/places, rate each one based on what you have seen, read or heard about them.

	Total Respondents	College Students
Search engines		
Very favorable	56%	52%
Somewhat favorable	32%	40%
Neither favorable nor unfavorable	9%	7%
Not very favorable	1%	1%
Not at all favorable	0%	0%
Physical library		
Very favorable	44%	47%
Somewhat favorable	35%	38%
Neither favorable nor unfavorable	16%	11%
Not very favorable	4%	3%
Not at all favorable	1%	0%
Physical bookstore		
Very favorable	38%	43%
Somewhat favorable	39%	41%
Neither favorable nor unfavorable	19%	14%
Not very favorable	2%	2%
Not at all favorable	1%	0%
Online library		
Very favorable	17%	27%
Somewhat favorable	29%	39%
Neither favorable nor unfavorable	46%	26%
Not very favorable	4%	5%
Not at all favorable	3%	2%
Online bookstore		
Very favorable	25%	27%
Somewhat favorable	33%	45%
Neither favorable nor unfavorable	35%	22%
Not very favorable	5%	6%
Not at all favorable	2%	0%

Source: *Perceptions of Libraries and Information Resources*, OCLC, 2005, question 1315.

Favorable Ratings for Online Library —
by College Students across all Regions

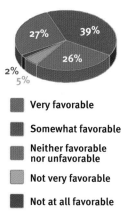

- Very favorable
- Somewhat favorable
- Neither favorable nor unfavorable
- Not very favorable
- Not at all favorable

Source: *Perceptions of Libraries and Information Resources*, OCLC, 2005, question 1315.

Favorable Ratings for Information Sources—
by Library Card Holders and Non-Card Holders across All Regions

Based on your overall impressions, please indicate how you would rate each source/place with respect to the information available. Even if you haven't used one or more of the sources/places, rate each one based on what you have seen, read or heard about them.

	Total Respondents	Library Card Holders	Non-Card Holders
Search engines			
Very favorable	56%	58%	52%
Somewhat favorable	32%	32%	33%
Neither favorable nor unfavorable	9%	9%	11%
Not very favorable	1%	1%	2%
Not at all favorable	0%	0%	1%
Physical library			
Very favorable	44%	51%	24%
Somewhat favorable	35%	33%	40%
Neither favorable nor unfavorable	16%	12%	28%
Not very favorable	4%	3%	6%
Not at all favorable	1%	1%	2%
Physical bookstore			
Very favorable	38%	42%	27%
Somewhat favorable	39%	37%	46%
Neither favorable nor unfavorable	19%	17%	22%
Not very favorable	2%	2%	3%
Not at all favorable	1%	1%	2%
Online library			
Very favorable	17%	21%	9%
Somewhat favorable	29%	31%	24%
Neither favorable nor unfavorable	46%	42%	56%
Not very favorable	4%	4%	6%
Not at all favorable	3%	2%	4%
Online bookstore			
Very favorable	25%	29%	16%
Somewhat favorable	33%	33%	31%
Neither favorable nor unfavorable	35%	31%	45%
Not very favorable	5%	5%	6%
Not at all favorable	2%	2%	3%

Source: *Perceptions of Libraries and Information Resources*, OCLC, 2005, question 1315.

please

let us study there longer!!!

20-year-old from Singapore

Source: *Perceptions of Libraries and Information Resources*, OCLC, 2005, question 1240, "If you could provide one piece of advice to your library, what would it be?"

Information Sources Considered

Search engines are the most often used information source.
They are also the information source most likely to be used the next time
respondents need information.

Survey respondents were asked what information sources they will consider the next time they need information. Ninety-one percent of respondents selected search engines as an information source they would consider, while 55 percent selected the bricks-and-mortar library and 42 percent selected the online library.

Search engines again are ranked as the "first choice" for information by 80 percent of all respondents. The library ranks a distant second with 11 percent and the online library third at 6 percent.

Information Sources Considered and First Choice—
by Total Respondents

Next time you need a source/place for information, which source or sources would you consider? Select all that apply.
And, which source/place would be your first choice?

Sources Considered	%	First Choice...	%
Search engines	91%	Search engines	80%
Library (physical)	55%	Library (physical)	11%
Online library	42%	Online library	6%
Bookstore (physical)	37%	Bookstore (physical)	2%
Online bookstore	30%	Online bookstore	2%

Source: *Perceptions of Libraries and Information Resources*, OCLC, 2005, questions 1325 and 1335.

Tables detailing information by region, U.S. age, college students and library card holder status are included in the tables in Appendix A.

First Choice for Information Source—
by College Students across all Regions

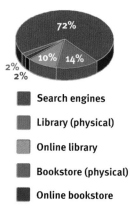

- Search engines
- Library (physical)
- Online library
- Bookstore (physical)
- Online bookstore

Source: *Perceptions of Libraries and Information Resources*, OCLC, 2005, question 1335.

Finding Worthwhile Information

Ninety-three percent of respondents at least agree
Google provides worthwhile information.

Seventy-eight percent at least agree
library Web sites provide worthwhile information.

93%
agree Google provides worthwhile information.

78%
agree library Web sites provide worthwhile information.

85%
agree Yahoo! provides worthwhile information.

Respondents were asked to rate the information from the following brands:

- About.com
- AllTheWeb.com
- AltaVista.com
- AOL Search
- Ask an expert (e.g., Homework Helper)
- Ask Jeeves.com
- Clusty.com
- Dogpile.com
- Excite.com
- Gigablast.com
- Google.com
- HotBot.com
- iWon.com
- Library Web sites
- LookSmart.com
- Lycos.com
- MSN Search
- Netscape Search
- Online librarian question services (Ask a librarian)
- Teoma.com
- Yahoo.com

Respondents who indicated any usage of the 21 brands were asked to rate the degree to which they agree or disagree that each brand they have used provides worthwhile information. Google, Yahoo!, MSN Search and Ask Jeeves top the list of brands providing worthwhile information.

Respondents who have used Google rate it highest, with 55 percent indicating that they *completely agree* that Google provides worthwhile information. Yahoo! and the library Web site are closely rated by the respondents who use those brands, at 34 percent and 33 percent respectively. MSN Search and Ask Jeeves round out the top five brands information consumers report to provide worthwhile information.

Forty-five percent of the college students across all regions *completely agree* that library Web sites provide worthwhile information, more so than any other segment in the study.

Significant variation in views about library Web sites was apparent across U.S. age groups. U.S. 14- to 17-year-olds are the least likely to *completely agree* that the library Web site provides worthwhile information compared to other U.S. age groups (20 percent). U.S. 18- to 24-year-olds and those over 65 are the most likely to *completely agree* that the library Web site provides worthwhile information among the U.S. age groups (over 40 percent).

Tables detailing worthwhile information, familiarity and usage for the 21 information brands by region are included in Appendix A.

Five Highest-Rated Information Brands with Worthwhile Information—by Total Respondents

Please rate the degree to which you agree or disagree that each electronic information source provides worthwhile information.

Base: Respondents who indicated usage of any of the list of 21 information brands.

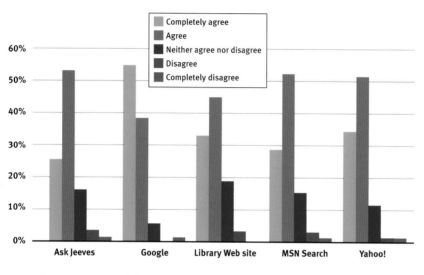

Source: *Perceptions of Libraries and Information Resources*, OCLC, 2005, question 670.

Five Highest-Ranked Information Brands with Worthwhile Information—by Total Respondents

Please rate the degree to which you agree or disagree that each electronic information source provides worthwhile information.

Base: Respondents who indicated usage of any of the list of 21 information brands.

	Ask Jeeves	Google	Library Web site	MSN Search	Yahoo!
Completely agree	25%	55%	33%	29%	34%
Agree	53%	38%	45%	52%	51%
Neither agree nor disagree	16%	6%	19%	15%	12%
Disagree	3%	0%	3%	3%	1%
Completely disagree	1%	1%	0%	1%	1%

Source: *Perceptions of Libraries and Information Resources*, OCLC, 2005, question 670.

Aim to become the **one-stop-shopping,** *authoritative and trustworthy source for infomation i.e the mother of all search engines.*

59-year-old from Canada

Source: *Perceptions of Libraries and Information Resources*, OCLC, 2005, question 1240, "If you could provide one piece of advice to your library, what would it be?"

Improve the web site more—

I like the catalog, but if it could reference some sort of rating system it would be even better—I was looking at a new author today who has many books, and I had to go to an internet computer, check on Amazon and see which books were most highly recommended, and go back to the catalog to see if they were available.

15-year-old from the United States

Source: *Perceptions of Libraries and Information Resources*, OCLC, 2005, question 1240, "If you could provide one piece of advice to your library, what would it be?"

Five Highest-Rated Information Brands with Worthwhile Information—
by Age of U.S. Respondents who "Completely Agree"

Please rate the degree to which you agree or disagree that each electronic information source provides worthwhile information.

(Only "Completely Agree" responses are graphed below.)

Base: Respondents who indicated usage of any of the list of 21 information brands.

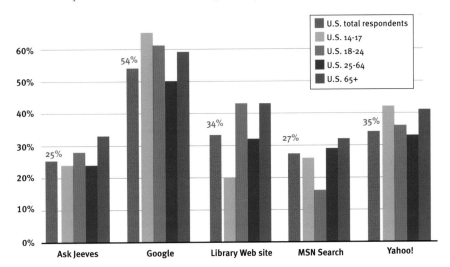

Source: *Perceptions of Libraries and Information Resources*, OCLC, 2005, question 670.

Worthwhile Information from the Library Web site—
All Respondents who "Completely Agree"

Please rate the degree to which you agree or disagree that each electronic information source provides worthwhile information.

(Only "Completely Agree" responses are graphed below.)

Base: Respondents who indicated usage of the library Web site from a list of 21 information brands.

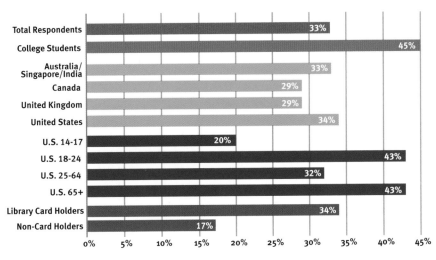

Source: *Perceptions of Libraries and Information Resources*, OCLC, 2005, question 670.

Library Electronic Resources

Respondents who use the library agree that electronic library information resources are worthwhile.

Respondents who use the library's electronic information sources are in general consensus that the library sources provide worthwhile information. The online library catalog, online reference materials, the library Web site and electronic magazines/journals rate highly as resources providing worthwhile information.

Although usage of many of the library electronic resources is relatively low, respondents indicated that the information provided was worthwhile. While only 6 percent of respondents have used an online librarian question service, 71 percent agree (*completely agree* or *agree*) this service provides worthwhile information.

Again, college students had higher ratings than the overall group.

- Seventy-two percent of college students *completely agree* or *agree* that online databases provide worthwhile information.

- Eighty-five percent of college students *completely agree* or *agree* that electronic magazines/journals provide worthwhile information. Roughly three-quarters of respondents from all geographic regions indicate they *completely agree* or *agree*.

Doing an **online search** *and request for material from the comfort of my home*

33-year-old from Canada

Source: *Perceptions of Libraries and Information Resources,* OCLC, 2005, question 807, "What is the first thing you think of when you think of a library?"

Worthwhile Information from the Library's Resources—
by Region of Respondent

Please rate the degree to which you agree or disagree that each electronic information source available through your primary library provides worthwhile information.

	Total Respondents	Australia Singapore India	Canada	United Kingdom	United States
Online library catalog					
Completely agree	39%	32%	39%	31%	43%
Agree	43%	50%	44%	50%	40%
Neither agree nor disagree	14%	15%	12%	16%	14%
Disagree	1%	1%	2%	2%	1%
Completely disagree	2%	2%	3%	1%	2%
Online reference materials					
Completely agree	34%	28%	40%	21%	36%
Agree	45%	55%	43%	53%	42%
Neither agree nor disagree	19%	17%	14%	22%	21%
Disagree	1%	0%	3%	2%	1%
Completely disagree	1%	1%	0%	2%	1%
Online librarian question service					
Completely agree	32%	29%	31%	22%	35%
Agree	39%	41%	36%	42%	39%
Neither agree nor disagree	26%	29%	25%	32%	24%
Disagree	2%	1%	6%	1%	1%
Completely disagree	2%	1%	3%	3%	1%
Library Web site					
Completely agree	31%	23%	30%	25%	34%
Agree	46%	52%	50%	52%	43%
Neither agree nor disagree	19%	21%	16%	20%	19%
Disagree	1%	2%	3%	1%	1%
Completely disagree	2%	2%	1%	2%	2%
Online databases					
Completely agree	28%	26%	24%	15%	31%
Agree	43%	48%	47%	55%	39%
Neither agree nor disagree	27%	25%	22%	27%	28%
Disagree	2%	0%	6%	3%	1%
Completely disagree	1%	0%	1%	0%	1%
Audiobooks (downloadable/digital)					
Completely agree	22%	13%	23%	18%	26%
Agree	43%	52%	38%	40%	41%
Neither agree nor disagree	33%	32%	34%	40%	31%
Disagree	2%	2%	4%	0%	1%
Completely disagree	1%	2%	0%	2%	1%
Electronic magazines/journals					
Completely agree	28%	27%	32%	33%	26%
Agree	48%	55%	50%	45%	46%
Neither agree nor disagree	22%	16%	13%	21%	26%
Disagree	1%	0%	3%	1%	0%
Completely disagree	2%	1%	1%	1%	2%
Electronic books (digital)					
Completely agree	20%	18%	26%	21%	18%
Agree	47%	53%	37%	44%	49%
Neither agree nor disagree	29%	26%	26%	34%	30%
Disagree	2%	1%	9%	0%	1%
Completely disagree	2%	2%	1%	1%	2%

Source: *Perceptions of Libraries and Information Resources*, OCLC, 2005, question 870.

Worthwhile Information from the Library's Resources—
by Age of U.S. Respondent

Please rate the degree to which you agree or disagree that each electronic information source available through your primary library provides worthwhile information.

	Total U.S. Respondents	U.S. 14-17	U.S. 18-24	U.S. 25-64	U.S. 65+
Online library catalog					
Completely agree	43%	29%	33%	50%	33%
Agree	40%	40%	41%	38%	52%
Neither agree nor disagree	14%	24%	24%	10%	12%
Disagree	1%	2%	1%	0%	0%
Completely disagree	2%	5%	1%	1%	2%
Online reference materials					
Completely agree	36%	23%	27%	44%	22%
Agree	42%	39%	40%	41%	52%
Neither agree nor disagree	21%	29%	31%	16%	24%
Disagree	1%	5%	1%	0%	0%
Completely disagree	1%	3%	1%	0%	2%
Online librarian question service					
Completely agree	35%	15%	11%	47%	25%
Agree	39%	44%	45%	34%	53%
Neither agree nor disagree	24%	33%	39%	19%	21%
Disagree	1%	1%	3%	0%	0%
Completely disagree	1%	7%	2%	0%	1%
Library Web site					
Completely agree	34%	17%	26%	39%	31%
Agree	43%	36%	44%	43%	52%
Neither agree nor disagree	19%	41%	28%	15%	11%
Disagree	1%	3%	1%	1%	3%
Completely disagree	2%	3%	1%	2%	2%
Online databases					
Completely agree	31%	18%	22%	38%	16%
Agree	39%	31%	37%	40%	43%
Neither agree nor disagree	28%	39%	39%	22%	39%
Disagree	1%	5%	0%	0%	1%
Completely disagree	1%	7%	1%	0%	1%
Audiobooks (downloadable/digital)					
Completely agree	26%	13%	8%	35%	11%
Agree	41%	21%	38%	41%	64%
Neither agree nor disagree	31%	54%	51%	24%	22%
Disagree	1%	4%	1%	0%	1%
Completely disagree	1%	8%	2%	0%	2%
Electronic magazines/journals					
Completely agree	26%	17%	22%	28%	28%
Agree	46%	37%	43%	48%	48%
Neither agree nor disagree	26%	35%	33%	22%	21%
Disagree	0%	3%	0%	0%	1%
Completely disagree	2%	9%	1%	1%	2%
Electronic books (digital)					
Completely agree	18%	7%	12%	23%	18%
Agree	49%	34%	36%	59%	38%
Neither agree nor disagree	30%	38%	51%	18%	41%
Disagree	1%	9%	0%	0%	0%
Completely disagree	2%	11%	1%	0%	4%

Source: *Perceptions of Libraries and Information Resources*, OCLC, 2005, question 870.

> *I love audio books,* they are a great resource for new moms.
>
> **23-year-old from the United States**

Source: *Perceptions of Libraries and Information Resources*, OCLC, 2005, question 1240, "If you could provide one piece of advice to your library, what would it be?"

Worthwhile Information from the Library's Resources—
by College Students across all Regions
Please rate the degree to which you agree or disagree that each electronic information source available through your primary library provides worthwhile information.

Worthwhile Information for Electronic Magazines/Journals—
by College Students across all Regions

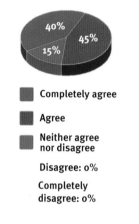

■ Completely agree

■ Agree

■ Neither agree nor disagree

Disagree: 0%

Completely disagree: 0%

Source: *Perceptions of Libraries and Information Resources*, OCLC, 2005, question 870.

	Total Respondents	College students
Online library catalog		
Completely agree	39%	44%
Agree	43%	39%
Neither agree nor disagree	14%	15%
Disagree	1%	2%
Completely disagree	2%	0%
Online reference materials		
Completely agree	34%	38%
Agree	45%	43%
Neither agree nor disagree	19%	18%
Disagree	1%	0%
Completely disagree	1%	0%
Online librarian question service		
Completely agree	32%	32%
Agree	39%	32%
Neither agree nor disagree	26%	36%
Disagree	2%	0%
Completely disagree	2%	0%
Library Web site		
Completely agree	31%	38%
Agree	46%	41%
Neither agree nor disagree	19%	20%
Disagree	1%	1%
Completely disagree	2%	0%
Online databases		
Completely agree	28%	36%
Agree	43%	36%
Neither agree nor disagree	27%	29%
Disagree	2%	0%
Completely disagree	1%	0%
Audiobooks (downloadable/digital)		
Completely agree	22%	24%
Agree	43%	38%
Neither agree nor disagree	33%	38%
Disagree	2%	0%
Completely disagree	1%	0%
Electronic magazines/journals		
Completely agree	28%	40%
Agree	48%	45%
Neither agree nor disagree	22%	15%
Disagree	1%	0%
Completely disagree	2%	0%
Electronic books (digital)		
Completely agree	20%	20%
Agree	47%	41%
Neither agree nor disagree	29%	37%
Disagree	2%	1%
Completely disagree	2%	0%

Source: *Perceptions of Libraries and Information Resources*, OCLC, 2005, question 870.

Part 2: Using the Library— In Person and Online

OCLC

Borrowing print books *is the top library activity for information consumers.*

41% *use the library* **at least once a year** *to get assistance with research.*

In the U.S., frequency of library use **declines with age.**

In Part 1, we reviewed survey findings related to respondents' frequency of use, familiarity and favorability toward a wide range of information sources, including the physical and online library.

In Part 2, we review responses to questions that probe further for respondents' use habits with regard to activities pursued at the library and through the online library. In particular, respondents were asked about their levels of familiarity and satisfaction with library-provided electronic information resources and where they seek help when they need assistance using library information resources. Finally, we review responses related to the evaluation of search engines and libraries against a set of performance attributes.

2.1 Activities at the Library

Borrowing print books, researching specific reference books and getting assistance with research are the top three library activities.

We asked respondents to indicate how frequently they use 20 different library resources. Results show that libraries are used to pursue activities in all 20 categories, but frequency of use varies considerably across types of resources and across regions and U.S age groups surveyed.

Eight of the most frequently used activities are reviewed. Please refer to Appendix A for detailed data on all 20 library activities by geographic region, U.S. age and college students.

Borrowing print books is the activity respondents used most frequently. Fifty-five percent of all respondents borrow print books *at least annually.* Frequency varied across regions. Respondents from the Australia/Singapore/India regions borrow print books most frequently with 61 percent reporting they borrow print books *at least annually.* Respondents from the U.K. borrow print books least frequently, at 51 percent *at least annually.*

Researching specific reference books is the second most frequent library activity conducted annually. Respondents from the Australia/Singapore/India regions report the highest use of specific reference books at 61 percent, with the U.K. respondents again reporting the lowest use at 45 percent *at least annually.*

Of the 20 library activities surveyed, using the computer/Internet ranked seventh in frequency of annual use. Twenty-nine percent of all respondents report they use the computer/Internet at a library *at least annually*. Forty-two percent of all respondents report they *never have used* a library to use a computer/Internet. Computer/Internet use in the library varies across U.S. age groups. While 62 percent of U.S. respondents 65 and over *never have used* the library for computer/Internet access, only 14 percent of U.S. youth age 14–17 *never have used* a library for this purpose. Sixty-four percent of U.S. respondents age 14–17 use the library for computer/Internet access *at least annually*.

Activities at the Library—by Region of Respondent

How frequently do you use your library for the following reasons?

Note: *At least monthly* is a rollup of daily, weekly and monthly.
At least annually is a rollup of several times a year and at least once a year.

	Total Respondents	Australia Singapore India	Canada	United Kingdom	United States
Borrow print books					
At least monthly	26%	35%	30%	23%	23%
At least annually	29%	26%	30%	28%	30%
Not even once a year	10%	7%	12%	7%	11%
Never have used	17%	13%	14%	19%	18%
Used to use, but no longer do	19%	19%	14%	22%	19%
Research specific reference books					
At least monthly	15%	22%	17%	14%	12%
At least annually	36%	39%	36%	31%	36%
Not even once a year	12%	8%	11%	10%	14%
Never have used	15%	9%	16%	15%	16%
Used to use, but no longer do	23%	22%	20%	29%	22%
Get assistance with research					
At least monthly	11%	17%	15%	10%	9%
At least annually	30%	34%	27%	25%	30%
Not even once a year	13%	9%	15%	9%	15%
Never have used	23%	20%	22%	30%	22%
Used to use, but no longer do	23%	21%	21%	25%	24%
Read/borrow best-seller					
At least monthly	16%	19%	17%	16%	16%
At least annually	23%	28%	25%	22%	23%
Not even once a year	11%	9%	12%	7%	12%
Never have used	31%	28%	30%	34%	32%
Used to use, but no longer do	17%	16%	15%	21%	17%
Get copies of articles/journals					
At least monthly	9%	18%	12%	8%	7%
At least annually	25%	27%	25%	18%	25%
Not even once a year	12%	11%	13%	8%	13%
Never have used	33%	25%	34%	44%	33%
Used to use, but no longer do	21%	19%	16%	23%	22%
Use online databases					
At least monthly	15%	21%	19%	9%	14%
At least annually	18%	17%	20%	10%	19%
Not even once a year	9%	8%	7%	6%	10%
Never have used	46%	39%	42%	61%	45%
Used to use, but no longer do	13%	15%	12%	14%	12%
Use the computer/Internet					
At least monthly	13%	17%	14%	10%	13%
At least annually	16%	17%	19%	11%	16%
Not even once a year	9%	8%	12%	6%	10%
Never have used	42%	36%	33%	54%	44%
Used to use, but no longer do	18%	21%	22%	19%	16%
Do homework/study					
At least monthly	12%	16%	13%	9%	11%
At least annually	15%	19%	18%	11%	14%
Not even once a year	8%	7%	6%	6%	10%
Never have used	27%	23%	22%	34%	27%
Used to use, but no longer do	39%	35%	40%	40%	39%

Source: *Perceptions of Libraries and Information Resources*, OCLC, 2005, question 840.

The library has no purpose in my life.

I guess it is more of a historical archive of old paper documents. Who knows?

50-year-old from Canada

Source: *Perceptions of Libraries and Information Resources*, OCLC, 2005, question 810, "What do you feel is the main purpose of the library?"

All associations with my library are positive

76-year-old from Canada

Source: *Perceptions of Libraries and Information Resources*, OCLC, 2005, question 812a, "Please list two positive associations with the library."

Frequency of annual use of the top eight library activities typically declines with age. U.S. 14- to 17-year-olds report that they borrow print books more frequently than other U.S. age groups, at 66 percent. U.S. respondents age 25–64 report lower usage and U.S. respondents age 65 and older report the least frequent print book borrowing at 49 percent. Sixty-eight percent of U.S. 14- to 17-year-old respondents report they research specific reference books *at least annually,* compared to 46 percent of U.S. respondents age 25-64. Read/borrow best-seller showed the most consistent use *at least annually* across U.S. age groups.

Activities at the Library—by Age of U.S. Respondent

How frequently do you use your library for the following reasons?

Note: *At least monthly* is a rollup of daily, weekly and monthly.
At least annually is a rollup of several times a year and at least once a year.

*Activities at the Library:
Borrow Print Books—*
**by College Students
across all Regions**

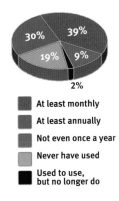

- At least monthly
- At least annually
- Not even once a year
- Never have used
- Used to use,
  but no longer do

Source: *Perceptions of Libraries and Information Resources,* OCLC, 2005, question 840.

	Total U.S. Respondents	U.S. 14-17	U.S. 18-24	U.S. 25-64	U.S. 65+
Borrow print books					
At least monthly	23%	32%	28%	22%	19%
At least annually	30%	34%	27%	30%	30%
Not even once a year	11%	8%	6%	12%	10%
Never have used	18%	21%	25%	15%	24%
Used to use, but no longer do	19%	5%	14%	21%	18%
Research specific reference books					
At least monthly	12%	27%	25%	10%	4%
At least annually	36%	41%	40%	36%	33%
Not even once a year	14%	11%	8%	14%	16%
Never have used	16%	16%	14%	15%	21%
Used to use, but no longer do	22%	6%	14%	25%	26%
Get assistance with research					
At least monthly	9%	23%	20%	7%	2%
At least annually	30%	35%	37%	28%	27%
Not even once a year	15%	10%	10%	16%	15%
Never have used	22%	28%	18%	22%	27%
Used to use, but no longer do	24%	6%	16%	27%	29%
Read/borrow best-seller					
At least monthly	16%	18%	15%	15%	17%
At least annually	23%	26%	18%	23%	24%
Not even once a year	12%	12%	13%	13%	11%
Never have used	32%	38%	45%	29%	30%
Used to use, but no longer do	17%	6%	9%	20%	16%
Get copies of articles/journals					
At least monthly	7%	16%	13%	6%	1%
At least annually	25%	29%	31%	26%	20%
Not even once a year	13%	11%	8%	14%	14%
Never have used	33%	40%	32%	29%	47%
Used to use, but no longer do	22%	5%	15%	25%	18%
Use online databases					
At least monthly	14%	21%	30%	12%	7%
At least annually	19%	32%	25%	17%	12%
Not even once a year	10%	10%	7%	12%	6%
Never have used	45%	31%	27%	45%	66%
Used to use, but no longer do	12%	6%	11%	14%	9%
Use the computer/Internet					
At least monthly	13%	34%	35%	10%	5%
At least annually	16%	30%	24%	14%	12%
Not even once a year	10%	12%	4%	11%	8%
Never have used	44%	14%	19%	48%	62%
Used to use, but no longer do	16%	10%	18%	17%	13%
Do homework/study					
At least monthly	11%	33%	34%	6%	0%
At least annually	14%	32%	25%	10%	11%
Not even once a year	10%	11%	7%	11%	6%
Never have used	27%	16%	12%	28%	39%
Used to use, but no longer do	39%	7%	22%	44%	43%

Source: *Perceptions of Libraries and Information Resources,* OCLC, 2005, question 840.

Monthly activity levels among college students are higher than total respondents in all but one category (read/borrow best-seller). Forty-two percent report researching specific reference books at the library *at least monthly,* 48 percent report using a library to do homework/study *at least monthly,* and 33 percent report getting assistance with research at a library *at least monthly.* Only 12 percent of these respondents report using a library to read/borrow best-sellers *at least monthly.*

Tables detailing activities at the library by region, U.S. age and college students are included in Appendix A.

Activities at the Library—by College Students across all Regions

How frequently do you use your library for the following reasons?
Note: *At least monthly* is a rollup of daily, weekly and monthly.
At least annually is a rollup of several times a year and at least once a year.

	Total Respondents	College Students
Borrow print books		
At least monthly	26%	39%
At least annually	29%	30%
Not even once a year	10%	9%
Never have used	17%	19%
Used to use, but no longer do	19%	2%
Research specific reference books		
At least monthly	15%	42%
At least annually	36%	41%
Not even once a year	12%	5%
Never have used	15%	8%
Used to use, but no longer do	23%	4%
Get assistance with research		
At least monthly	11%	33%
At least annually	30%	35%
Not even once a year	13%	9%
Never have used	23%	19%
Used to use, but no longer do	23%	4%
Read/borrow best-seller		
At least monthly	16%	12%
At least annually	23%	19%
Not even once a year	11%	8%
Never have used	31%	58%
Used to use, but no longer do	17%	3%
Get copies of articles/journals		
At least monthly	9%	32%
At least annually	25%	37%
Not even once a year	12%	6%
Never have used	33%	19%
Used to use, but no longer do	21%	7%
Use online databases		
At least monthly	15%	44%
At least annually	18%	26%
Not even once a year	9%	5%
Never have used	46%	22%
Used to use, but no longer do	13%	3%
Use the computer/Internet		
At least monthly	13%	45%
At least annually	16%	24%
Not even once a year	9%	4%
Never have used	42%	20%
Used to use, but no longer do	18%	8%
Do homework/study		
At least monthly	12%	48%
At least annually	15%	29%
Not even once a year	8%	6%
Never have used	27%	9%
Used to use, but no longer do	39%	7%

A library should primarily provide books and study resources. Music and DVDs are cool, but popular titles should not be carried since they can be rented from the video shop for very little. *I don't believe that lending Finding Nemo* should be part of a public library's charter.

33-year-old from Australia

Source: *Perceptions of Libraries and Information Resources,* OCLC, 2005, question 1240, "If you could provide one piece of advice to your library, what would it be?"

Source: *Perceptions of Libraries and Information Resources,* OCLC, 2005, question 840.

Comparing Libraries and Bookstores

Respondents favor libraries over bookstores for free Internet access, free materials and special programs. They favor bookstores for coffee shops, current materials and meeting their friends.

Respondents were asked to compare a library to a bookstore against a list of activities and attributes. The data show that respondents' libraries are considered more suitable than local bookstores on eight of 11 activities/attributes. Seventy-one percent of all respondents feel the library is more suitable than their local bookstore in providing comfortable seating, and 86 percent feel the library is more suitable than local bookstores in providing access to free entertainment. Respondents feel that the local bookstore is more a suitable source of current materials than their library.

U.S. young adults age 18 to 24 rated bookstores as more suitable for access to music than did total respondents. They were split on whether the library or bookstore had a more friendly environment.

Tables detailing data for responses by region, U.S. age, college students and library card holder are included in Appendix A.

Provide a more **bookstore** **environment** *for free and more people will come*

24-year-old from the United States

Source: *Perceptions of Libraries and Information Resources,* OCLC, 2005, question 1240, "If you could provide one piece of advice to your library, what would it be?"

Suitability of the Library and the Bookstore for Specific Activities—**by Total Respondents**

Comparing the library to your local bookstore, which do you feel provides a more suitable environment for activities/materials in regard to the following?

Libraries are more suitable than bookstores for...	Bookstores are more suitable than libraries for...
Free access to the Internet: 95%	Coffee/snack shop: 83%
Free materials: 95%	More current materials: 60%
Special programs: 89%	It's where my friends are: 57%
Access to free entertainment: 86%	
Book club/story hour: 77%	
Comfortable seating/meeting area: 71%	
Friendly environment: 64%	
Access to music: 62%	

Source: *Perceptions of Libraries and Information Resources,* OCLC, 2005, question 1230.

*Suitability of the Library and the Bookstore
for Specific Activities*—**by U.S. 18- to 24-year-olds**

Comparing the library to your local bookstore, which do you feel provides a more
suitable environment for activities/materials in regard to the following?

Note: *Friendly environment* appears in both columns because respondents were split on whether
the library or bookstore had a more friendly environment.

Libraries are more suitable than bookstores for...	Bookstores are more suitable than libraries for...
Free materials: 92%	Coffee/snack shop: 89%
Free access to the Internet: 91%	Find more current materials: 71%
Access to free entertainment: 82%	It's where my friends are: 61%
Special programs: 81%	Access to music: 55%
Book club/story hour: 62%	Friendly environment: 50%
Comfortable seating/meeting area: 59%	
Friendly environment: 50%	

Source: *Perceptions of Libraries and Information Resources*, OCLC, 2005, question 1230.

2.2 Awareness of Library Electronic Resources

*Awareness of electronic databases and electronic materials at the library is
low. Awareness of library Web sites and online library catalogs is high.*

Respondents were asked to indicate if their library provides various types of electronic
resources. Results indicate that awareness among respondents is low for most of
the library's electronic resources. For example, 58 percent of all respondents are *not
sure* if their library offers access to online databases.

Of the eight library electronic resources evaluated, respondents show the highest
level of awareness for the library Web site and online library catalog. At least 60
percent of respondents are aware of these resources. Awareness of the online
library catalog is highest among Canadian respondents at 74 percent and lowest
among respondents from the U.K. at 45 percent.

A slight majority (55 percent) of respondents are aware that their library has online
reference materials.

In the other five categories, most respondents are *not sure* if the library has the
electronic resources. For example, only 38 percent of respondents indicate the
library has audiobooks, and just 34 percent indicate they are aware that their library
has electronic magazines/journals.

*Advertise
what you
offer more*

*for general public.
If you don't have
kids or are not
studying—you
don't often know
what the library
offers*

33-year-old from Australia

Source: *Perceptions of Libraries and
Information Resources*, OCLC, 2005,
question 1240, "If you could provide
one piece of advice to your library,
what would it be?"

Awareness of Library Resources—by Region of Respondent

Please indicate which electronic information sources your primary library has.

	Total Respondents	Australia Singapore India	Canada	United Kingdom	United States
Library Web site					
Yes, library has these	61%	67%	72%	45%	60%
No, library does not have	6%	8%	5%	7%	5%
Not sure	33%	25%	23%	48%	35%
Online library catalog					
Yes, library has these	60%	69%	74%	45%	58%
No, library does not have	5%	6%	5%	6%	5%
Not sure	35%	25%	21%	48%	38%
Online reference materials					
Yes, library has these	55%	57%	60%	44%	55%
No, library does not have	4%	7%	5%	6%	3%
Not sure	41%	36%	34%	50%	42%
Audiobooks (downloadable/digital)					
Yes, library has these	38%	42%	40%	33%	37%
No, library does not have	8%	10%	8%	9%	8%
Not sure	54%	48%	52%	58%	55%
Online databases					
Yes, library has these	37%	40%	41%	24%	39%
No, library does not have	5%	8%	5%	6%	4%
Not sure	58%	53%	54%	69%	57%
Electronic magazines/journals					
Yes, library has these	34%	42%	38%	23%	34%
No, library does not have	7%	8%	9%	10%	5%
Not sure	58%	50%	53%	67%	60%
Electronic books (digital)					
Yes, library has these	32%	38%	39%	24%	31%
No, library does not have	8%	10%	8%	9%	7%
Not sure	60%	51%	53%	67%	62%
Online librarian question service					
Yes, library has these	27%	32%	30%	20%	27%
No, library does not have	10%	13%	11%	10%	9%
Not sure	63%	56%	59%	69%	64%

Source: *Perceptions of Libraries and Information Resources*, OCLC, 2005, question 850.

Varied source of information and entertainment in the form of books, periodicals, computers, audio and visual sources in the form of CDs, etc.

51-year-old from England

Source: *Perceptions of Libraries and Information Resources*, OCLC, 2005, question 807, "What is the first thing you think of when you think of a library?"

Overall, the level of awareness of electronic library resources among U.S. respondents varies with age. U.S. 18- to 24-year-olds are more aware of the library's electronic information sources compared to U.S. respondents 25 and older. Seventy-five percent of U.S. 18- to 24-year-olds indicate the library has an online catalog, as compared to 55 percent of U.S. respondents age 25-64. Eighty-one percent of U.S. 18- to 24-year-olds indicate the library has a Web site as compared to 57 percent of U.S. respondents age 25–64.

U.S. respondents 65 and older have the lowest level of awareness of library electronic resources. At least half of these respondents are not aware of seven of the eight electronic resources. It is worth reminding the reader that this survey was administered electronically and all respondents had access to the Internet.

Awareness of Library Resources—by Age of U.S. Respondent

Please indicate which electronic information sources your primary library has.

	Total U.S. Respondents	U.S. 14-17	U.S. 18-24	U.S. 25-64	U.S. 65+
Library Web site					
Yes, library has these	60%	73%	81%	57%	53%
No, library does not have	5%	8%	4%	5%	3%
Not sure	35%	19%	15%	39%	44%
Online library catalog					
Yes, library has these	58%	73%	75%	55%	47%
No, library does not have	5%	7%	7%	4%	3%
Not sure	38%	20%	18%	41%	50%
Online reference materials					
Yes, library has these	55%	68%	74%	52%	47%
No, library does not have	3%	7%	6%	2%	3%
Not sure	42%	25%	20%	45%	50%
Audiobooks (downloadable/digital)					
Yes, library has these	37%	37%	46%	36%	36%
No, library does not have	8%	19%	11%	7%	3%
Not sure	55%	44%	43%	57%	61%
Online databases					
Yes, library has these	39%	43%	58%	37%	34%
No, library does not have	4%	10%	6%	3%	3%
Not sure	57%	47%	36%	61%	63%
Electronic magazines/journals					
Yes, library has these	34%	36%	60%	31%	27%
No, library does not have	5%	20%	8%	4%	4%
Not sure	60%	44%	32%	66%	69%
Electronic books (digital)					
Yes, library has these	31%	28%	47%	30%	26%
No, library does not have	7%	22%	12%	5%	4%
Not sure	62%	50%	41%	66%	70%
Online librarian question service					
Yes, library has these	27%	26%	40%	24%	26%
No, library does not have	9%	26%	12%	8%	6%
Not sure	64%	48%	48%	68%	69%

advertise a bit more; until this survey I didn't really realize that a library *might have music, movies, and audio books to borrow.*

24-year-old from the United States

Source: *Perceptions of Libraries and Information Resources,* OCLC, 2005, question 1240, "If you could provide one piece of advice to your library, what would it be?"

Source: *Perceptions of Libraries and Information Resources,* OCLC, 2005, question 850.

College students across all geographic regions show high levels of awareness of library electronic resources across all eight categories and closely mirror the level of awareness indicated by U.S. 18- to 24-year-olds.

Just remember that

students are less informed

about the resources of the library than ever before because they are competing heavily with the Internet.

20-year-old from the United States

Source: *Perceptions of Libraries and Information Resources,* OCLC, 2005, question 1240, "If you could provide one piece of advice to your library, what would it be?"

Awareness of Library Resources—
by College Students across all Regions
Please indicate which electronic information sources your primary library has.

	Total Respondents	College Students
Library Web site		
Yes, library has these	61%	87%
No, library does not have	6%	5%
Not sure	33%	8%
Online library catalog		
Yes, library has these	60%	86%
No, library does not have	5%	6%
Not sure	35%	8%
Online reference materials		
Yes, library has these	55%	71%
No, library does not have	4%	5%
Not sure	41%	23%
Audiobooks (downloadable/digital)		
Yes, library has these	38%	43%
No, library does not have	8%	12%
Not sure	54%	44%
Online databases		
Yes, library has these	37%	62%
No, library does not have	5%	6%
Not sure	58%	31%
Electronic magazines/journals		
Yes, library has these	34%	62%
No, library does not have	7%	6%
Not sure	58%	32%
Electronic books (digital)		
Yes, library has these	32%	47%
No, library does not have	8%	11%
Not sure	60%	42%
Online librarian question service		
Yes, library has these	27%	45%
No, library does not have	10%	13%
Not sure	63%	42%

Source: *Perceptions of Libraries and Information Resources,* OCLC, 2005, question 850.

2.3 Using Library Electronic Information Resources

Regular use of library electronic resources is low, particularly among U.S. respondents age 65 and older.

Respondents' monthly use of online databases, electronic magazines/journals, online reference materials, electronic books, online librarian question services and audiobooks is less than 25 percent.

The data show distinctly different patterns of frequency of use by the age of U.S. respondents. U.S. respondents over the age of 65 are the most likely to report they *never have used* several electronic resource categories. Twenty-seven percent of these respondents *never have used* the online library catalog, 68 percent *never have used* electronic magazines/journals and 65 percent *never have used* online databases.

By comparison, U.S. 18- to 24-year-olds are the most likely of all U.S. respondents to have used the online library catalog with 71 percent reporting use *at least annually*. Fifty-seven percent in this age segment report they use online databases *at least annually*.

Use of library electronic resources among college students *at least annually* is 63 percent or higher in six of the eight categories. Eighty-six percent of college students report using the library Web site *at least annually* and 85 percent of them report using the online catalog *at least annually*. Over 50 percent use the library Web site *at least monthly*.

College students report low annual use of online librarian question services and audiobooks, 51 percent and 48 percent respectively.

68%

of U.S. respondents 65 and older have never used an electronic magazine/ journal.

68%

of U.S. youth age 14–17 use an online library catalog at least once a year.

86%

of college students use the library Web site at least annually.

Usage of Library Electronic Resources—
by Region of Respondent

Which of the following library electronic information sources have you ever
used from your primary library and how often do you use them?

Base: Respondents who indicated their primary library has the following electronic information
resources. Note: *At least monthly* is a rollup of daily, weekly and monthly.
At least annually is a rollup of several times a year and at least once a year.

	Total Respondents	Australia Singapore India	Canada	United Kingdom	United States
Online library catalog					
At least monthly	28%	37%	35%	17%	25%
At least annually	36%	36%	36%	36%	36%
Not even once a year	8%	4%	7%	8%	10%
Never have used	21%	12%	15%	29%	23%
Used to use, but no longer do	8%	11%	7%	10%	7%
Library Web site					
At least monthly	28%	38%	33%	17%	30%
At least annually	34%	32%	36%	34%	36%
Not even once a year	10%	7%	11%	6%	12%
Never have used	18%	16%	13%	34%	18%
Used to use, but no longer do	8%	7%	7%	10%	5%
Online reference materials					
At least monthly	17%	23%	27%	12%	14%
At least annually	35%	33%	33%	27%	34%
Not even once a year	8%	7%	8%	8%	11%
Never have used	29%	21%	24%	35%	32%
Used to use, but no longer do	11%	14%	9%	19%	9%
Electronic magazines/journals					
At least monthly	19%	31%	22%	20%	14%
At least annually	28%	24%	34%	23%	28%
Not even once a year	7%	5%	9%	4%	7%
Never have used	37%	30%	28%	43%	41%
Used to use, but no longer do	9%	10%	7%	10%	10%
Online databases					
At least monthly	18%	24%	25%	10%	15%
At least annually	28%	25%	30%	23%	27%
Not even once a year	12%	12%	12%	9%	13%
Never have used	35%	28%	29%	48%	37%
Used to use, but no longer do	8%	11%	5%	10%	7%
Online librarian question service					
At least monthly	11%	18%	13%	11%	9%
At least annually	30%	38%	31%	33%	25%
Not even once a year	12%	8%	12%	6%	15%
Never have used	38%	27%	41%	40%	41%
Used to use, but no longer do	8%	9%	3%	9%	9%
Electronic books (digital)					
At least monthly	13%	22%	13%	11%	10%
At least annually	17%	19%	22%	13%	17%
Not even once a year	10%	8%	12%	9%	11%
Never have used	54%	42%	51%	63%	57%
Used to use, but no longer do	5%	8%	3%	3%	6%
Audiobooks (downloadable/digital)					
At least monthly	8%	17%	8%	2%	7%
At least annually	17%	14%	20%	11%	18%
Not even once a year	9%	7%	14%	8%	8%
Never have used	60%	53%	51%	70%	62%
Used to use, but no longer do	7%	8%	7%	9%	6%

Source: *Perceptions of Libraries and Information Resources*, OCLC, 2005, question 855.

Usage of Library Electronic Resources—
by Age of U.S. Respondent

Which of the following library electronic information sources have you ever used from your primary library and how often do you use them?

Base: Respondents who indicated their primary library has the following electronic information resources. Note: *At least monthly* is a rollup of daily, weekly and monthly. *At least annually* is a rollup of several times a year and at least once a year.

	Total U.S. Respondents	U.S. 14-17	U.S. 18-24	U.S. 25-64	U.S. 65+
Online library catalog					
At least monthly	25%	34%	29%	23%	20%
At least annually	36%	34%	42%	34%	39%
Not even once a year	10%	14%	6%	11%	8%
Never have used	23%	16%	15%	25%	27%
Used to use, but no longer do	7%	4%	9%	7%	5%
Library Web site					
At least monthly	30%	29%	38%	29%	18%
At least annually	36%	39%	33%	36%	38%
Not even once a year	12%	14%	10%	12%	11%
Never have used	18%	14%	8%	18%	30%
Used to use, but no longer do	5%	5%	9%	5%	3%
Online reference materials					
At least monthly	14%	22%	18%	13%	3%
At least annually	34%	43%	45%	31%	28%
Not even once a year	11%	11%	11%	10%	13%
Never have used	32%	20%	20%	34%	46%
Used to use, but no longer do	9%	4%	7%	10%	9%
Electronic magazines/journals					
At least monthly	14%	26%	22%	12%	3%
At least annually	28%	20%	41%	27%	13%
Not even once a year	7%	14%	6%	7%	10%
Never have used	41%	34%	27%	41%	68%
Used to use, but no longer do	10%	6%	6%	13%	5%
Online databases					
At least monthly	15%	23%	23%	15%	1%
At least annually	27%	31%	34%	27%	19%
Not even once a year	13%	16%	10%	14%	9%
Never have used	37%	27%	25%	36%	65%
Used to use, but no longer do	7%	2%	8%	8%	4%
Online librarian question service					
At least monthly	9%	32%	17%	4%	5%
At least annually	25%	24%	26%	26%	28%
Not even once a year	15%	11%	10%	16%	20%
Never have used	41%	30%	41%	43%	39%
Used to use, but no longer do	9%	2%	6%	11%	8%
Electronic books (digital)					
At least monthly	10%	24%	19%	7%	3%
At least annually	17%	14%	25%	14%	20%
Not even once a year	11%	9%	13%	10%	12%
Never have used	57%	48%	40%	62%	61%
Used to use, but no longer do	6%	4%	3%	7%	4%
Audiobooks (downloadable/digital)					
At least monthly	7%	22%	8%	3%	6%
At least annually	18%	9%	19%	20%	13%
Not even once a year	8%	12%	10%	8%	6%
Never have used	62%	52%	60%	62%	70%
Used to use, but no longer do	6%	4%	2%	8%	5%

Source: *Perceptions of Libraries and Information Resources*, OCLC, 2005, question 855.

When I think of the library, I think of an **abundance of information on all topics.** *I would rather research from a library or print source than the Internet.*

17-year-old from the United States

Source: *Perceptions of Libraries and Information Resources*, OCLC, 2005, question 807, "What is the first thing you think of when you think of a library?"

Usage of Library Electronic Resources—
by College Students across all Regions

Which of the following library electronic information sources have you ever
used from your primary library and how often do you use them?

Base: Respondents who indicated their libraries have the following electronic information resources.
Note: *At least monthly* is a rollup of daily, weekly and monthly. *At least annually* is a rollup
of several times a year and at least once a year.

	Total Respondents	College Students
Online library catalog		
At least monthly	28%	47%
At least annually	36%	38%
Not even once a year	8%	2%
Never have used	21%	10%
Used to use, but no longer do	8%	4%
Library Web site		
At least monthly	28%	56%
At least annually	34%	30%
Not even once a year	10%	6%
Never have used	18%	6%
Used to use, but no longer do	8%	2%
Online reference materials		
At least monthly	17%	38%
At least annually	35%	41%
Not even once a year	8%	4%
Never have used	29%	14%
Used to use, but no longer do	11%	3%
Electronic magazines/journals		
At least monthly	19%	49%
At least annually	28%	33%
Not even once a year	7%	3%
Never have used	37%	12%
Used to use, but no longer do	9%	3%
Online databases		
At least monthly	18%	42%
At least annually	28%	33%
Not even once a year	12%	7%
Never have used	35%	15%
Used to use, but no longer do	8%	2%
Online librarian question service		
At least monthly	11%	17%
At least annually	30%	34%
Not even once a year	12%	7%
Never have used	38%	41%
Used to use, but no longer do	8%	1%
Electronic books (digital)		
At least monthly	13%	34%
At least annually	17%	29%
Not even once a year	10%	10%
Never have used	54%	25%
Used to use, but no longer do	5%	2%
Audiobooks (downloadable/digital)		
At least monthly	8%	16%
At least annually	17%	32%
Not even once a year	9%	7%
Never have used	60%	40%
Used to use, but no longer do	7%	4%

Source: *Perceptions of Libraries and Information Resources*, OCLC, 2005, question 855.

Can be over-
whelming

*with all the different
ways there are to find
resource materials.
Does not contain
information that can
be found on a website.*

28-year-old from Canada

Source: *Perceptions of Libraries and
Information Resources*, OCLC, 2005, question 812b, "Please list two negative associations with the library."

2.4 Seeking Assistance in Using Library Resources

Most respondents do not seek assistance when using library electronic resources.

Most respondents indicated they have not sought help (64 percent) when using library resources. Respondents from the U.K. are least likely to seek help at 25 percent, and respondents from the Australia/Singapore/India regions are the most likely to seek help at 44 percent.

Assistance in Using the Library—by Region of Respondent

Did you ever seek help when using your library's electronic resources or when searching for information at your library?
Base: Respondents who have used the library, either walk-in or online.

	Total Respondents	Australia Singapore India	Canada	United Kingdom	United States
Yes, have sought help when using library's electronic resources or searching at library	36%	44%	39%	25%	35%
No	64%	56%	61%	75%	65%

Source: *Perceptions of Libraries and Information Resources*, OCLC, 2005, question 1035.

Responses indicate little variability across age groups when seeking help with using library resources. Forty-one percent of U.S. 14- to 17-year-olds have sought help and 41 percent of U.S. respondents 65 and older have sought help. U.S. 25- to 64-year-olds are the least likely to seek assistance at 33 percent.

Assistance in Using the Library—by Age of U.S. Respondent

Did you ever seek help when using your library's electronic resources or when searching for information at your library?
Base: Respondents who have used the library, either walk-in or online.

	Total U.S. Respondents	U.S. 14-17	U.S. 18-24	U.S. 25-64	U.S. 65+
Yes, have sought help when using library's electronic resources or searching at library	35%	41%	40%	33%	41%
No	65%	59%	60%	67%	59%

Source: *Perceptions of Libraries and Information Resources*, OCLC, 2005, question 1035.

To have the resources made easier for people to use. I find that it is extremely **hard to find** *what you are looking for* **without** *the assistance of the* **librarian.**

28-year-old from Canada

Source: *Perceptions of Libraries and Information Resources*, OCLC, 2005, question 1240, "If you could provide one piece of advice to your library, what would it be?"

College students are more likely than any other segment surveyed to seek help when using library resources. Even among this group, more than half responded they do not seek help.

Assistance in Using the Library—
by College Students across all Regions

Did you ever seek help when using your library's electronic resources
or when searching for information at your library?

Base: Respondents who have used the library, either walk-in or online.

	Total Respondents	College Students
Yes, have sought help when using library's electronic resources or searching at library	36%	46%
No	64%	54%

Source: *Perceptions of Libraries and Information Resources,* OCLC, 2005, question 1035.

Sources of Help at the Library

When respondents seek help at the library,
librarians are the clear choice.

Thirty-six percent of total respondents indicated they have sought help using library resources. Overwhelmingly, respondents from all geographic regions and across U.S. age groups indicate the librarian is the first choice when seeking assistance at the library.

First Source of
Help at the Library—
by Total Respondents

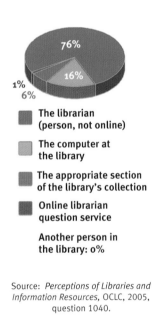

The librarian (person, not online)

The computer at the library

The appropriate section of the library's collection

Online librarian question service

Another person in the library: 0%

Source: *Perceptions of Libraries and Information Resources,* OCLC, 2005, question 1040.

*First Source of Help at the Library—*by Region of Respondent

What is the first source you typically go to for help with your problem?

Base: Respondents who sought help at the library.

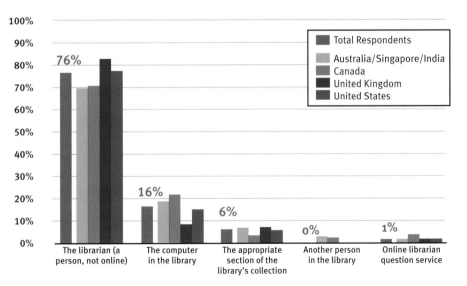

Source: *Perceptions of Libraries and Information Resources,* OCLC, 2005, question 1040.

2.5 Familiarity with the Library Web Site

Overall, not knowing the Web site exists is the main reason respondents do not use the library Web site. U.S. youth and young adults ages 14–24 indicate that they do not use the library Web site because other sites have better information.

As library Web sites are the main point of access to libraries' catalogs and resources, survey respondents were asked specifically about their familiarity with library Web sites. In Section 1.2 we reported that 46 percent of all respondents are *extremely familiar* or *very familiar* with the library and 17 percent of all respondents are *extremely familiar* or *very familiar* with the online library. In Part 2.3, we reported that 18 percent of respondents *never have used* a library Web site.

For respondents who reported they have never visited an online library Web site, "I did not know the Web site existed/does not exist" is the primary reason cited for lack of use. Fifty-five percent report they did not know the library Web site exists or say it does not exist. Lack of awareness is highest among respondents from the U.K. and lowest among Canadian respondents.

To bring out a library website
with a whole lot of information...
27-year-old from India

Source: *Perceptions of Libraries and Information Resources,* OCLC, 2005, question 1240, "If you could provide one piece of advice to your library, what would it be?"

Reasons for Never Using the Online Library Web Site— by Region of Respondent

Why haven't you ever used the online library Web site?
Base: Respondents who indicated they do not visit the library online.

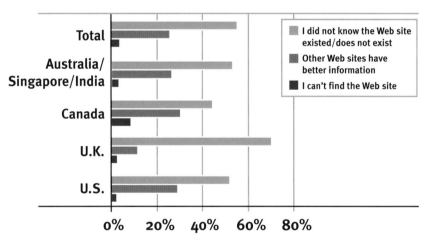

Legend:
- I did not know the Web site existed/does not exist
- Other Web sites have better information
- I can't find the Web site

Source: *Perceptions of Libraries and Information Resources,* OCLC, 2005, question 1090.

Of U.S. respondents who do not use the library Web site, younger respondents age 14 to 24 are more likely to respond that other Web sites have better information, despite data that show people in this age segment use library resources more than any other age segment (see Part 2.1).

Accessing the Library from the Web—
by College Students across all Regions

Have you ever started your search for information using a search engine and ended up at a library Web site?

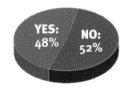

YES: 48% NO: 52%

If yes... did you use the library Web site?

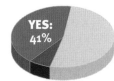

YES: 41%

NO: 7%

If yes, did the library Web site fulfill your information needs?

10%
27%
4%

27%: YES
but I also had to use other resources

10%: YES
the only resource I needed to use

4%: NO
not enough information available

Source: *Perceptions of Libraries and Information Resources,* OCLC, 2005, questions 1005, 1010, 1015.

Reasons for Never Using the Online Library Web Site—
by Age of U.S. Respondent

Why haven't you ever used the online library Web site?
Base: Respondents who indicated they do not visit the library online, question 815.

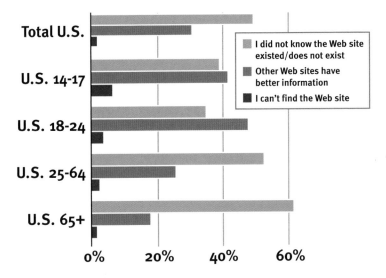

Total U.S.
U.S. 14-17
U.S. 18-24
U.S. 25-64
U.S. 65+

- I did not know the Web site existed/does not exist
- Other Web sites have better information
- I can't find the Web site

0%   20%   40%   60%

Source: *Perceptions of Libraries and Information Resources,* OCLC, 2005, question 1090.

Most college students know the library Web site exists. Those who do not use the library Web site respond that other Web sites have better information (44 percent).

Reasons for Never Using the Online Library Web Site—
by College Students across all Regions

Why haven't you ever used the online library Web site?
Base: Respondents who indicated they do not visit the library online, question 815.

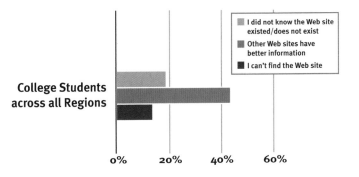

College Students across all Regions

- I did not know the Web site existed/does not exist
- Other Web sites have better information
- I can't find the Web site

0%   20%   40%   60%

Source: *Perceptions of Libraries and Information Resources,* OCLC, 2005, question 1090.

2.6 The Internet Search Engine, the Library and the Librarian

Libraries are seen as more trustworthy/credible and as providing more accurate information than search engines. Search engines are seen as more reliable, cost-effective, easy to use, convenient and fast.

Earlier in this report, we reviewed data that show search engines are the preferred starting place for survey respondents when searching for information. Respondents were asked to compare search engines and libraries against a set of seven performance attributes.

Libraries are rated higher than search engines along two of the seven performance attributes: *trustworthy/credible* sources of information and *accurate*. Sixty percent of all respondents indicate libraries are best described using the attribute *trustworthy/credible information,* and 56 percent indicate that libraries are best described using the attribute *accurate (quality information).*

Search engines are rated higher than libraries by respondents in five of the seven performance attributes: *reliability, cost effectiveness, ease of use, convenience* and *speed.* Eighty-five percent of respondents indicate search engines are best described by the attribute *ease of use,* 89 percent indicate search engines are best described by the attribute *convenient,* and 92 percent indicate search engines are best described by the attribute *fast.*

That librarians were

among the first

to move information electronically and to use computers effectively and efficiently to serve their customers.

73-year-old from the United States

Source: *Perceptions of Libraries and Information Resources,* OCLC, 2005, question 807, "What is the first thing you think of when you think of a library?"

Attributes of the Library and the Search Engine—
by Total Respondents

Comparing an online or physical library to a search engine, please indicate which source is best described by the following.

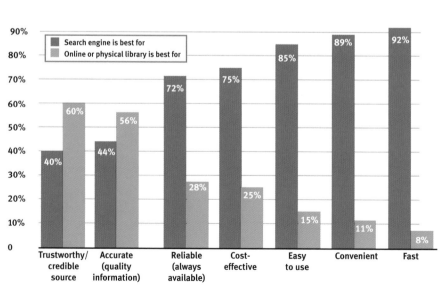

Source: *Perceptions of Libraries and Information Resources,* OCLC, 2005, question 1355.

Librarians and the Search Process

Respondents who have used a librarian for assistance agree that librarians add value to the search process.

In Part 2.4 we reviewed data reporting the percent of respondents who have sought help from a librarian when looking for information or using electronic information resources. Those survey respondents who have used the assistance of a librarian were also asked to rate the degree to which they agree or disagree that the librarian adds value to the search process.

Seventy-seven percent of all respondents *completely agree* or *agree* that the librarian adds value to the search process. Respondents from the U.K. are more likely to *completely agree* or *agree* the librarian adds value to the search process (at 95 percent).

Librarians Add Value to the Search Process— ## by Region of Respondent

Please rate the degree to which you agree or disagree that the librarian adds value to the information search process.
Base: Respondents who have used a librarian.

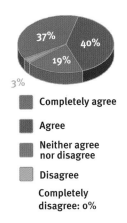

Librarian Adds Value to the Search Process— ## by Total Respondents

- Completely agree
- Agree
- Neither agree nor disagree
- Disagree
- Completely disagree: 0%

Source: *Perceptions of Libraries and Information Resources,* OCLC, 2005, question 1070.

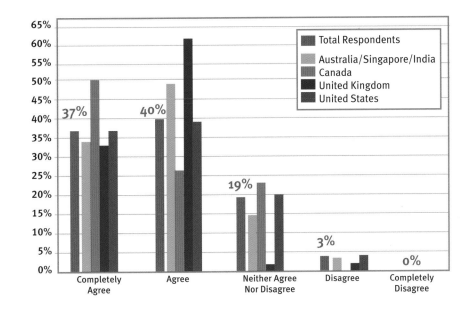

Source: *Perceptions of Libraries and Information Resources,* OCLC, 2005, question 1070.

U.S. respondents show variation according to age segment in how they rate the value the librarian adds to the search process. Overall, 76 percent of all U.S. respondents *completely agree* or *agree* that the librarian adds value. U.S. respondents 65 and older are much more likely to *completely agree* that the librarian adds value to the search process (70 percent) and U.S. 14- to 17-year-olds are the least likely to *completely agree* (22 percent).

Librarians Add Value to the Search Process—
by Age of U.S. Respondent

Please rate the degree to which you agree or disagree that the librarian adds value
to the information search process.

Base: Respondents who have used a librarian.

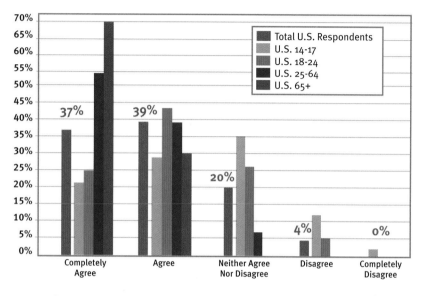

Legend:
- Total U.S. Respondents
- U.S. 14-17
- U.S. 18-24
- U.S. 25-64
- U.S. 65+

Source: *Perceptions of Libraries and Information Resources,* OCLC, 2005, question 1070.

Librarians Add Value to the Search Process—
by College Students across all Regions

Please rate the degree to which you agree or disagree that the librarian adds
value to the information search process.

Base: Respondents who have used a librarian.

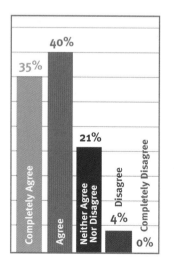

Source: *Perceptions of Libraries and Information Resources,* OCLC, 2005, question 1070.

They have what I need, or can get it. *Wonderfully helpful librarians*

60-year-old from the United States

Source: *Perceptions of Libraries and Information Resources,* OCLC, 2005, question 812a, "Please list two positive associations with the library."

Comparing Assistance—Search Engines and Librarians

Respondents who indicated they have used a search engine to assist in searching for information and who also indicated they have sought assistance from a librarian in the process of using library electronic resources or in searching for information were then asked to compare that assistance. Forty-three percent of all respondents indicate the assistance they received from a librarian was the same as the assistance provided by a search engine. U.S. respondents are the most likely to indicate *assistance from a librarian was better* than that of a search engine, with respondents from the Australia/Singapore/India regions being the least likely.

43%

indicate that assistance received from a librarian was the same as the assistance received from search engines.

Assistance from Search Engines and Librarians— by Region of Respondent

Please compare the assistance you received from a librarian to that of the assistance from a search engine on a 5-point scale.

Base: Respondents who have used a librarian and a search engine.

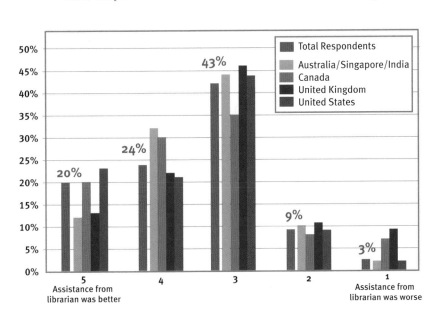

Source: *Perceptions of Libraries and Information Resources*, OCLC, 2005, question 1065.

Satisfaction with Search Engines and Librarians

Quality and quantity of information are top determinants of a satisfactory information search.

Survey respondents who indicated they have used the assistance of a librarian and a search engine were asked to indicate their levels of satisfaction with the information provided, the quantity of information received, the speed with which the search was conducted, and their overall search experience.

Satisfaction with the overall experience of searching has a strong correlation to the quality and quantity of information returned in the search process. There is also a moderate correlation between the overall experience of using a search engine and the speed of conducting the search. These correlations indicate that the attributes of quality, quantity and speed are contributing factors to respondents' *overall experience* rating.

The *overall experience* of using the assistance of a librarian also has strong correlations with the responses for quality and quantity of information provided and moderate correlation between overall experience and speed of conducting the search.

Tables detailing data for responses by region, U.S. age, college students and library card holders across all regions are included in Appendix A.

Satisfaction with the Librarian and the Search Engine—
by Total Respondents

Based on the most recent search you conducted through [search engine used most recently], how satisfied were you in each of the following areas?

Base: Respondents who have used a search engine.

Based on your most recent experience seeking assistance from a librarian for help with a search or locating information, how satisfied were you in each of the following areas?

Base: Respondents who have used a librarian.

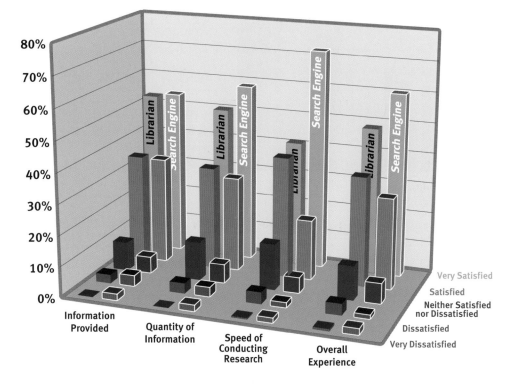

Source: *Perceptions of Libraries and Information Resources,* OCLC, 2005, questions 665 and 1050.

Satisfaction with the Information Provided

Librarians and search engines both provide quality information.

Eighty-eight percent of survey respondents indicated they were *very satisfied* or *satisfied* with the information provided from their most recent search conducted with the assistance of a librarian. Eighty-nine percent indicated they were *very satisfied* or *satisfied* with the information provided from their most recent search using a search engine. Very few (less than 8 percent) respondents were dissatisfied with the information received during their most recent information search.

very helpful,

friendly, knowledgeable, resourceful, easy to use, always available, free

37-year-old from Canada

Source: *Perceptions of Libraries and Information Resources*, OCLC, 2005, question 807, "What is the first thing you think of when you think of a library?"

Satisfaction with the Information Provided—
by Total Respondents

Based on the most recent search you conducted through [search engine used most recently], how satisfied were you with the information provided?
Base: Respondents who have used a search engine.

Based on your most recent experience seeking assistance from a librarian for help with a search or locating information, how satisfied were you with the information provided?
Base: Respondents who have used a librarian.

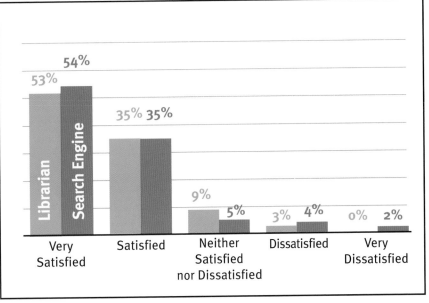

Source: *Perceptions of Libraries and Information Resources*, OCLC, 2005, questions 665 and 1050.

Satisfaction with the Quantity of Information Provided

Respondents are slightly more satisfied with the quantity of information provided by search engines than by librarians.

Eighty-four percent of respondents indicated they were *very satisfied* or *satisfied* with the quantity of information provided from their most recent search using the assistance of a librarian. Eighty-nine percent of respondents indicated they were *very satisfied* or *satisfied* with the amount of information provided in their most recent search using a search engine.

Satisfaction with the Quantity of Information Provided— by Total Respondents

Based on the most recent search you conducted through [search engine used most recently], how satisfied were you with the quantity of information provided?
Base: Respondents who have used a search engine.

Based on your most recent experience seeking assistance from a librarian for help with a search or locating information, how satisfied were you with the quantity of information provided?
Base: Respondents who have used a librarian.

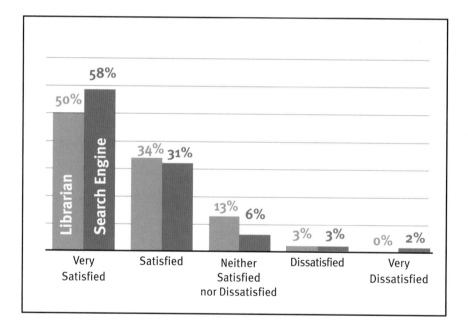

Source: *Perceptions of Libraries and Information Resources*, OCLC, 2005, questions 665 and 1050.

there is no toilet in my library so getting information **must be quick** *there needs to be more seats for the disabled*

57-year-old from England

Source: *Perceptions of Libraries and Information Resources*, OCLC, 2005, question 812b, "Please list two negative associations with the library."

Satisfaction with the Speed of Conducting the Search

Respondents are significantly more satisfied with the speed of conducting the search using search engines.

Satisfaction with the speed of conducting the search is the attribute for which there is the largest difference between a search engine and a librarian. Seventy-two percent of respondents were *very satisfied* with the speed of conducting research using a search engine, while 41 percent of respondents were *very satisfied* with the speed of conducting research with a librarian.

Satisfaction with the Speed of Conducting the Search— by Total Respondents

Based on the most recent search you conducted through [search engine used most recently], how satisfied were you with the speed of conducting the search?
Base: Respondents who have used a search engine.

Based on your most recent experience seeking assistance from a librarian for help with a search or locating information, how satisfied were you with the speed of conducting the search?
Base: Respondents who have used a librarian.

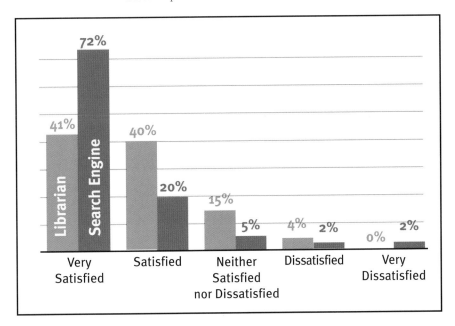

Source: *Perceptions of Libraries and Information Resources*, OCLC, 2005, questions 665 and 1050.

Satisfaction with the Overall Experience

Overall, more respondents are very satisfied with searches using search engines than they are with librarian-assisted searches.

Ninety percent of respondents were satisfied *(very satisfied* or *satisfied)* with the overall experience of using a search engine. Sixty percent of respondents were *very satisfied* with the overall experience of using a search engine compared to 48 percent of respondents who were *very satisfied* with the overall experience of using the assistance of a librarian.

If it just provides internet services, I can get that at home.

Needs to advertise/ inform

that it has access to all of the most up-to-date reliable research sources or can get them easily.

40-year-old from Canada

Source: *Perceptions of Libraries and Information Resources*, OCLC, 2005, question 1240, "If you could provide one piece of advice to your library, what would it be?"

Satisfaction with the Overall Experience—
by Total Respondents

Based on the most recent search you conducted through [search engine used most recently], how satisfied were you with the overall experience?

Base: Respondents who have used a search engine.

Based on your most recent experience seeking assistance from a librarian for help with a search or locating information, how satisfied were you with the overall experience?

Base: Respondents who have used a librarian.

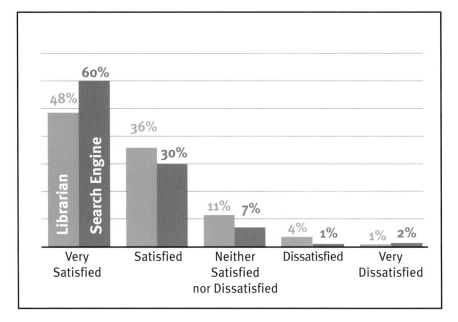

Source: *Perceptions of Libraries and Information Resources*, OCLC, 2005, questions 665 and 1050.

2.7 Keeping Up-to-Date with Library Resources

Almost half of all respondents keep up with resources available at the library by calling or coming into the library. One-third do not keep up with library resources.

Forty-eight percent of all respondents indicate they *call or walk in the library* to keep current with the resources of the library. Responses across geographic regions are relatively consistent. Twenty-five percent of all respondents keep current by using a *library Web site*, and 33 percent indicate they do not keep up with resources available at the library.

Keeping Up-to-Date with Library Resources— by Region of Respondent

How do you typically keep abreast of the resources available to you at your library?
(Select all that apply.)

	Total Respondents	Australia Singapore India	Canada	United Kingdom	United States
Call or walk in the library	48%	53%	53%	47%	46%
I don't keep up with resources available	33%	26%	28%	39%	35%
Library Web site	25%	32%	33%	12%	24%
Point of use materials (signs/fliers/posters at the library)	22%	23%	28%	20%	21%
Community/local paper	20%	24%	23%	18%	19%
Friends/neighbors/relatives	18%	19%	22%	10%	18%
E-mail lists	10%	18%	12%	7%	8%
School bulletin boards	6%	6%	9%	4%	6%

Source: *Perceptions of Libraries and Information Resources*, OCLC, 2005, question 1215.

advertise more

to the public in the local papers

46-year-old from England

Source: *Perceptions of Libraries and Information Resources*, OCLC, 2005, question 1240, "If you could provide one piece of advice to your library, what would it be?"

U.S. respondents keep up-to-date with library resources differently across age groups. Those 65 and older are more likely than other U.S. age segments to *call or walk in the library* (48 percent) or reference a *community or local paper* (37 percent). Only 19 percent indicate they keep current by using the *library Web site*. Thirty-nine percent of U.S. 18- to 24-year-olds indicate they *call or walk in the library*. Only 9 percent indicate they reference a *community or local paper* to keep up-to-date with library resources compared to 32 percent of this age segment who use the *library Web site* to keep up-to-date.

College students use both the *library Web site* and library visits to keep up-to-date with library resources.

Keeping Up-to-Date on Library Resources—
by Age of U.S. Respondent

How do you typically keep abreast of the resources available to you at your library? (Select all that apply.)

	Total U.S. Respondents	U.S. 14-17	U.S. 18-24	U.S. 25-64	U.S. 65+
Call or walk in the library	46%	40%	39%	47%	48%
I don't keep up with resources available	35%	36%	36%	35%	32%
Library Web site	24%	19%	32%	24%	19%
Point of use materials (signs/fliers/posters at the library)	21%	15%	24%	21%	20%
Community/local paper	19%	5%	9%	18%	37%
Friends/neighbors/relatives	18%	18%	20%	18%	18%
E-mail lists	8%	7%	11%	8%	6%
School bulletin boards	6%	15%	15%	5%	0%

Source: *Perceptions of Libraries and Information Resources*, OCLC, 2005, question 1215.

I would suggest the library

reach out to teens

and 20 somethings. They are the group that uses the library least.

24-year-old from the United States

Source: *Perceptions of Libraries and Information Resources*, OCLC, 2005, question 1240, "If you could provide one piece of advice to your library, what would it be?"

Keeping Up-to-Date on Library Resources—
by College Students across all Regions

How do you typically keep abreast of the resources available to you at your library? (Select all that apply.)

	Total Respondents	College Students
Call or walk in the library	48%	48%
I don't keep up with resources available	33%	26%
Library Web site	25%	49%
Point of use materials (signs/fliers/posters at the library)	22%	25%
Community/local paper	20%	9%
Friends/neighbors/relatives	18%	18%
E-mail lists	10%	19%
School bulletin boards	6%	21%

Source: *Perceptions of Libraries and Information Resources*, OCLC, 2005, question 1215.

Across all geographic regions, 58 percent of library card holders *call or walk in the library* as their primary means of keeping abreast of available library resources as compared to 21 percent of non-card holders. Fifty-eight percent of non-card holders indicate that they *do not keep up with resources available*, compared to 23 percent of library card holders.

Keeping Up-to-Date on Library Resources—
by Library Card Holder Status across all Regions

How do you typically keep abreast of the resources available
to you at your library? (Select all that apply.)

58%

of non-card holders don't keep abreast of library resources.

	Total Respondents	Library Card Holders	Non-Card Holders
Call or walk in the library	48%	58%	21%
I don't keep up with resources available	33%	23%	58%
Library Web site	25%	31%	7%
Point of use materials (signs/fliers/posters at the library)	22%	27%	10%
Community/local paper	20%	22%	14%
Friends/neighbors/relatives	18%	18%	16%
E-mail lists	10%	11%	8%
School bulletin boards	6%	7%	4%

Source: *Perceptions of Libraries and Information Resources*, OCLC, 2005, question 1215.

Part 3: The Library Brand

"Books" is the library brand.

In Parts 1 and 2 of this report, we reviewed data related to respondents' use of libraries and their familiarity with and favorability toward a variety of information sources, including libraries and their resources. We reviewed the frequency of use of library services, how respondents keep up-to-date with library services and respondents' satisfaction levels with those services.

In Part 3, we move from reviewing usage and familiarity of information sources to reporting responses related to perceptions and trust. Ubiquitous access to content is in its infancy and there is much to learn about how information consumers make choices and form preferences about electronic resources and services. How do information consumers assess and value electronic information? What, and who, do they trust? What mindshare does the "Library" hold compared to other information resources and services available to those with access to the Internet? The survey data provide some insight.

Information consumers are looking for "worthwhile" information.

Respondents were asked to rate the specific criteria they used to evaluate and verify electronic resources. The top three evaluation criteria used by respondents are that the source *provides worthwhile information,* that it *provides free information* and that it *provides credible/trustworthy information.*

Respondents rely on themselves to judge if an electronic source is trustworthy. Common sense and personal knowledge are the top verification criteria. Respondents also verify information trustworthiness based on *reputation of the company* and by *finding the information on multiple sites/cross-referencing.* Respondents believe free information is trustworthy and overwhelmingly do not trust information more if they have to pay for it. Few have paid for information.

Information consumers trust information from both libraries and search engines.

We explored the question of product "fit" by asking respondents to tell us how well they felt different information sources fit with their lifestyle. Ease of product use and consumption or "fit" is often a key driver of both current and future use. Respondents feel search engines are a perfect fit with their lifestyle. Libraries fit but are not a perfect fit.

We examined respondents' perceptions of the library and library information resources by asking an open-ended question about top-of-mind associations with libraries and positive and negative associations. Across all regions surveyed, respondents associate libraries first and foremost with "books." There is no runner-up. Respondents provided thousands of positive and negative associations about libraries. Overall, respondents provided more positive than negative associations. Top positive associations are related to library products—books, materials, computers, etc. The majority of negative associations were also related to products and offerings, followed by facilities.

Respondents were asked what they felt was the "main purpose of the library." While about a third of respondents indicated they felt the main purpose of the library is "books," the majority of respondents (53 percent) feel that the library's main purpose is "information."

3.1 The Value of Electronic Information Resources

"Provides worthwhile information" is the top criterion respondents use when selecting electronic information. "Free" is also an important factor.

Respondents use multiple criteria to determine the value of electronic information sources. Contrary to what is often attributed as the primary benefit of digital information access, speed of information delivery is not the most critical factor respondents use to evaluate electronic information resources. Three criteria were selected more frequently than speed. Seventy-seven percent of total respondents typically select an information source based on whether the source *provides worthwhile information*. Respondents also base their decision on if the source *provides free information* (72 percent) and *ease of use* (65 percent).

Recommendations are used by just 28 percent of respondents as a criterion for selecting an electronic information source.

to provide a

free community resource centre

40-year-old from Australia

Source: *Perceptions of Libraries and Information Resources,* OCLC, 2005, question 810, "What do you feel is the main purpose of the library?"

Evaluating Information Sources—by Total Respondents

How do you decide which electronic information source to use?
(Select all that apply.)

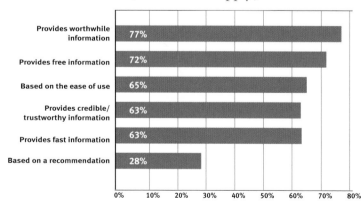

Provides worthwhile information	77%
Provides free information	72%
Based on the ease of use	65%
Provides credible/ trustworthy information	63%
Provides fast information	63%
Based on a recommendation	28%

Source: *Perceptions of Libraries and Information Resources,* OCLC, 2005, question 715.

Provides worthwhile information is the top criterion to evaluate an information source for all regions surveyed except the U.K., where *provides free information* is the most frequently selected criterion (70 percent).

Evaluating Information Sources—by Region of Respondent

How do you decide which electronic information source to use?
(Select all that apply.)

	Total Respondents	Australia Singapore India	Canada	United Kingdom	United States
Provides worthwhile information	77%	82%	84%	67%	76%
Provides free information	72%	73%	69%	70%	73%
Based on the ease of use	65%	68%	62%	62%	66%
Provides credible/trustworthy information	63%	66%	67%	51%	65%
Provides fast information	63%	69%	62%	64%	61%
Based on a recommendation	28%	34%	30%	26%	26%

Source: *Perceptions of Libraries and Information Resources*, OCLC, 2005, question 715.

Provides worthwhile information is also the highest-rated factor in determining the value of electronic resources across U.S. age groups. The relative importance of *ease of use* as a decision factor increases with age and was cited as a selection criterion slightly more often than credible/trustworthy information for respondents age 25 and over.

Evaluating Information Sources—by Age of U.S. Respondent

How do you decide which electronic information source to use?
(Select all that apply.)

	Total U.S. Respondents	U.S. 14-17	U.S. 18-24	U.S. 25-64	U.S. 65+
Provides worthwhile information	76%	71%	77%	77%	74%
Provides free information	73%	67%	74%	73%	73%
Based on the ease of use	66%	58%	62%	68%	68%
Provides credible/trustworthy information	65%	56%	66%	65%	67%
Provides fast information	61%	61%	60%	61%	58%
Based on a recommendation	26%	22%	30%	27%	22%

Source: *Perceptions of Libraries and Information Resources*, OCLC, 2005, question 715.

Evaluating Information Sources— by College Students across all Regions

How do you decide which electronic information source to use?
(Select all that apply.)

	Total Respondents	College Students
Provides worthwhile information	77%	82%
Provides free information	72%	73%
Based on the ease of use	65%	64%
Provides credible/trustworthy information	63%	73%
Provides fast information	63%	62%
Based on a recommendation	28%	36%

Source: *Perceptions of Libraries and Information Resources*, OCLC, 2005, question 715.

3.2 Judging the Trustworthiness of Information

Respondents rely on themselves to judge if electronic information is trustworthy.

Respondents indicate they use a variety of criteria to select an electronic resource. As noted in Part 3.1, 63 percent of all respondents indicate that *provide credible, trustworthy information* is a key evaluation criterion.

To understand more about the criteria respondents use to judge the trustworthiness of electronic information, respondents who selected this criterion were asked to indicate how they judge trustworthiness. Eighty-six percent of all respondents indicate they use *personal knowledge/common sense* to determine trustworthiness. Three other criteria were selected by over half of respondents. These include the *reputation of the company/organization*, the ability to *find the information on multiple sites/cross-reference* and *recommendation from a trusted source*. Only 1 percent of respondents indicate that electronic information is trustworthy *because it costs money*.

U.S. respondents age 14–24 use the *professional appearance of the site* to judge trustworthiness more than other U.S. age group, roughly twice as much as U.S. respondents age 25 and over.

College students rely on *personal knowledge/common sense* and the ability to *find the information on multiple sites/cross-reference* as their top methods of evaluating trustworthiness.

endless references
assistance in finding accurate information

25-year-old from Australia

Source: *Perceptions of Libraries and Information Resources*, OCLC, 2005, question 812a, "Please list two positive associations with the library."

Factors in Determining Trustworthiness of Information— by Region of Respondent

How do you judge if electronic information is trustworthy?
Base: Respondents selecting "provides credible/trustworthy information" in question 715.

	Total Respondents	Australia Singapore India	Canada	United Kingdom	United States
Based on personal knowledge/common sense	86%	89%	86%	86%	85%
Based on the reputation of the company/organization	75%	72%	86%	73%	73%
Find the information on multiple sites/cross-referencing	65%	62%	64%	57%	67%
Recommendation from a trusted source	59%	61%	72%	56%	55%
Based on the professional appearance of the site	28%	30%	28%	21%	28%
Based on the author	26%	26%	35%	15%	26%
The fact that it costs money	1%	1%	2%	1%	1%
Other	3%	4%	4%	1%	2%

Source: *Perceptions of Libraries and Information Resources*, OCLC, 2005, question 725.

Factors in Determining Trustworthiness of Information—
by Age of U.S. Respondent

How do you judge if electronic information is trustworthy?

Base: Respondents selecting "provides credible/trustworthy information" in question 715.

	Total U.S. Respondents	U.S. 14-17	U.S. 18-24	U.S. 25-64	U.S. 65+
Based on personal knowledge/common sense	85%	83%	78%	88%	82%
Based on the reputation of the company/organization	73%	79%	64%	75%	72%
Find the information on multiple sites/cross-referencing	67%	72%	69%	69%	57%
Recommendation from a trusted source	55%	59%	60%	55%	51%
Based on the professional appearance of the site	28%	46%	45%	26%	16%
Based on the author	26%	29%	34%	25%	20%
The fact that it costs money	1%	3%	1%	0%	0%
Other	2%	3%	4%	2%	1%

Source: *Perceptions of Libraries and Information Resources*, OCLC, 2005, question 725.

Factors in Determining Trustworthiness of Information—
by College Students across all Regions

How do you judge if electronic information is trustworthy?

Base: Respondents selecting "provides credible/trustworthy information" in question 715.

	Total Respondents	College Students
Based on personal knowledge/common sense	86%	83%
Based on the reputation of the company/organization	75%	69%
Find the information on multiple sites/cross-referencing	65%	71%
Recommendation from a trusted source	59%	68%
Based on the professional appearance of the site	28%	42%
Based on the author	26%	46%
The fact that it costs money	1%	2%
Other	3%	3%

Source: *Perceptions of Libraries and Information Resources*, OCLC, 2005, question 725.

3.3 Trust in Library Resources and Search Engines

Libraries and search engines both provide trustworthy information.

Sixty-nine percent of respondents feel that information from a search engine is at the same level of trustworthiness as a library information source. Twenty-two percent believe that information received from a library is more trustworthy than information received from a search engine and 9 percent indicated they believe it is less trustworthy than search engines.

Ask Jeeves, Google and Yahoo! all have approximately the same relative level of trustworthiness compared to a library's information sources. Note that even though use varies considerably among brands of search engines (see Part 1.2), the level of trustworthiness of the three most used brands is nearly equal.

Respondents from the U.K. and the U.S. are the most likely to view the trustworthiness of libraries and search engines similarly. Canadian respondents indicated the highest level of trust in libraries.

Trustworthiness of Library Sources vs. Search Engines— by Total Respondents

Thinking about your usage of your library and the things you like and dislike about it, is the information you get from the library sources more or less trustworthy compared to the information you can get from search engines?

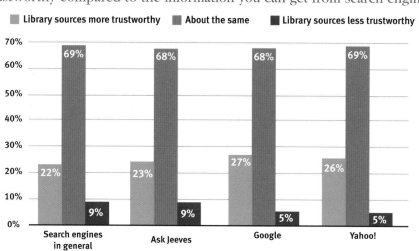

Source: *Perceptions of Libraries and Information Resources,* OCLC, 2005, question 1205.

69%

feel libraries and search engines provide the same level of trustworthiness.

Trustworthiness of Library Sources vs. Search Engines— by Region of Respondent

Thinking about your usage of your library and the things you like and dislike about it, is the information you get from the library sources more or less trustworthy compared to the information you can get from search engines?

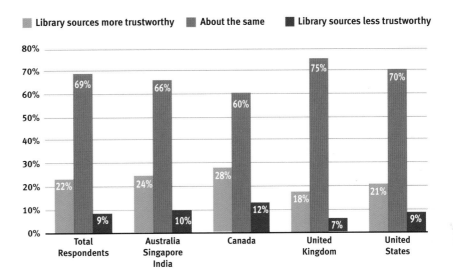

Source: *Perceptions of Libraries and Information Resources,* OCLC, 2005, question 1205.

Results indicate that younger U.S. respondents (14- to 24-year-olds) were significantly more likely to respond that the library resources are *less trustworthy* than search engines among all U.S. age groups. The U.S. 25- to 64-year-olds and U.S. respondents 65 and older who rate the library sources *more trustworthy* than search engines do so at a margin of about three to one over those who rate it *less trustworthy.*

Although search engines have been in general use for a relatively short period of time, over 70 percent of all U.S. respondents over the age of 25, including those over 65, believe they provide the same level of trustworthiness as information providers that libraries do.

Trustworthiness of Library Sources vs. Search Engines— by Age of U.S. Respondent

Thinking about your usage of your library and the things you like and dislike about it, is the information you get from the library sources more or less trustworthy compared to the information you can get from search engines?

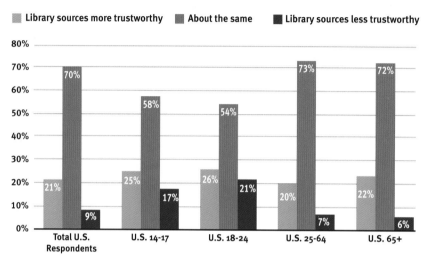

Source: *Perceptions of Libraries and Information Resources*, OCLC, 2005, question 1205.

Almost a third of college students indicate a higher level of trust in library resources than in search engines. Fifty-three percent rate search engines' information to be about the same level of trustworthiness as the libraries' sources. There is no significant difference in the attitudes toward trustworthiness of library card holders as compared to non-card holders.

Trustworthiness of Library Sources vs. Search Engines— by College Students, Library Card Holders and Non-Card Holders

Thinking about your usage of your library and the things you like and dislike about it, is the information you get from the library sources more or less trustworthy compared to the information you can get from search engines?

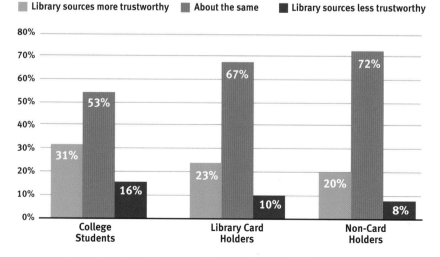

Source: *Perceptions of Libraries and Information Resources*, OCLC, 2005, question 1205.

> **A library is vital** in order to get information. I trust and love libraries. The web cannot take over because **the library is sacred.**
>
> **18-year-old from the United States**

Source: *Perceptions of Libraries and Information Resources*, OCLC, 2005, question 810, "What do you feel is the main purpose of the library?"

3.4 Free vs. For-Fee Information

Respondents do not trust information they have to purchase more than free information.

The survey examined another aspect of trust by examining if respondents trust an electronic information source more if they have to pay for the information. Ninety-three percent of the total U.S. respondents said *No,* they do not trust the information more if they pay for it. This attitude was consistent across all geographic regions surveyed and library card holder status.

U.S. 14- to 17-year-olds are more likely than other U.S. age segments to trust an information source more if they have to pay for the information. Almost 20 percent of U.S. 14- to 17-year-olds indicate a higher trust level in an information source when there is a cost for the information.

Free vs. For-Fee Information— by Total Respondents

Would you trust an electronic information source more if you have to pay for the information compared to a free source?

No **Yes**

Source: *Perceptions of Libraries and Information Resources*, OCLC, 2005, question 755.

*Free vs. For-Fee Information—*by Region of Respondent

Would you trust an electronic information source more if you have to pay for the information compared to a free source?

	Total Respondents	Australia Singapore India	Canada	United Kingdom	United States
No	92%	88%	94%	88%	93%
Yes	8%	12%	6%	12%	7%

Source: *Perceptions of Libraries and Information Resources*, OCLC, 2005, question 755.

Free vs. For-Fee Information— by Age of U.S. Respondent

Would you trust an electronic information source more if you have to pay for the information compared to a free source?

	Total U.S. Respondents	U.S. 14-17	U.S. 18-24	U.S. 25-64	U.S. 65+
No	93%	81%	87%	95%	92%
Yes	7%	19%	13%	5%	8%

Source: *Perceptions of Libraries and Information Resources*, OCLC, 2005, question 755.

Free vs. For-Fee Information— by College Students across all Regions

Would you trust an electronic information source more if you have to pay for the information compared to a free source?

	Total Respondents	College Students
No	92%	90%
Yes	8%	10%

Source: *Perceptions of Libraries and Information Resources*, OCLC, 2005, question 755.

Free vs. For-Fee Information—
by Library Card Holders across all Regions

Would you trust an electronic information source more if you have to pay
for the information compared to a free source?

	Total Respondents	Library Card Holders	Non-Card Holders
No	92%	92%	90%
Yes	8%	8%	10%

Source: *Perceptions of Libraries and Information Resources*, OCLC, 2005, question 755.

Paying for Information via an Electronic Information Source

The majority of respondents have never paid for information.

The survey asked respondents to indicate if they have ever paid for information from
an electronic information source. Eighty-seven percent indicated they have not.

While few respondents have paid for information from an electronic information
source, of those who have, nearly a third or more have purchased a registration
to a Web site, a subscription or an article (51 percent, 38 percent and 26 percent,
respectively).

Free vs. For-Fee Information—
by Total Respondents

Have you ever paid for information from an electronic information source?
What did you buy?

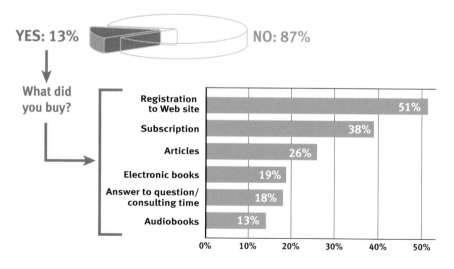

Source: *Perceptions of Libraries and Information Resources*, OCLC, 2005, questions 625 and 630.

Free information from a trusted source.

A large quantity of books to be read for enjoyment.

19-year-old from the United States

Source: *Perceptions of Libraries and Information Resources*, OCLC, 2005, question 812a, "Please list two positive associations with the library."

The survey also asked respondents who have purchased information from an electronic information source if the future frequency of purchasing would be more, less or about the same. Fifty-nine percent of the respondents report frequency will remain the same, 25 percent say frequency will be less and 16 percent say frequency will be more. Anticipated increased use of free information was generally consistent across all geographic regions and all U.S. age groups surveyed.

Information Purchases in the Future—
by Region of Respondent

Do you anticipate you will be paying more frequently, less frequently, or about the same frequency for electronic information in the future?

	Total Respondents	Australia Singapore India	Canada	United Kingdom	United States
More frequently	16%	17%	16%	15%	11%
About the same	59%	56%	57%	67%	54%
Less frequently	25%	27%	27%	19%	34%

Source: *Perceptions of Libraries and Information Resources,* OCLC, 2005, question 635.

Free vs. For-Fee Verbatim Comments

Would you trust an electronic information source more if you have to pay for the information compared to a free source?

Respondents provided 1,873 comments to an open-ended question asking why they would or would not trust an electronic source more if they had to pay for the information. Responses indicate a wide range of perceptions and expectations with regard to for-fee information, from an expectation that for-fee information is more likely to be trustworthy because it is likely more scrutinized prior to release, to opinions that because so much free information is readily available it is hard to justify any payment.

The traditional notion that higher price equals higher quality appears to not hold true for information as a commodity. There is a clear theme expressed through the comments that information should be free and available to all.

Note: All verbatim comments presented as entered by survey respondents, including spelling, grammatical and punctuation errors.

*If I knew that the source was reputable (e.g., New York Times)
it would probably be worth it.*

17-year-old from the United States

If you trust information from a free source why wouldn't you trust information from a source where you had to pay? Because I cross reference, I would only pay for information if I needed the extra data.

68-year-old from Australia

I also exercise my own judgement and cross referencing with friends and teachers. Having to pay for the information does not make the information more or less trust worthy.

33-year-old from Singapore

Because information should be free for everyone to know, I can very easily get in my car and drive to the library to see find the information without having to pay for it. Because you can get info from the library for free.

16-year-old from the United States

I would think it would be safe to assume that if you have to pay for something it would be trustworthy and true. The information being provided probably needs to meet certain criteria and costs them money; therefore they need to charge to release the information. Opposed to free information, anyone can provide information whether it's trustworthy or not without having to meet certain criteria.

24-year-old from the United States

Something paid for results in value.

Often free gets what one pays for.

48-year-old from Canada

Source: *Perceptions of Libraries and Information Resources,* OCLC, 2005, question 760, "Would you trust an electronic information source more if you have to pay for the information compared to a free source? Why is that?"

All my life before electronic info I was able to get info I needed without paying for it....

why start now?

78-year-old from the United States

Source: *Perceptions of Libraries and Information Resources,* OCLC, 2005, question 760, "Would you trust an electronic information source more if you have to pay for the information compared to a free source? Why is that?"

I do not think that I should have to pay for information that I can get freely from other sources on the internet or at the local library for free.

40-year-old from the United Kingdom

are you saying if information is free, it's not to be trusted!!!!!!!!

52-year-old from the United Kingdom

Too many free sources from free websites to libraries to radio to broadcast to get information, I think it would be almost impossible to justify paying for what so many sources offer for free both online and offline.

35-year-old from the United States

Would you trust my survey responses more if you had to pay me for it? :) Having to pay, while it psychologically leverages you to commit to the experience more, doesn't validate the veracity of the information gained through the transaction experience. The two things are independent.

38-year-old from Australia

3.5 Validating Information

Respondents most often cross-reference other Web sites to validate electronic information.

Sixty-five percent of respondents judge the trustworthiness of electronic information sources by cross-referencing to other sources (see Part 3.2).

The survey explored cross-referencing as a method of information validation. Survey respondents were given a list of possible cross-referencing sources and asked to select all that they use.

Over 80 percent of total respondents use *other Web sites with similar information* as a validation tool. *Print material* is selected as a cross-reference source by 68 percent of all respondents.

Librarians are rated as the least-used cross-referencing source for validation, at 16 percent of all respondents. Use of the librarian to validate electronic information was considerably higher for college students and U.S. youth. Twenty-six percent of U.S. 14- to 17-year-olds use *librarians* to validate information and 36 percent of college students use the librarian.

Looking and reading an entire book

takes too long

when the specific information can be gained online in a matter of minutes. Cross referencing takes a lot of time and effort.

38-year-old from the United States

Source: *Perceptions of Libraries and Information Resources*, OCLC, 2005, question 812b, "Please list two negative associations with the library."

Cross-referencing Sources to Validate Information— by Total Respondents

What other source(s) do you use to validate the information?
Base: Respondents selecting "find the information
on multiple sites/cross-referencing" in question 725.

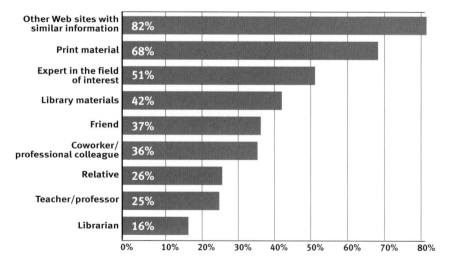

Source: *Perceptions of Libraries and Information Resources*, OCLC, 2005, question 735.

Regional differences were observed, although using *other Web sites with similar information* to validate information was the top choice across all geographic regions surveyed. Nine percent of respondents from the U.K. use a *teacher or professor* to validate information compared to 32 percent of Canadians and 25 percent of total respondents. U.S. respondents are least likely to use a librarian (14 percent).

The use of *library materials* as cross-referencing sources to validate information is relatively consistent across regions, ranging from roughly 40 to 50 percent. Again, the use of *library materials* as sources to validate information is higher among college students at 64 percent.

I need to go get a card! As it is a good place to cross reference items. I do enjoy reading book's!

70-year-old from the United States

Source: *Perceptions of Libraries and Information Resources,* OCLC, 2005, question 807, "What is the first thing you think of when you think of a library?"

Cross-referencing Sources to Validate Information— by Region of Respondent

What other source(s) do you use to validate the information?
Base: Respondents selecting "find the information on multiple sites/cross-referencing" in question 725.

	Total Respondents	Australia Singapore India	Canada	United Kingdom	United States
Other Web sites with similar information	82%	86%	78%	82%	82%
Print material	68%	68%	76%	53%	68%
Expert in the field of interest	51%	63%	54%	46%	48%
Library materials	42%	45%	48%	39%	40%
Friend	37%	46%	48%	39%	32%
Coworker/professional colleague	36%	38%	47%	39%	33%
Relative	26%	30%	35%	20%	24%
Teacher/professor	25%	28%	32%	9%	26%
Librarian	16%	19%	22%	15%	14%

Source: *Perceptions of Libraries and Information Resources,* OCLC, 2005, question 735.

Cross-referencing Sources to Validate Information— by Age of U.S. Respondent

What other source(s) do you use to validate the information?
Base: Respondents selecting "find the information on multiple sites/cross-referencing" in question 725.

	Total U.S. Respondents	U.S. 14-17	U.S. 18-24	U.S. 25-64	U.S. 65+
Other Web sites with similar information	82%	79%	78%	85%	75%
Print material	68%	63%	65%	70%	61%
Expert in the field of interest	48%	40%	51%	51%	36%
Library materials	40%	47%	58%	37%	36%
Friend	32%	54%	35%	29%	34%
Coworker/professional colleague	33%	10%	21%	41%	15%
Relative	24%	34%	33%	20%	29%
Teacher/professor	26%	70%	60%	16%	19%
Librarian	14%	26%	32%	10%	10%

Source: *Perceptions of Libraries and Information Resources,* OCLC, 2005, question 735.

Cross-referencing Sources to Validate Information—
by College Students across all Regions

What other source(s) do you use to validate the information?

Base: Respondents selecting "find the information on multiple sites/cross-referencing" in question 725.

	Total Respondents	College Students
Other Web sites with similar information	82%	80%
Print material	68%	76%
Expert in the field of interest	51%	59%
Library materials	42%	64%
Friend	37%	35%
Coworker/professional colleague	36%	37%
Relative	26%	29%
Teacher/professor	25%	78%
Librarian	16%	36%

Source: *Perceptions of Libraries and Information Resources*, OCLC, 2005, question 735.

Cross-referencing Sources to Validate Information—
by Library Card Holders across all Regions

What other source(s) do you use to validate the information?

Base: Respondents selecting "find the information on multiple sites/cross-referencing" in question 725.

	Total Respondents	Library Card Holders	Non- Card Holders
Other Web sites with similar information	82%	84%	76%
Print material	68%	72%	53%
Expert in the field of interest	51%	53%	43%
Library materials	42%	50%	13%
Friend	37%	37%	37%
Coworker/professional colleague	36%	37%	35%
Relative	26%	26%	27%
Teacher/professor	25%	30%	10%
Librarian	16%	19%	4%

Source: *Perceptions of Libraries and Information Resources*, OCLC, 2005, question 735.

Trusted Sources for Recommendations

Experts, other Web sites and print materials are the top trusted sources for validating information. Two percent of respondents consult librarians when seeking help from a trusted source.

While 65 percent of respondents judge the trustworthiness of electronic resources by *finding information on multiple sites/cross-referencing,* 59 percent of respondents indicate they use *recommendations from a trusted source.* We asked this subset of respondents to identify who or what is their most trusted source they typically use. Nine options were provided and respondents were asked to select one. Nineteen percent of respondents use an *expert in the field of interest* as the trusted source they typically use to help judge if electronic information is trustworthy. *Other Web sites with similar information* are used by 17 percent of respondents. *Librarians* were selected as a trusted source for validating information by 2 percent of respondents.

College students rely on their *teachers and professors* as trusted sources to validate information, more than any other source. Library card holders tend to show the smallest amount of variation among sources they trust to validate information.

Respondents use a wide range of trusted sources to validate electronic information and show regional differences. Twenty-three percent of respondents from the U.K. trust *coworkers,* which is double that of the 11 percent of total respondents. Conversely, only 9 percent of U.S. respondents use *coworkers* as sources of validation.

U.S. 14- to 17-year-olds name *teachers and professors* as their trusted sources to validate electronic information. Two percent of college students across all regions use *librarians* as their trusted source for validation. U.S. respondents age 65 and older use *experts, print materials* and *relatives* as their top trusted sources of validation for electronic information.

Trusted Sources for Validating Information— by Total Respondents

Who or what is that trusted source you most typically use?

Base: Respondents selecting "recommendation from a trusted source" in question 725.

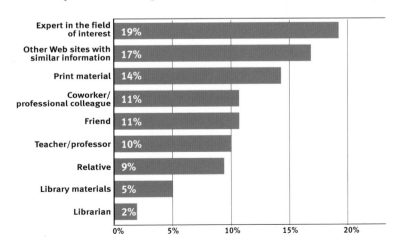

Source: *Perceptions of Libraries and Information Resources,* OCLC, 2005, question 745.

Trusted Sources for Validating Information—
by Region of Respondent

Who or what is that trusted source you most typically use?
Base: Respondents selecting "recommendation from a trusted source" in question 725.

	Total Respondents	Australia Singapore India	Canada	United Kingdom	United States
Expert in the field of interest	19%	23%	19%	15%	19%
Other Web sites with similar information	17%	18%	16%	14%	17%
Print material	14%	15%	8%	9%	16%
Friend	11%	13%	16%	10%	9%
Coworker/professional colleague	11%	11%	12%	23%	9%
Teacher/professor	10%	6%	11%	8%	11%
Relative	9%	6%	8%	10%	10%
Library materials	5%	5%	6%	5%	5%
Librarian	2%	2%	1%	4%	1%

Source: *Perceptions of Libraries and Information Resources*, OCLC, 2005, question 745.

Trusted Sources for Validating Information—
by Age of U.S. Respondent

Who or what is that trusted source you most typically use?
Base: Respondents selecting "recommendation from a trusted source" in question 725.

	Total U.S. Respondents	U.S. 14-17	U.S. 18-24	U.S. 25-64	U.S. 65+
Expert in the field of interest	19%	9%	4%	23%	20%
Other Web sites with similar information	17%	10%	13%	19%	12%
Print material	16%	14%	7%	17%	21%
Friend	9%	17%	8%	8%	10%
Coworker/professional colleague	9%	0%	4%	12%	4%
Teacher/professor	11%	33%	40%	4%	6%
Relative	10%	9%	10%	7%	21%
Library materials	5%	2%	10%	5%	1%
Librarian	1%	4%	2%	1%	1%

Source: *Perceptions of Libraries and Information Resources*, OCLC, 2005, question 745.

Trusted Sources for Validating Information—
by College Students across all Regions

Who or what is that trusted source you most typically use?
Base: Respondents selecting "recommendation from a trusted source" in question 725.

	Total Respondents	College Students
Expert in the field of interest	19%	9%
Other Web sites with similar information	17%	15%
Print material	14%	13%
Friend	11%	3%
Coworker/professional colleague	11%	2%
Teacher/professor	10%	45%
Relative	9%	4%
Library materials	5%	6%
Librarian	2%	2%

Source: *Perceptions of Libraries and Information Resources*, OCLC, 2005, question 745.

Unlimited resources and cross-reference abilities.

17-year-old from the United States

Source: *Perceptions of Libraries and Information Resources*, OCLC, 2005, question 812a, "Please list two positive associations with the library."

The trusted source most typically used to validate electronic information resources varied depending on whether the respondents are library card holders or not. Non-card holders select *coworkers* as their trusted source more often than library card holders do (21 percent compared to 9 percent.) Non-card holders typically do not select *library materials* or *librarians* as their trusted sources.

Trusted Sources for Validating Information— by Total Respondents, Library Card Holders and Non-Card Holders across all Regions

Who or what is that trusted source you most typically use?

Base: Respondents selecting "recommendation from a trusted source" in question 725.

	Total Respondents	Library Card Holders	Non-Card Holders
Expert in the field of interest	19%	18%	25%
Other Web sites with similar information	17%	16%	18%
Print material	14%	16%	6%
Friend	11%	10%	14%
Coworker/professional colleague	11%	9%	21%
Teacher/professor	10%	12%	3%
Relative	9%	8%	10%
Library materials	5%	6%	0%
Librarian	2%	2%	0%

Source: *Perceptions of Libraries and Information Resources*, OCLC, 2005, question 745.

3.6 Libraries—Positive and Negative Associations

"Books" and "information" are the highest positive associations with libraries. "Customer/User services" yielded the highest number of negative associations.

Survey respondents were asked to provide—in their own words—two positive and two negative associations about libraries. 3,034 respondents provided 5,271 positive comments (an average of 1.74 comments per respondent) and 2,985 respondents provided 4,793 negative comments (an average of 1.61 comments per respondent).

Verbatim responses were grouped into four categories: Products and Offerings, Customer/User Service, Staff and Facility/Environment. These primary categories were used to group both positive and negative associations. As the following graph indicates, respondents' positive and negative comments are matched across the four categories. Respondents had strong positive associations with books; respondents also had strong negative associations with books.

Overall, the positive associations of libraries for survey respondents are ones libraries have long been valued for: providing freely available materials and facilities that support individual inquiry. Many of the negative associations relate to the availability and conditions of the materials and facilities.

Over 3,100 positive associations with products and offerings were provided by respondents. This category yielded the most positive associations. Comments relating to products and offerings also were the most frequently cited negative associations, at 35 percent. The negative associations include unavailable or out-of-date items/information, unavailable or out-of-date computers and limited variety in the collection.

Other frequently cited negative associations relate to facilities and environment, at 26 percent. Most frequently cited were noise levels (too loud or too quiet), being too crowded, limited parking and the need to travel to the library.

Negative customer/user service associations outnumber positive customer/user service associations. Limited library hours were the most cited negative association. Fees, inflexible return policies and other policy concerns were cited frequently.

U.S. respondents over age 65 had the strongest positive associations with library staff among U.S. respondents, while young people in the U.S. age 14–17 had the strongest negative associations with library staff.

For the full data tables, please see Appendix A.

when they don't have the book you need

that darn dewey thing

15-year-old from the United States

Source: *Perceptions of Libraries and Information Resources*, OCLC, 2005, question 812b, "Please list two negative associations with the library."

Positive and Negative Associations of Libraries—
by Total Respondents

Please list two positive and two negative associations with the library.

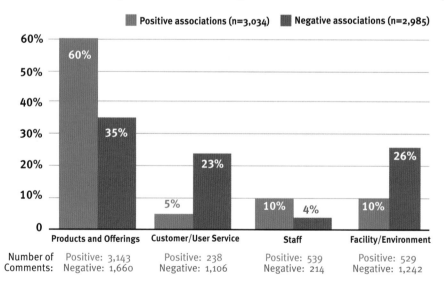

■ Positive associations (n=3,034)   ■ Negative associations (n=2,985)

	Products and Offerings	Customer/User Service	Staff	Facility/Environment
Positive	60%	5%	10%	10%
Negative	35%	23%	4%	26%

Number of Comments:	Positive: 3,143 Negative: 1,660	Positive: 238 Negative: 1,106	Positive: 539 Negative: 214	Positive: 529 Negative: 1,242

Source: *Perceptions of Libraries and Information Resources*, OCLC, 2005, question 812.

The data show relative consistency across regions, with strong consistency for the positive associations. Negative associations are slightly more varied. For example, Canadian respondents registered more negative comments about customer/user service than other regions, and respondents for the U.K. registered more negative comments about the facilities and the environment.

Positive associations with regard to library staff and customer/user service were offered more often by U.S. respondents age 65 and over than by U.S. respondents in any other age group. U.S. respondents 14 to 17 years old had the highest positive association with books than any other U.S. age group at 22 percent, while 13 percent reported *books* as a negative association.

Positive Associations of Libraries—by Region of Respondent

Please list two positive associations with the library.

	Total Respondents	Australia Singapore India	Canada	United Kingdom	United States
Products and Offerings					
Books	18%	16%	17%	21%	18%
Information	14%	16%	14%	14%	14%
Materials	9%	9%	10%	12%	9%
Free	8%	8%	7%	11%	8%
Computers	3%	2%	3%	3%	4%
Resources	3%	3%	4%	2%	4%
Easy	3%	4%	4%	4%	3%
Staff					
Staff	10%	9%	10%	10%	11%
Facility/Environment					
Environment	10%	11%	9%	7%	11%
Customer/User Service					
Service	5%	5%	6%	4%	4%

Source: *Perceptions of Libraries and Information Resources*, OCLC, 2005, question 812a.

Positive Associations of Libraries—
by Age of U.S. Respondent

Please list two positive associations with the library.

	Total U.S. Respondents	U.S. 14-17	U.S. 18-24	U.S. 25-64	U.S. 65+
Products and Offerings					
Books	18%	22%	16%	18%	13%
Information	14%	14%	18%	13%	13%
Materials	9%	7%	7%	12%	13%
Free	8%	8%	8%	9%	4%
Computers	4%	4%	5%	4%	3%
Resources	4%	3%	5%	5%	2%
Easy	3%	2%	3%	3%	3%
Staff					
Staff	11%	8%	9%	11%	17%
Facility/Environment					
Environment	11%	12%	11%	9%	8%
Customer/User Service					
Service	4%	4%	2%	4%	6%

Source: *Perceptions of Libraries and Information Resources*, OCLC, 2005, question 812a.

Positive Associations

Note: All verbatim comments presented as entered by survey respondents, including spelling, grammatical and punctuation errors.

Products and Offerings

Books: 18 percent of respondents provided positive associations related to books. These comments included free books, many or a variety of books, borrowing books, good books, available or accessible books, browsing books and current books.

Information: 14 percent of respondents included positive thoughts related to information, including free information, accurate/trustworthy information, reliable information, access to information, current information and comprehensive information.

Materials: 9 percent of respondents offered comments associated with library materials, such as a variety or many materials available, free materials and borrowing materials.

Free: 8 percent of the respondents have positive associations related to the concept of "free" or "free access."

Computers: 3 percent of the positive comments related to computer or Internet access.

Resources: 3 percent of the positive associations were associated with access to free or a variety of resources.

Easy to access/find: 3 percent of the respondents provided positive statements about the ease of accessing or finding information or resources.

Libraries are embracing computer technology and now offer library users the best of both worlds when they visit. They can borrow conventional books, magazines and newspapers and they can also log on to the computer system and find lots of information there. Teachers and school administrators still advocate the use of libraries and encourage their students to visit, so I think libraries will be here for a while yet.
41-year-old from Canada

most of the information and reseach available are trustworthy
29-year-old from Singapore

Generally Free (Inter)National cooperation
27-year-old from Canada

books. classics, in depth research. facility, the way to obtain hard to get information.
73-year-old from the United Kingdom

Facility/Environment

10 percent of the respondents have positive associations of the library related to the:

- Quiet environment
- Friendly and comfortable surroundings
- Work environment

Can access info in tangible form - ie can pick it up and look at it. can go there for peace and quiet if you need to study without distractions
26-year-old from the United Kingdom

source of learning
they have become more child friendly
33-year-old from the United Kingdom

Positive Associations (cont.)

Note: All verbatim comments presented as entered by survey respondents, including spelling, grammatical and punctuation errors.

Staff

10 percent of respondents provided positive comments related to the library staff, including:

- Helpful
- Friendly
- Knowledgeable
- Available

lots of information helpful staff
14-year-old from the United States

learn always & almost all references needed.
71-year-old from India

There are many sources of information available through the library, and the people there are always very friendly. It is also a very community oriented thing.
16-year-old from the United States

Customer/User Service

5 percent of the respondents have positive associations of the service provided by libraries. Some of the positive associations are:

- The online catalog
- The practice of being open to the public
- Interlibrary loan and library "linking"
- The ability to self-service and search
- The option to browse and borrow materials
- The way libraries are organized
- The hours libraries are open

Recreation for 75 years of my life
Resource for education purposes
82-year-old from the United States

The possible ability to aquire information that may not be available from other souces. the option of alternative medium types, ie cd, dvd, video, etc
71-year-old from Australia

A form of entertainment. A knowledgable place.
44-year-old from Singapore

1.Any one can get infromation about all subject in library generally. 2. Its the cheapist means to get knowledge.
35-year-old from India

Negative Associations of Libraries—
by Region of Respondent

Please list two negative associations with the library.

	Total Respondents	Australia Singapore India	Canada	United Kingdom	United States
Products and Offerings					
Books	13%	16%	14%	14%	11%
Materials	10%	10%	12%	8%	10%
Information	7%	9%	8%	6%	6%
Time-consuming	3%	4%	3%	1%	3%
Computers	2%	2%	2%	2%	3%
Facility/Environment					
Environment	11%	11%	8%	15%	11%
Travel there	7%	8%	7%	6%	7%
Not convenient	5%	5%	5%	5%	5%
Dull	2%	1%	1%	4%	2%
Customer/User Service					
Service	23%	19%	28%	20%	23%
Staff					
Staff	4%	3%	2%	4%	5%

Source: *Perceptions of Libraries and Information Resources*, OCLC, 2005, question 812b.

Negative Associations of Libraries—
by Age of U.S. Respondent

Please list two negative associations with the library.

	Total U.S. Respondents	U.S. 14-17	U.S. 18-24	U.S. 25-64	U.S. 65+
Products and Offerings					
Books	11%	13%	12%	10%	10%
Materials	10%	9%	10%	8%	8%
Information	6%	4%	9%	6%	5%
Time-consuming	3%	4%	4%	2%	2%
Computers	3%	3%	3%	1%	4%
Facility/Environment					
Environment	11%	12%	14%	9%	11%
Travel there	7%	5%	5%	10%	11%
Not convenient	5%	4%	3%	7%	5%
Dull	2%	5%	3%	9%	0%
Customer/User Service					
Service	23%	23%	23%	26%	21%
Staff					
Staff	5%	9%	5%	3%	4%

Source: *Perceptions of Libraries and Information Resources*, OCLC, 2005, question 812b.

Negative Associations

Note: All verbatim comments presented as entered by survey respondents, including spelling, grammatical and punctuation errors.

Products and Offerings

Books: 13 percent of the respondents had negative associations with the library books, including that they are:

- Not available
- Difficult to access
- Heavy to carry
- Not what is needed

- Not current
- Not taken care of or are dirty
- Of limited variety

Other comments suggested that there are too many books and that the respondents have to return the books to the library.

Materials: 10 percent of the negative comments related to library materials, including:

- The limited variety
- Are hard to access/find/use
- Are not what's needed
- Are not circulated

- Not available
- Are not current
- Are not taken care of/dirty

Information: 7 percent of the respondents made negative comments regarding information, including:

- Hard to access/find/use
- Not available
- Too much

- Not current
- Not what is needed
- Limited variety

Computers: 2 percent of the respondents have negative associations regarding:

- Outdated computers
- Use of the Internet filters

- Computers that are not available

Time-consuming: 3 percent of respondents made negative comments indicating that use of the library is time-consuming.

old people, old books, fines, outdated information, archaic research tool
17-year-old from the United States

Sometimes it is very hard to find the books. Sometimes it is difficult to find someone to help.
21-year-old from the United States

I always have to ask information about where to look for the information I need. It is too difficult to find it by myself, because there is so much information.... I could waste too much time looking for it.
80-year-old from the United States

we get to pay charges to renew the same book. Many books have the pages torn out, esp. the good recipes.
48-year-old from Singapore

really old old books.
24-year-old from Singapore

Nothing negative about a library. It just can't compete with individuals using computers to get information. The trip to the computer is a few seconds, where the trip to the library is measured in minutes.
43-year-old from the United States

Negative Associations (cont.)

Note: All verbatim comments presented as entered by survey respondents, including spelling, grammatical and punctuation errors.

Facility/Environment

11 percent offered negative comments about the library environment, including:

- Too quiet
- Limited parking
- Dirty
- Too noisy
- Too small
- Homeless people
- Too crowded
- Confusing layout
- Not safe

Travel there: 7 percent of respondents have negative associations with travel to the library.

Dull: 2 percent of the respondents indicated that libraries are dull.

Not convenient: 5 percent of the respondents commented that the library is not convenient.

Perceived as a hidebound and stuffy entity where silence is golden. Large institution which can be somewhat intimidating for poeple who are not confidant with learning or exploring.
43-year-old from Australia

homeless people / bad bathrooms
43-year-old from the United States

HAVE TO LEAVE THE HOME TO GET THIS INFORMATION
60-year-old from the United Kingdom

Customer/User Service

23 percent of the respondents provided negative associations related to:

- Limited or poor hours of operation
- Fees and policies associated with using the library
- Stringent return dates and other limits on circulation
- Use of the online catalog
- Poor service

Fines
Hassle of keeping card
21-year-old from the United States

Poor selection of books
Inconvenient opening hours
34-year-old from the United Kingdom

Staff

4 percent of the respondents indicated negative associations related to the library staff, including:

- Unfriendly
- Not knowledgeable
- Unavailable
- Not helpful

Unfriendly staff, having to wait a long time for a book or do not have it in any library and have to wait for them to get a loan from outside the area.
40-year-old from the United Kingdom

Moody librarians! Insufficient books on certain topics
40-year-old from Australia

not to much help, you feel like you should know how it all works and if you don't they sometimes don't seem to want to help you. To quiet, sometimes you have to work in groups and you always feel like you can't talk
30-year-old from Canada

3.7 Lifestyle Fit

Respondents are reading less and using the library less since they started using the Internet.

Watching television, using the library, reading books and *reading the newspaper* are the top four activities respondents report doing less frequently since they began using the Internet. Fourteen percent of respondents say they visit with family and friends less often.

Tables detailing decreased activities due to Internet use by region, U.S. age, college students and library card holders are included in Appendix A.

33%
use the library less often since they started using the Internet.

Decreased Activities Due to Internet Use—by Total Respondents

What activities do you engage in less often since you began using the Internet?

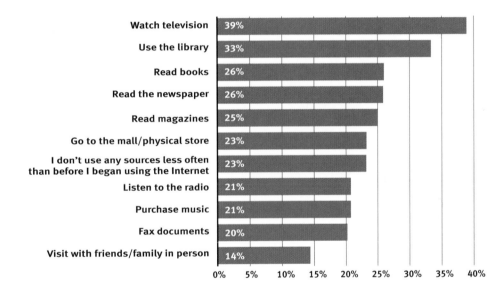

Activity	Percentage
Watch television	39%
Use the library	33%
Read books	26%
Read the newspaper	26%
Read magazines	25%
Go to the mall/physical store	23%
I don't use any sources less often than before I began using the Internet	23%
Listen to the radio	21%
Purchase music	21%
Fax documents	20%
Visit with friends/family in person	14%

Source: *Perceptions of Libraries and Information Resources*, OCLC, 2005, question 415.

Information Sources and Lifestyle Fit

Over half of respondents say search engines fit perfectly with their lifestyle.

Understanding how compatible a product or service is to a consumer's lifestyle and consumption habits can provide interesting insights into how a consumer may use that product or a competing product or service in the future.

Respondents rated search engines, libraries, online libraries, bookstores and online bookstores as information sources that did, or did not, fit with their lifestyle.

Fifty-five percent of all respondents feel search engines *fit perfectly* with their lifestyles, and 90 percent of respondents feel search engines are a *good* to *perfect fit*. Forty-nine percent feel the library is a *good* to *perfect fit*. U.S. respondents 65 and older rate search engines' lifestyle fit substantially lower than younger age groups.

Library card holders expressed a higher level of *perfect lifestyle fit* for all information sources than non-card holders. Library card holders were four times more likely than non-card holders to see libraries as a perfect lifestyle fit.

Information Sources by Lifestyle Fit—
by Total Respondents

Thinking of each information source and your information needs and lifestyles, would you say it...?

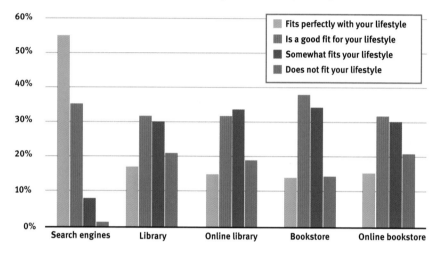

Legend:
- Fits perfectly with your lifestyle
- Is a good fit for your lifestyle
- Somewhat fits your lifestyle
- Does not fit your lifestyle

Source: *Perceptions of Libraries and Information Resources,* OCLC, 2005, question 1345.

Information Sources with Perfect Lifestyle Fit—
by Region of Respondent

Thinking of each information source and your information needs and lifestyles, would you say it *fits perfectly with your lifestyle?*

	Total Respondents	Australia Singapore India	Canada	United Kingdom	United States
Search engines	55%	62%	55%	53%	54%
Library	17%	17%	18%	12%	18%
Online library	15%	16%	18%	11%	15%
Bookstore	14%	13%	16%	9%	15%
Online bookstore	16%	15%	17%	16%	16%

Source: *Perceptions of Libraries and Information Resources,* OCLC, 2005, question 1345.

Layout of the library should be more

lifestyle based and user friendly.

It should offer its patrons the wow factor from the instance you walk in the door that this is the place you want to be in and have the comfort and ease to locate what you are after and feel at home and want to spend time there, quality and quantity.

40-year-old from Australia

Source: *Perceptions of Libraries and Information Resources,* OCLC, 2005, question 1240, "If you could provide one piece of advice to your library, what would it be?"

My schedule
rarely fits
their
schedule.

**21-year-old from the
United States**

Source: *Perceptions of Libraries and Information Resources,* OCLC, 2005, question 812b, "Please list two negative associations with the library."

Information Sources with Perfect Lifestyle Fit—
by Age of U.S. Respondent

Thinking of each information source and your information needs and lifestyles, would you say it *fits perfectly with your lifestyle?*

	Total U.S. Respondents	U.S. 14-17	U.S. 18-24	U.S. 25-64	U.S. 65+
Search engines	54%	52%	54%	58%	38%
Library	18%	17%	17%	17%	22%
Online library	15%	10%	14%	16%	10%
Bookstore	15%	16%	17%	15%	11%
Online bookstore	16%	10%	19%	18%	10%

Source: *Perceptions of Libraries and Information Resources,* OCLC, 2005, question 1345.

Information Sources with Perfect Lifestyle Fit—
by College Students across all Regions

Thinking of each information source and your information needs and lifestyles, would you say it *fits perfectly with your lifestyle?*

	Total Respondents	College Students
Search engines	55%	64%
Library	17%	24%
Online library	15%	30%
Bookstore	14%	21%
Online bookstore	16%	24%

Source: *Perceptions of Libraries and Information Resources,* OCLC, 2005, question 1345.

Information Sources with Perfect Lifestyle Fit—
by Library Card Holders across all Regions

Thinking of each information source and your information needs and lifestyles, would you say it *fits perfectly with your lifestyle?*

	Library Card Holders	Non-Card Holders
Search engines	57%	52%
Library	22%	5%
Online library	18%	7%
Bookstore	15%	10%
Online bookstore	18%	11%

Source: *Perceptions of Libraries and Information Resources,* OCLC, 2005, question 1345.

Online Libraries and Lifestyle Fit

Ninety percent of respondents see search engines as a good lifestyle fit. Nearly half see online libraries as a good lifestyle fit.

Although both information sources are Internet-based, substantially more respondents rate search engines as a *perfect fit* than online libraries. Fifteen percent of total respondents say the online library *fits perfectly* with their lifestyle. Fifty-five percent rate search engines as a *perfect fit*. College students indicate the best fit with the online library, with 30 percent of them stating that it *fits perfectly* with their lifestyles.

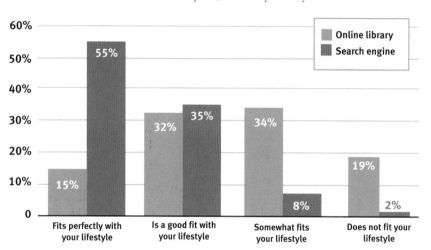

Online Libraries Compared to Search Engines—
by Total Respondents

Thinking of each information source and your information needs and lifestyles, would you say it...?

Source: *Perceptions of Libraries and Information Resources*, OCLC, 2005, question 1345.

Online Libraries and the Lifestyle Fit—
by College Students across all Regions

- Fits perfectly with your lifestyle
- Is a good fit with your lifestyle
- Somewhat fits your lifestyle
- Does not fit with your lifestyle

Source: *Perceptions of Libraries and Information Resources*, OCLC, 2005, question 1345.

3.8 Books—the Library Brand

The library brand is "books."

Books, books, books, rows and rows of books, stacks of books, tables filled with books, people holding books, people checking out books. Libraries are all about books. That is what I think and that is what I will always think.

41-year-old from Canada

Plenty of books, movies, cds and other media that I have access to free of charge. It's great!

16-year-old from the United States

In the introduction to this report, we noted that one of the most important goals of the project is to begin to provide a clearer understanding of the "Library" brand.

What do information consumers think about libraries? How do information consumers identify libraries in the growing universe of alternatives? What is the "Library" brand image from the viewpoint of the online information consumer?

"Brand" is derived from the Old Norse word "brandr," which means "to burn," as brands were the means by which owners of livestock marked their animals to identify them.[1] The American Marketing Association defines "brand image" as "the perception of a brand in the minds of persons. The brand image is a mirror reflection (though perhaps inaccurate) of the brand personality or product being. It is what people believe about a brand—their thoughts, feelings, expectations."[2]

We asked a variety of questions in this survey to help us collect information about the library's brand image, and about the information consumer's thoughts, feelings and expectations.

We asked the open-ended question: "What is the first thing you think of when you think of a library?" 3,785 verbatim comments from 3,163 respondents were grouped by main theme. Roughly 70 percent of respondents, across all geographic regions and U.S. age groups, associate library first and foremost with *books*. There was no runner-up.

Tables detailing data on top-of-mind associations with libraries by region, U.S. age, college students and library card holders are in Appendix A.

1. Kevin Lane Keller, *Strategic Brand Management: Building, Measuring and Managing Brand Equity,* (Upper Saddle River, NJ: Prentice Hall, Inc., 1998), 2.
2. http://www.marketingpower.com/mg-dictionary.php?Searched=1&SearchFor=brand%20image (accessed October 15, 2005).

First (Top-of-mind) Association with the Library—
by Total Respondents

What is the first thing you think of when you think of a library?

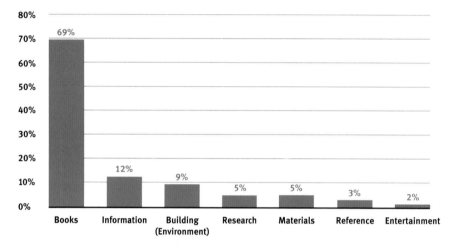

Source: *Perceptions of Libraries and Information Resources*, OCLC, 2005, question 807.
Note: The percentage is based on the number of comments received divided by the number of respondents.
Some respondents chose to provide more than one response, and all responses were included.

First (Top-of-mind) Association with the Library—
by Region of Respondent

What is the first thing you think of when you think of a library?

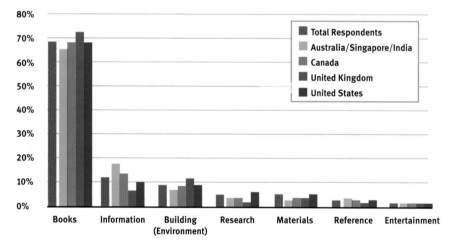

Source: *Perceptions of Libraries and Information Resources*, OCLC, 2005, question 807.
Note: The percentage is based on the number of comments received divided by the number of respondents.
Some respondents chose to provide more than one response, and all responses were included.

Books,
in fact it's the
only thing
I think of
when thinking about
a library.

69-year-old from England

Source: *Perceptions of Libraries and Information Resources*, OCLC, 2005, question 807, "What is the first thing you think of when you think of a library?"

First (Top-of-mind) Association with the Library— by Age of U.S. Respondent

What is the first thing you think of when you think of a library?

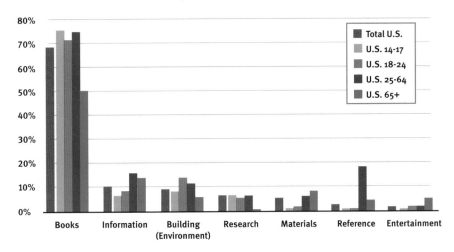

Source: *Perceptions of Libraries and Information Resources*, OCLC, 2005, question 807.
Note: The percentage is based on the number of comments received divided by the number of respondents. Some respondents chose to provide more than one response, and all responses were included.

Great access to a multitude of books—

I buy favorites but have a much broader range of book availability, including some I wish to only read once or those I need specific information from,through the library.

51-year-old from the United States

Source: *Perceptions of Libraries and Information Resources*, OCLC, 2005, question 807, "What is the first thing you think of when you think of a library?"

Brand Associations

"Free," "access" and "information" were occasionally mentioned.

The responses from the 3,163 respondents were also analyzed for secondary themes or descriptors that could lend understanding of library brand image. The words "book" or "books" were mentioned 2,152 times. The word "information" was the top-of-mind recall 291 times. "Free" was mentioned 70 times. Other descriptors mentioned infrequently included access, the physical building, the librarian and library as "a place for information," but the overwhelming response is that the "library brand equals books."

Words often used by librarians to describe libraries and library services include "trust," "privacy," "authoritative information," "quality information," "education," "learning," "community" and "access." We reviewed the over 3,500 verbatim responses from 3,163 respondents to the question "What is the first thing you think of when you think of a library?" to see how many times "trust," "quality," "authoritative," "education" and "privacy" and other often used library attributes were mentioned as the top-of-mind library image.

The words *trust, authoritative* and *privacy* were never mentioned. *Community* was mentioned in one response. *Quality* was mentioned twice. *Education* was mentioned four times; *learning* was mentioned nine times. *Free* was mentioned 70 times. *Books* were mentioned 2,152 times.

We also analyzed brand associations by looking at the respondents' open-ended positive and negative associations. This set of questions was asked in the library section of the survey. (See Part 3.6: "List two positive and two negative associations with the library.")

We reviewed word count to identify potential brand image associations against the same list of traditional library attributes. Total mentions were as follows:

Positive Library Associations Word Count

- Authoritative – 0
- Quality – 1
- Privacy – 2
- Trust – 14
- Community – 21
- Education – 25
- Entertainment – 36
- Learning – 89
- Internet/Web – 91
- Knowledge – 92
- Research – 155
- Access – 264
- Free – 652
- Information – 727
- Books – 1,106

Again, *books* surfaced as the leading positive association. It was mentioned by 37 percent of respondents who provided positive association comments. *Information* and *free* were mentioned in approximately 24 percent and 21 percent of responses, respectively.

So why the overwhelming brand image of library as *books?*

As mentioned in the introduction, *Environmental Scan* discussions with librarians over the past two years have often surfaced a view that a potential reason for the disconnect between the user's perception of libraries as books and the librarian's association with a much broader set of products and services is a lack of user education. Many have expressed a feeling that today's information consumer is just not aware of what is currently available at libraries. The survey data would support the assertion that library users are not aware of many electronic library resources. As reported in Part 2, online information consumers are unaware or unfamiliar with many of the products and services currently available at the library. Fifty-eight percent of total respondents do not know that libraries offered electronic journals. Fifty-eight percent are not aware that libraries provide online databases. Thirty-three percent did not know their libraries have Web sites.

Why are information consumers so uninformed? Seventy-two percent hold a library card. Is the lack of awareness of the libraries' online electronic resources a cause or an effect of the view of the library brand as a book provider? Are respondents (all of whom took the survey online) not aware that the library has a Web site or electronic databases because they do not expect or look for the libraries to be more than books?

Books,

though I know they have other media available

55-year-old from Canada

Source: *Perceptions of Libraries and Information Resources,* OCLC, 2005, question 807, "What is the first thing you think of when you think of a library?"

We analyzed the top-of-mind brand association of the library for the subset of respondents who indicated that they are *extremely familiar* or *very familiar* with the physical library (see Part 2). 1,557 respondents or 46 percent of total survey respondents indicated that they were *very familiar* or *extremely familiar* with the library. Top-of-mind brand image of the library for this subset of respondents yielded the following word associations:

Old book smell.

Not a bad thing though, it's comforting!

23-year-old from the United States

Source: *Perceptions of Libraries and Information Resources,* OCLC, 2005, question 807, "What is the first thing you think of when you think of a library?"

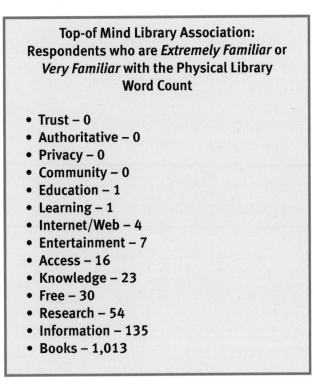

Top-of Mind Library Association:
Respondents who are *Extremely Familiar* or *Very Familiar* with the Physical Library
Word Count

- **Trust – 0**
- **Authoritative – 0**
- **Privacy – 0**
- **Community – 0**
- **Education – 1**
- **Learning – 1**
- **Internet/Web – 4**
- **Entertainment – 7**
- **Access – 16**
- **Knowledge – 23**
- **Free – 30**
- **Research – 54**
- **Information – 135**
- **Books – 1,013**

For this same subset of respondents (those who are *extremely familiar* or *very familiar* with the physical library), we also analyzed their usage patterns of library electronic resources.

The survey results suggest that the respondents who indicate they are *very familiar* or *extremely familiar* with libraries use library electronic resources more frequently than total respondents.

We reviewed the top-of-mind library image for this group of respondents who indicate they are *extremely familiar* or *very familiar* with and use library resources. Their brand image of libraries is "books." Over 60 percent of responses included the word "book" or "books."

Based on the results of the survey, the library brand—across geographic regions, across U.S. ages, across those who use the library often—is books.

A Sample of Respondents' Verbatim Comments:

What is the first thing you think of when you think of a library?

Tables detailing a larger sample of verbatim responses are included in Appendix B.

Note: All verbatim comments presented as entered by survey respondents, including spelling, grammatical and punctuation errors.

The first thing that I think of when I think of 'library' is the broad range of resources it offers, such as internet access, periodicals, and of course, books.
47-year-old from the United States

Equality. Libraries more than any other institution make the access of information available to anyone who wants it. Libraries run literacy programs, have volunteers teach ESL courses, Give open access joyfully to all the literatue, art, periodicals and plain old 'how to' instructions. Give access to Natural History, Music. Libraries are the treasure of our Civilization. AND They are the great equalizers. The first time I used a computer was in a library. THe first thing I think of when I think of a library is MAGIC!
61-year-old from Canada

Boring.
33-year-old from the United Kingdom

The wealth of knowledge that resides in books.
17-year-old from the United States

Peace and quiet.
41-year-old from the United Kingdom

It's in the centre of the town where I live and it's difficult to get to, i.e., no nearby free parking. I think it's an old fashioned way of getting information.
60-year-old from the United Kingdom

Quiet.
32-year-old from Australia

The librarian hushing everyone .
17-year-old from the United States

A Sample of Respondents' Verbatim Comments (continued):

What is the first thing you think of when you think of a library?

Note: All verbatim comments presented as entered by survey respondents, including spelling, grammatical and punctuation errors.

Provide information, knowledge, resources and relaxation to

everyone and anyone

who needs it. It also helps a person to upgrade oneself.

31-year-old from Singapore

Source: *Perceptions of Libraries and Information Resources*, OCLC, 2005, question 807, "What is the first thing you think of when you think of a library?"

Great place to get a book I am interested in.
45-year-old from Australia

last place I want to go for info
68-year-old from the United States

Quiet, books, boring, helpful.
17-year-old from the United States

difficult to find what you really need without spending hours looking.
32-year-old from the United Kingdom

Pleasure.
46-year-old from the United Kingdom

An study place for students.
18-year-old from the United States

Good collection of fiction and non-fiction books.
23-year-old from the United States

A large building with books on all subjects.
65-year-old from the United States

Need to be quiet, need to hunt around for what you want, lots of leg work.
39-year-old from Canada

Enjoyment.
72-year-old from the United States

Great access to a multitude of books-I buy favorites but have a much broader range of book availability, including some I wish to only read once or those I need specific information, from the library.
51-year-old from the United States

3.9 Brand Potential—Libraries, Books and Information

The majority of respondents indicated that the main purpose of libraries was broader than books.

To be an 'information station'.
57-year-old from the United States

Getting book, studying material for school or college, using a computer if you don't own one.
69-year-old from the United States

Books and lending.
38-year-old from Canada

As important as it is to know what your brand image is today, it is equally important to understand brand potential. What are the possibilities? Can brand image be changed or expanded? Can brand image be "refreshed?" What potential exists for expanding the "Library" brand beyond books?

To explore "Library" brand potential, we asked respondents to look beyond first impression and indicate what they felt is the purpose (mission) of the library.

Slightly over half of respondents (53 percent) indicated that they feel the main purpose of the library is *information*. Thirty-one percent of respondents indicated that the main purpose of the library is *books*.

Responses were generally consistent across both region and age. Respondents from the United Kingdom were more likely to link the main purpose of the library to *books* (42 percent) than respondents from other geographic regions. Australia/Singapore/India residents indicated *books* as the main purpose of the library less than respondents from all other regions, at 22 percent.

U.S. respondents 65 and over indicated *information* as the main purpose of the library more than any other age group, at 62 percent. At 45 percent, U.S. respondents age 14–17 selected *information* less than other age groups. They indicated *books* as the main purpose of the library more than any other age group (at 40 percent).

Tables detailing the library's main purpose by region, U.S. age, college students and library card holders are included in Appendix A.

53%
feel the main purpose of the library is information

Main Purpose of the Library—
by Total Respondents

What do you feel is the main purpose of the library?

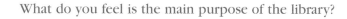

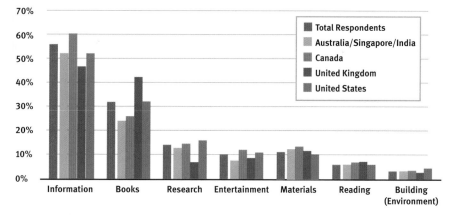

Source: *Perceptions of Libraries and Information Resources,* OCLC, 2005, question 810.

Main Purpose of the Library—by Region of Respondent

What do you feel is the main purpose of the library?

Source: *Perceptions of Libraries and Information Resources,* OCLC, 2005, question 810.

Main Purpose of the Library—
by Age of U.S. Respondent

What do you feel is the main purpose of the library?

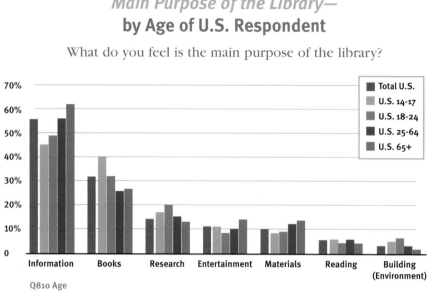

Q810 Age

Source: *Perceptions of Libraries and Information Resources*, OCLC, 2005, question 810.

An information and entertainment resource center.

48-year-old from Canada

Source: *Perceptions of Libraries and Information Resources*, OCLC, 2005, question 810, "What do you feel is the main purpose of the library?"

Responses to the question "What do you feel is the main purpose of the library?" varied in both content and length. Some responses were one- or two-word replies; others were lengthy answers indicating more than one main purpose of the library.

Responses such as "provide resources for learning and research and to provide books for one's enjoyment" (16-year-old from the U.S.) indicate a multidimensional view of the purpose of the library. Learning, research, books and enjoyment are all mentioned. The majority of respondents indicated that their view of the main purpose of the library was broader than just books. When books were mentioned, other activities or services were also frequently mentioned.

to allow

everyone

the opportunity and access to

resource information and reading

46-year-old from Canada

Source: *Perceptions of Libraries and Information Resources*, OCLC, 2005, question 810, "What do you feel is the main purpose of the library?"

Again, when we reviewed the 3,161 responses by word count against the list of traditional brand attributes, we see similar attributes mentioned but with higher frequency for many attributes. *Information*—1,290 mentions related to the main purpose compared to 727 mentions for top-of-mind, *education*—87 mentions compared to 25 mentions and *research*—420 mentions compared to 155 mentions. *Community* was mentioned 98 times in response to the library's main purpose. This represents less than 1 percent of the responses, but four times more than either top-of-mind or positive library associations.

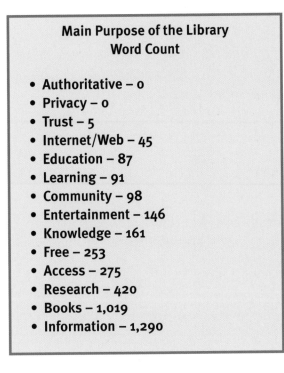

**Main Purpose of the Library
Word Count**

- **Authoritative – 0**
- **Privacy – 0**
- **Trust – 5**
- **Internet/Web – 45**
- **Education – 87**
- **Learning – 91**
- **Community – 98**
- **Entertainment – 146**
- **Knowledge – 161**
- **Free – 253**
- **Access – 275**
- **Research – 420**
- **Books – 1,019**
- **Information – 1,290**

Attributes that were not frequently mentioned in any set of brand association responses (the top-of-mind, positive associations or main purpose responses) are *privacy, Internet* or *Web* and *trust*.

The data suggest that, when prompted, many online information consumers can see a role for libraries beyond books. Information is seen as that expanded role for libraries by the largest number of respondents.

A Sample of Respondents' Verbatim Comments:

What is the main purpose of the library?

Tables detailing a larger sample of verbatim responses are included in Appendix B.

Note: All verbatim comments presented as entered by survey respondents, including spelling, grammatical and punctuation errors.

To provide and give people access to information.

28-year-old from Canada

A central source for the general public to be able to access many things, including the borrowing of books, reference material, computer access and daily/weekly newspapers/magazines. Also a great learning environment for children.

50-year-old from Australia

Books and information for free.

17-year-old from the United States

For people who cannot afford things like computers and books to have free access to information. That is something that is necessary in a free and open society.

22-year-old from the United States

Provide resources for learning and research and to provide books for one's enjoyment.

16-year-old from the United States

Serve as a centralized information repository.

21-year-old from the United States

To provide access to materials needed for personal and research purposes. A public library has a bit different of a function within the community, to enhance intergroup understandings and encourage or facilitate growth etc. Academic libraries need to have print materials and electronic resources, as well as professional librarians to assist researchers.

29-year-old from Canada

Provide both electronic and hard copy information on topics both factual and fictional. A local point in which to store the information.

45-year-old from Australia

Part 4: Respondents' Advice to Libraries

85% *agree the library is a place to learn.*

Keep keeping up! You are an invaluable resource/facility in the community. Without you, many people's opportunity/desire to learn & develop would be greatly diminished (think Billy Connelly & Michael Caine's love of libraries)

26-year-old from Australia

A smile goes a long way. The environment, including the friendliness of the staff, makes a difference for me.

18-year-old from Canada

A search engine of their own.

36-year-old from Canada

52% *agree their library's content/ collection meets their needs.*

Advertise.

17-year-old from the United States

Respondents were asked to indicate their level of agreement with a set of phrases and characteristics to determine how information consumers see the libraries' role in today's society. When prompted, respondents agree (*completely agree* or *agree*) that libraries serve many community roles, including a place to learn, a place to read and support literacy, a place for free computer/Internet access and a place to promote childhood learning and development.

Respondents were also asked to rate their library service across six service dimensions ranging from librarian assistance to technology. Less than 25 percent of respondents *completely agree* that libraries meet their needs on any single dimension.

As the wrap-up to the survey, respondents were offered the opportunity to provide— in their own words—one piece of advice to libraries. We received over 3,000 responses. Part 4.3 includes a summary of the verbatim comments. We have included a broader sample of verbatim comments in Appendix B.

4.1 The Library's Role in the Community

When prompted, respondents agree that libraries serve many community roles.

Respondents were asked to rate the library on 14 attributes that describe potential community roles that a library could provide. Over 50 percent of respondents *agree* or *completely agree* that their library provides 12 of the 14 community services surveyed.

Eighty-five percent of all respondents agree *(completely agree* or *agree)* that the library is perceived to be a *place to learn.*

Eighty percent or more of all respondents also agree that the library is a *place to read* and *make needed information freely available.*

Respondents were least likely to recognize their library as *supporting nonnative speakers* or as *a place to meet and socialize with friends.*

More **computer stations,** *able to bring in your own computer and hook up to internet*

17-year-old from the United States

Source: *Perceptions of Libraries and Information Resources,* OCLC, 2005, question 1240, "If you could provide one piece of advice to your library, what would it be?"

Library's Role in the Community— ## by Total Respondents

Please rate the degree to which you agree or disagree with the following statements about your library's role in the community.

Note: This graph shows the *completely agree* and *agree* responses.

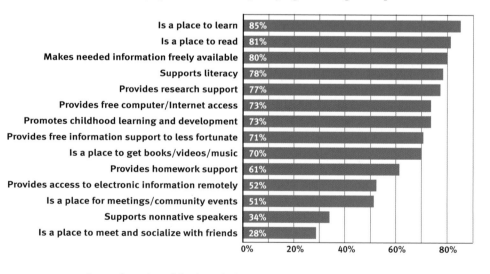

Is a place to learn	85%
Is a place to read	81%
Makes needed information freely available	80%
Supports literacy	78%
Provides research support	77%
Provides free computer/Internet access	73%
Promotes childhood learning and development	73%
Provides free information support to less fortunate	71%
Is a place to get books/videos/music	70%
Provides homework support	61%
Provides access to electronic information remotely	52%
Is a place for meetings/community events	51%
Supports nonnative speakers	34%
Is a place to meet and socialize with friends	28%

Source: *Perceptions of Libraries and Information Resources,* OCLC, 2005, question 1210.

In the U.S., 14- to 17-year-olds and 18- to 24-year-olds are significantly more likely to be *neutral* in their agreement that their library:

- *makes needed information freely available*
- *supports literacy*
- *provides free information to support those less fortunate*
- *promotes childhood learning and development*

Eighty-three percent of U.S. respondents perceive the library *as a place to learn.* This perception varies considerably by age. Sixty-nine percent of U.S. 14- to-17-year olds hold this perception as compared to an overwhelming 94 percent of U.S. respondents age 65 and over.

Free access
for all people
Programs
for children.

41-year-old from Australia

Source: *Perceptions of Libraries and Information Resources,* OCLC, 2005, question 812a, "Please list two positive associations with the library."

Agreement that the "Library is a Place to Learn"— by Age of U.S. Respondent

Please rate the degree to which you agree or disagree with the statement, "The library is a place to learn."

Note: This graph shows the *completely agree* and *agree* responses.

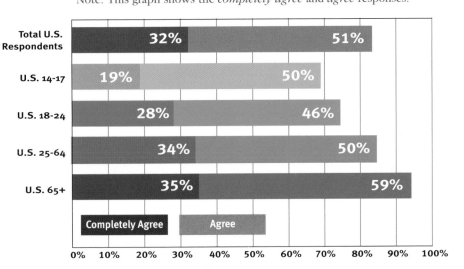

Source: *Perceptions of Libraries and Information Resources,* OCLC, 2005, question 1210.

Respondents indicate that they are aware of the availability of free computer and Internet access at the library across all geographic regions surveyed. Seventy-three percent of respondents *completely agree* or *agree* that their library *provides free computer/Internet access*.

Libraries and Free Computer/Internet Access— by Region of Respondent

Please rate the degree to which you agree or disagree with the statement, "The library provides free computer/Internet Access."
Note: This graph shows the *completely agree* and *agree* responses.

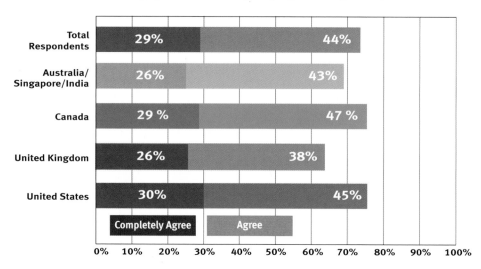

Source: *Perceptions of Libraries and Information Resources*, OCLC, 2005, question 1210.

4.2 Rating Library Services

Sixty-five percent of respondents agree that assistance from a librarian is available when needed.

Fifty-four percent agree that library technology meets their needs.

The survey asked respondents to rate their library's performance across six service dimensions ranging from librarian support to content to resource availability. While less than 25 percent of respondents *completely agree* their library provides these services, the majority at least agree (*completely agree* or *agree*) that most services meet their needs.

Sixty-five percent of respondents agree (*completely agree* or *agree)* that the *assistance of a librarian is available when needed.* This level of agreement is consistent among all geographic regions and U.S. age groups.

Roughly half (48 percent) of respondents are neutral or disagree that their content and collection needs are met.

Books improve your
life, by inspiring,
teaching, keeping
you involved and
interested, and

FREE TO
THINK.

LITERACY and being
informed raise the
standard of living of
individuals and
societies.

41-year-old from the
United States

Source: *Perceptions of Libraries and
Information Resources*, OCLC, 2005,
question 812a, "Please list two
positive associations with the
library."

Librarian and Library Services—
by Total Respondents

Please rate the degree to which you agree or disagree
with the following statements about your library.

Note: This graph shows the *completely agree* and *agree* responses.

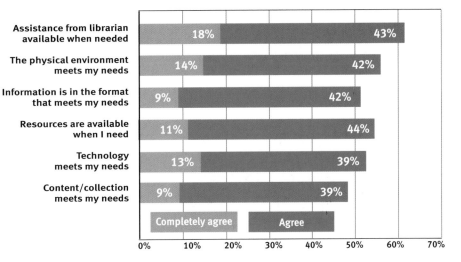

Source: *Perceptions of Libraries and Information Resources*, OCLC, 2005, question 1207.

Librarian and Library Services—
by U.S. 14- to 17-year-olds

Please rate the degree to which you agree or disagree
with the following statements about your library.

Note: This graph shows the *completely agree* and *agree* responses.

Source: *Perceptions of Libraries and Information Resources*, OCLC, 2005, question 1207.

4.3 Advice to Libraries

Respondents had opinions on all aspects of library staff, products and services, and facilities.

Respondents were invited to offer one piece of advice to libraries as a wrap-up to the survey. Some respondents offered more than one piece of advice and others declined to comment. 3,026 comments were received from 2,968 respondents. We categorized the advice into the following five themes: products and offerings, customer/user service, facility/environment, staff and satisfaction.

Tables detailing advice for libraries by region and U.S. age are included in Appendix A.

Advice for the Library—by Region of Respondent

If you could provide one piece of advice to your library, what would it be?
Note: This graph shows the percentage of respondents who offered advice related to the following themes: products and offerings, customer/user service, facility/environment, staff and satisfaction.

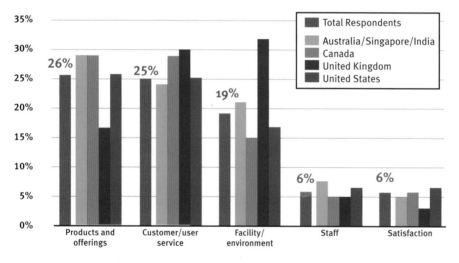

Source: *Perceptions of Libraries and Information Resources*, OCLC, 2005, question 1240.

The advice received covered a wide range of topics across a wide range of library services. We have summarized the advice received under each broad theme from products and offerings to staffing. A sample of the verbatim advice concludes this section. A larger sample of verbatim responses is included in Appendix B.

Respondents' Advice
If you could give one piece of advice to the library, what would it be?

Note: All verbatim comments presented as entered by survey respondents, including spelling, grammatical and punctuation errors.

Products and Offerings

Add to collection: 13 percent of total respondents advised libraries to add materials to their collections.

- Add more copies of books and other materials so that best-sellers and other popular materials would circulate faster.
- Add additional titles and other materials to the collection.
- Add new resources to the collection, such as audiobooks.
- Add new information, such as genealogy materials.

Update collection: 7 percent of total respondents suggested that libraries update their collection with new books, materials, information and other resources.

Computers: 5 percent of total respondents advised that libraries should add or update their computers.

Online catalogs: 1 percent suggested making local library catalogs more user-friendly and improving search capabilities.

Get more copies of current and classic bestsellers, then sell off the books to reduce inventory when they are no longer in as high demand.
29-year-old from Singapore

Needs a broad range of things, such as Audio Books and Comic books. Also needs more up to date books, new releases.
17-year-old from Australia

Please have more genealogy research materials available.
72-year-old from the United States

Have more internet terminals
28-year-old from Singapore

A more flexible lending programme, particularly allowing longer lending periods if the resource/book isn't being asked for by someone else...
54-year-old from the United Kingdom

e-mail reminders warning when books are due
19-year-old from the United States

Hold events which attract people back into the libraries such as book club evenings
43-year-old from the United Kingdom

Maintenance and upkeep of books to be improved.
62-year-old from India

Respondents' Advice

Note: All verbatim comments presented as entered by survey respondents, including spelling, grammatical and punctuation errors.

Customer/User Service:

Service: **16 percent** of total respondents provided advice related to the service.

- Extend the hours of operation.
- Reexamine the "rules" and fines/fees associated with using library materials.
- Offer the ability to reserve materials online.
- Make renewals easier.
- Offer longer lending periods for materials.
- Eliminate the fees for photocopies.

Promote: **6 percent** of total respondents advised libraries to increase their promotion and advertising.

Access: **4 percent** of total respondents suggested that libraries increase access to the collections, both physically for the disabled and virtually to allow easier remote access.

Run the library like a bookstore.
55-year-old from the United States

Provide a guide—I have no idea how to find books that I need in the library without feeling really stupid.
18-year-old from the United States

Open 24 hours all days
54-year-old from Singapore

I think this survey is right on track. The libraries should look at community spaces like Starbucks and Borders, and should also look at the value of online material like Google, and they should try to be more relevant in the current age.
51-year-old from the United States

Have hours like booksellers
49-year-old from the United States

Review the current search catalog system as it is hard to find material relevant to the topic you search for.
18-year-old from Australia

Have a No Late Fee policy like Blockbuster.
49-year-old from the United States

Have a beginners class for using the library and computer systems. Better prepared at the beginning ensures better usage.
51-year-old from the United States

To bring out a library website with a whole lot of information. free access to the internet. Bring about new Technologies. Weekly career related programmes. Latest books, magazines and various journals...
27-year-old from India

Respondents' Advice

Note: All verbatim comments presented as entered by survey respondents, including spelling, grammatical and punctuation errors.

Facility/Environment

Environment: 19 percent of respondents provided advice related to the physical library environment or facility.

- Increase the amount of seating and make it more comfortable.
- Expand the facility.
- Make the environment more inviting and up-to-date.
- Add café or snack shop.
- Decrease the noise level.

Increase the **organization** and reshelve materials more quickly.

Improve the lighting.

Improve the parking.

Add or update restroom facilities.

Place catalog computers on the second and third floors, so I will not have to run up and down the staircases everytime a call number does not bring a book up.
17-year-old from the United States

Brighter lights
15-year-old from the United States

Keep the areas warm
57-year-old from the United Kingdom

Our library needs music!!
14-year-old from the United States

Please install toilets
57-year-old from the United Kingdom

Acquire better parking.
38-year-old from Canada

Stop making it feel like church.
47-year-old from the United Kingdom

Do something about the bums and transients
24-year-old from the United States

Respondents' Advice

Note: All verbatim comments presented as entered by survey respondents, including spelling, grammatical and punctuation errors.

Staff

6 percent of total respondents provided advice regarding the library staff.
- Have friendlier staff.
- Increase the number of staff to help library users.
- Hire more helpful and knowledgeable staff.

Turf out the present city council. Political support is imperative.
45-year-old from Canada

Our library staff is very busy and help is difficult to get while there. I always have felt that I am an imposition if I ask a question. This needs to change to a more friendly environment to encourage more visits.
61-year-old from the United States

Train the staff to be friendlier and have better customer service.
35-year-old from the United States

Have friendly staff who explain how the library works/is laid out to anyone who seems unfamiliar with libraries.
58-year-old from Australia

Don't be so uptight about kids hanging out in the library.
17-year-old from the United States

Respondents' Advice

Satisfaction

6 percent of total respondents indicated that they were satisfied with the library and the services offered.

Keep up the good work
Mentioned 61 times by respondents ranging in age from 15 to 82 from Australia, Canada, United Kingdom and the United States

Keep it up, I appreciate everything you do.
16-year-old from the United States

I cannot think of one thing I have wanted or needed that the library has not supplied
80-year-old from the United States

I really think our library is well done. No complaints.
17-year-old from the United States

Keep up the great work. I have no complaints, Would like to see more people try using the libray website.
80-year-old from the United States

I don't have any advice. Our public libary is great.
38-year-old from Australia

Part 5: Libraries—A "Universal" Brand?

Patterns of
familiarity,
usage and
awareness
of library resources
were generally
consistent across
regions surveyed.

Perceptions, usage rates and advice shared by respondents were generally consistent across all regions surveyed.

One of the noteworthy findings of the survey is the general consistency and uniformity of responses across geographic regions. While statistical differences certainly exist in survey responses, responses indicated a "universal" view of the library across regions surveyed. Responses about awareness, familiarity and usage of electronic resources showed consistent views across all geographic regions surveyed. Respondents indicate similar levels of favorability and trust of both libraries and search engines while "library" brand image and brand potential show common themes and similarities across the regions surveyed.

A series of the graphs used in other parts of this report have been duplicated on the next two pages to illustrate this observation. A quick scan of these charts highlights this pattern of uniform response.

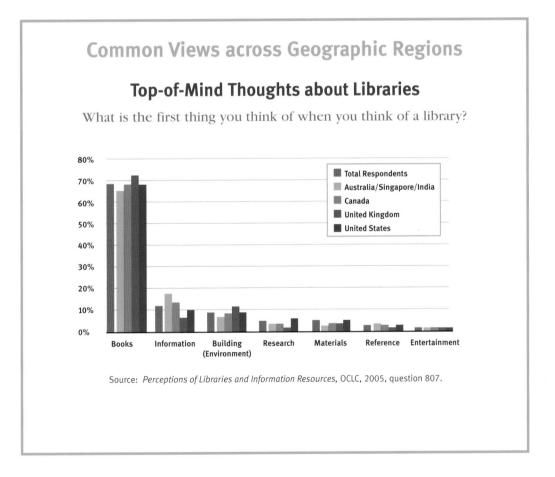

Common Views across Geographic Regions

Top-of-Mind Thoughts about Libraries

What is the first thing you think of when you think of a library?

Legend:
- Total Respondents
- Australia/Singapore/India
- Canada
- United Kingdom
- United States

Source: *Perceptions of Libraries and Information Resources*, OCLC, 2005, question 807.

Common View Across Geographic Regions

Positive Associations with the Library
Please list two positive associations with the library.

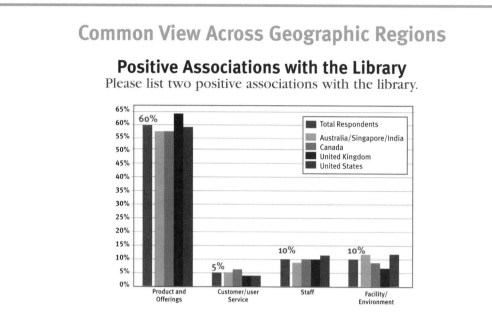

Source: *Perceptions of Libraries and Information Resources*, OCLC, 2005, question 812a.

Negative Associations with the Library
Please list two negative associations with the library.

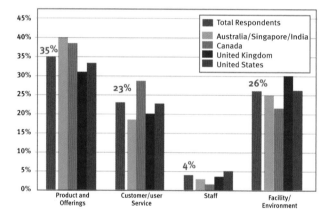

Source: *Perceptions of Libraries and Information Resources*, OCLC, 2005, question 812b.

Main Purpose of the Library
What do you feel is the main purpose of the library?

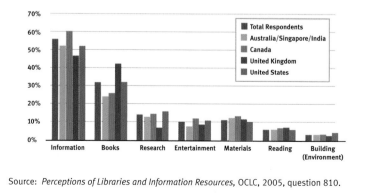

Source: *Perceptions of Libraries and Information Resources*, OCLC, 2005, question 810.

Common View Across Geographic Regions

Trustworthiness of the Library's Sources vs. Search Engines

Thinking about your usage of your primary library and the things you like and dislike about it, is the information you get from library sources more or less trustworthy compared to information you can get from search engines?

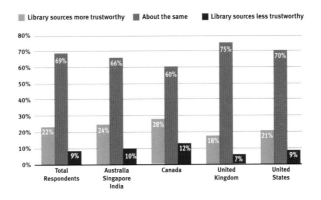

Source: *Perceptions of Libraries and Information Resources*, OCLC, 2005, question 1205.

Reasons for Never Using the Online Library Web Site

Why haven't you used the online library Web site?

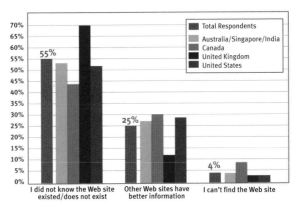

Source: *Perceptions of Libraries and Information Resources*, OCLC, 2005, question 1090.

Lifestyle Fits Perfectly with the Online Library

The chart below indicates the percentage of respondents by geographic region who agreed that the online library is a perfect fit with their information needs and lifestyles.

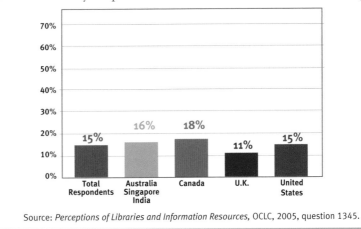

Source: *Perceptions of Libraries and Information Resources*, OCLC, 2005, question 1345.

Conclusion

Perceptions of Libraries and Information Resources: A Report to the OCLC Membership is intended to provide OCLC staff, the OCLC membership and the information community-at-large data on the perceptions and practices of the information consumer and how libraries are positioned in the infosphere they use.

This report is the result of a need to better understand the interests, habits and behaviors of people using libraries in a time of information abundance. We concluded *The 2003 OCLC Environmental Scan* by suggesting—based on the patterns and trends we identified and highlighted—that the place libraries hold today is no longer as distinct as it once was.

Libraries, many of their resources and services, and the information experts who work in libraries appeared to be increasingly less visible to today's information consumer. But we could not say with any certainty how extensive or how permanent this apparent shift had become, for, as we noted in the introduction to this report, there are no recent, large-scale use studies to draw on.

We have compiled a database of over 270,000 information consumer views, habits and recommendations from over 3,300 people in six countries. The database contains over 20,000 verbatim views about the library, Internet resources, library services and the "Library" brand. We have not identified and analyzed all aspects of the data for this report—this research data will be a source for ongoing exploration— but we have discovered much more about the practices and perceptions of these information consumers. A summary of the findings and a few conclusions and observations follow.

My library of the future,
will use technology,
to allow great books that are locked away
to be seen by you and me.

The great libraries of Alexandria,
and the monasteries of Rome,
will reveal hidden treasures
in the comfort of your home.

For each book will be scanned,
electronically of course,
and a hologram created,
it's the new modern force!

From *My Vision,*
a poem by "Kirstie,"
a Weatherhead (U.K.) High School student
[2003]

The full poem is reproduced in
The 2003 OCLC Environmental Scan, p.97.

Report Findings

...on Information Consumers' Perceptions and Habits

- Respondents use **search engines** to begin an information search (84 percent). **One percent** begin an information search on a **library Web site**. *(Part 1.2)*

- **Quality and quantity of information are top determinants** of a satisfactory information search. Search engines are rated higher than librarians. *(Part 2.6)*

- The criterion selected by most information consumers to evaluate electronic resources is that the information is ***worthwhile***. ***Free*** is a close second. ***Speed*** has less impact. *(Parts 3.1 and 3.4)*

- Respondents do not trust purchased information more than free information. The verbatim comments suggest a **high expectation of free information.** *(Part 3.4)*

- Library users like to self-serve. Most **respondents do not seek assistance** when using library resources. *(Part 2.4)*

- Library card holders **use information resources more** than non-card holders, and they are more favorably disposed to libraries than non-card holders. *(Parts 1.1, 1.4 and 3.7)*

- **Age matters sometimes. Sometimes it doesn't.** Responses are sometimes consistent across U.S. age groups, suggesting age-independent preferences and practices. Familiarity with e-mail is an example. In other areas, responses vary considerably by the age of the respondents. For example, young U.S. respondents are much less likely than those over 65 to agree librarians add value to the information search process. *(Part 2.6 and all Parts)*

- The survey **results are generally consistent across the geographic regions** surveyed. Responses from the United Kingdom showed the largest range of variations from other regions surveyed. *(Part 5 and all Parts)*

Report Findings

...on Libraries

- Information consumers **use the library.** They use the library less and read less since they began using the Internet. The majority of respondents anticipate their usage of libraries will be flat in the future. *(Parts 1.1 and 3.7)*

- **Borrowing print books** is the library service used most. *(Part 2.1)*

- "Books" is the **library brand.** There is no runner-up. *(Part 3.8)*

- Most information consumers **are not aware of,** nor do they use, most libraries' **electronic information resources.** *(Parts 1 and 2)*

- **College students** have the **highest rate of library use** and broadest use of library resources, both physical and electronic. *(Parts 1 and Part 2)*

- **Only 10 percent** of college students **indicated that their library's collection fulfilled their information needs** after accessing the library Web site from a search engine.

- The majority of information consumers are aware of many library community services and of the role the library plays in the larger community. Most respondents agree **the library is a place to learn.** *(Part 4.1)*

- Comments from respondents provide clear directions for physical libraries: be clean, bright, comfortable, warm and **well-lit;** be staffed by **friendly people;** have hours that fit their lifestyles; and **advertise services.** Find ways to get material to people, rather than making them come to the library. *(Appendix B)*

...on Alternatives to Libraries

- Information consumers like to **self-serve.** They use **personal knowledge** and common sense to judge if electronic information is trustworthy. They **cross-reference other sites** to validate their findings. *(Parts 3.2 and 3.5)*

- **Ninety percent** of respondents are satisfied with their most recent search for information using a **search engine**. Satisfaction with the overall search experience has a strong correlation to the quality and quantity of information returned in the search process. *(Part 2.6)*

- People trust what they find using search engines. They also trust information from libraries. They **trust them about the same.** *(Part 3.3)*

- **Search engines fit** the information consumer's lifestyle better than physical or online libraries. The majority of U.S. respondents, age 14 to 64, see search engines as a perfect fit. *(Part 3.7)*

Conclusions and Observations

What was confirmed

As discussed briefly in the introduction of the report, many findings of the survey do not surprise as much as they confirm the trends we highlighted in *The 2003 OCLC Environmental Scan*.

The survey results confirm that libraries are used by information seekers. The number of people holding library cards is compelling and most information seekers use library services at least annually. Libraries are used for borrowing books, access to reference books and research assistance. Respondents shared many positive associations with these traditional resources as well as with the library space itself. When asked to give advice, many respondents suggested increasing the library's quantity and variety of traditional information resources—"more books" was often cited—as well as the number of hours libraries are open. Respondents clearly want to be able to visit the library, but they want the services to be more convenient.

The results confirm, too, that the majority of information seekers are not making much use of the array of electronic resources (online magazines, databases and reference assistance, for example) libraries make available to their communities. Very few respondents use such resources regularly and the majority of respondents are not aware that their libraries have these electronic resources. Most do not use the library Web site where access to electronic resources is made available. College students are the exception. College students use electronic resources at significantly higher rates and are the most familiar with what libraries have to offer.

Results confirm that respondents are aware that libraries are "wired" and many use the computers in libraries to access the Internet and to use Internet resources. The majority of high school and college students use library computers regularly.

The survey confirms the findings of many other studies: that there is widespread use of Internet information resources. Respondents regularly use search engines, e-mail and instant messaging to obtain and share information. Many use these tools daily; most use them weekly or monthly. Subject-based Web sites, online news services, blogs and RSS feeds are all used, even if only minimally. The library is not the first or only stop for many information seekers. Search engines are the favorite place to begin a search and respondents indicate that Google is the search engine most recently used to begin their searches.

The information resource market—tools, content and access—is growing, not shrinking, providing more options and more choices to people using the Web to search for information and content. Information consumers are willing to experiment with new resources and incorporate them into their expanding repertoire of information tools. People continue to read, but they do it less as they add other

To gather as much literature and information as possible in one place, and to **share that wealth of resources with that community.** *It is important to have a place where anyone can go to learn (be it news, research, films and music, fiction, or non-fiction*

23-year-old from the United States

Source: *Perceptions of Libraries and Information Resources*, OCLC, 2005, question 810, "What do you feel is the main purpose of a library?"

ways of consuming information and content to their lives. Libraries are seen as a place for traditional resources (books, reference materials and research assistance) and to get access to the Internet. The results of this survey confirm that libraries are not seen as the top choice for access to electronic resources.

Awareness, usage and preference trends held fairly consistently across the geographic regions surveyed and across U.S. age groups. While differences in age group or geographic preferences are observed, general trends hold constant. Online information consumers surveyed are "universally" using the Internet, rather than the library, to access electronic information resources.

What was revealed

The survey revealed how information consumers make choices about electronic information resources; and how they evaluate those resources and make decisions about the quality, trustworthiness and monetary worth of resources available from libraries and generally on the open Web.

While it is easy to assume that search engines are the top choice of information consumers because of the speed with which information can be delivered, the study revealed that speed is not the only, and not the primary, reason search engines are the preferred starting point for today's information consumer. Quality and quantity of information delivered are the highest determinants of overall information search satisfaction. Respondents indicated that search engines deliver better quality and quantity of information than librarian-assisted searching—and at greater speed. As more and more content becomes digital and directly accessible via search engines, quantity will increase. The amount of quality information, overall, is also likely to increase.

Information consumers trust information they get from libraries, and they trust the information they get from search engines. The survey revealed that they trust them almost equally. While all U.S. age groups surveyed indicated trust across both sources, young people in the United States ages 14 to 24 show the greatest level of trust for information received via search engines. How much of this trust could be attributed to greater familiarity and frequent use of Web-based electronic resources? Most U.S. youth are not familiar with library electronic resources, but are very familiar with search engines, e-mail and chat. As more content becomes directly accessible via search engines, familiarity with more and different types of digital content is likely to increase. Will trust continue to increase too?

The survey highlighted that not only are information consumers happy to self-serve, they are confident that they can serve themselves well. When asked how they judge the trustworthiness of information, "common sense/ personal knowledge" was the top method used. Eighty-six percent of respondents feel confident they have the personal knowledge to evaluate information resources. When they want to validate information, they self-serve again, by searching another Web site that contains similar information (82 percent). This self-reliance was also reflected in respondents' use of the library. Most library users say they have not asked for help using any library resources, either at the physical or the virtual library. As more and more content becomes digital and accessible via the Internet, the number of information sources available for both information discovery and validation is likely to increase, fueling increased confidence and self-reliance.

Information consumers feel that information should be free. Most respondents will not pay for information and some who do (25 percent) expect that they will pay for information less frequently in the future. It is also clear that information seekers do not believe that higher priced information equals higher quality information. That the library provides access to "free" material is well-known. But the majority of users are not aware that free electronic information is available via their library. As many respondents are not familiar with, or infrequently use, the library Web site, the free library information is not accessed. The verbatim comments in Appendix B provide evidence of respondents' appreciation of free material as well as their frustrations with trying to access them and having to come to the library to use them. Information consumers want, and expect to use, more and more "free" and unfettered information in the future.

Survey respondents are generally satisfied with libraries and librarians, but most do not plan to increase their use of libraries. Many of them, particularly teenagers, use the library less since they began using the Internet. Verbatim comments reveal strong attachments to libraries as places, but many of these positive associations are nostalgic in nature and focused on books. As one respondent from the United States commented "...as a child I loved to go downstairs to the children's section and read books there and take them out. I loved the smell of old books." This attachment to the traditional nature and purpose of libraries is an asset all libraries share. It is not clear that this attachment extends, or will extend, to electronic resources or that it will have a significant impact on an information consumer's choice of information sources in the future.

Respondents do indeed have strong attachments to the idea of the "Library" but clearly expressed dissatisfaction with the service experience of the libraries they use. Poor signage, inhospitable surroundings, unfriendly staff, lack of parking, dirt, cold, hard-to-use systems and inconvenient hours were mentioned many, many times by respondents. The overall message is clear: improve the physical experience of using libraries.

We learned that respondents have much to say, when asked, about their libraries, the people who staff them and the services. This suggests that libraries have an opportunity to learn much more than was revealed in this report about the perceptions of the people in their communities by conducting local polls and open-ended surveys.

keep it current and keep it free

44-year-old from Canada

Source: *Perceptions of Libraries and Information Resources,* OCLC, 2005, question 1240, "If you could provide one piece of advice for your library, what would it be?"

The Library Brand

One of the most important goals of the project was to obtain a clearer understanding of the "Library" brand in 2005. How do information consumers think about libraries today? How do information consumers identify libraries in the growing universe of alternatives? What is the "Library" brand image?

What is the library's identity in the minds of information seekers? By a huge margin respondents feel that "library" is synonymous with "books." When asked about their first spontaneous impression of libraries, information consumers reply, "Books."

Familiarity, trust and quality—these are intangible traits often summed up by the word "brand." All brands from search engines to cars to libraries are either familiar or not, trusted or not, provide top quality or not. We tested these brand concepts in the survey.

We asked about familiarity. Libraries are very familiar as book providers. Search engines are very familiar as electronic information providers. We reviewed the concept of trust. The lines are fuzzy. Libraries and search engines are trusted almost equally. We asked about quality. Respondents see both libraries/librarians and search engines as providers of quality information. Again, the lines are blurred. In a tie, the data suggests the nod would go to search engines.

a building with books

35-year-old from Wales

Source: *Perceptions of Libraries and Information Resources,* OCLC, 2005, question 807, "What is the first thing you think of when you think of a library?"

The "Library" brand is dominant in one category—books. It would be delightful to assume that when respondents say "books," what they really mean to say is that books, in essence, stand for those intangible qualities of information familiarity, information trust and information quality. The data did not reveal it. We looked hard. We reviewed thousands of responses to the open-ended questions that inquired about positive library associations and library purpose. We searched for words and phrases that included mentions of "quality," "trust," "knowledge," "learning," "education," etc. We found mentions of each, but they were relatively few in number. "Books" dominated—across all regions surveyed and across all age groups.

In addition to being familiar, trusted and high-quality, strong brands must be relevant. Relevance is the degree to which people believe a brand meets their needs. In the survey we tested for relevancy and lifestyle fit. Over half of respondents said that search engines perfectly fit their lifestyle. Seventeen percent said libraries are a perfect fit. Over 20 percent said libraries do not fit their lifestyle. Of the activities that respondents are doing less since they began using the Internet, watching television was number one (39 percent) and using the library was number two (33 percent). Reading books, the dominant brand domain of the library, was third at 26 percent. That library resources and librarians add value to information search was not disputed by respondents, but the data suggest that the relevancy and lifestyle fit of that value are in question.

In a world where the sources of information and the tools of discovery continue to proliferate and increase in relevance to online information consumers, the brand differentiation of the library is still books. The library has not been successful in leveraging its brand to incorporate growing investments in electronic resources and library Web-based services.

Can the brand be expanded or updated to be more relevant, to be more than books? While this is a very difficult question to explore in a single survey, we briefly tested the concept. We asked respondents to identify what they felt was the "main purpose" of the library. What could/should the "Library" brand be? While a third of respondents still indicated "books" as the main purpose, over 50 percent of respondents feel "information" is the main purpose of the library. These views held fairly constant across all regions surveyed. U.S. youth were more inclined to view books as the library's main purpose; those 25 and older had a stronger feeling that the main purpose of the library is information.

The study suggests that the potential exists to stretch the "Library" brand beyond books. More study is required.

The similarity of perceptions about libraries and their resources across respondents from six countries is striking. It suggests that libraries are seen by information consumers as a common solution, a single organization—one entity with many outlets—constant, consistent, expected. The "Library" is, in essence, a global brand: a brand dominated by nostalgia and reinforced by common experience.

This global, nostalgic perception should give the library community reason to be concerned, but it also provides a solid base from which to leverage value, and create change, on a large scale. When change is needed, scale can be incredibly useful. In a world where information is rapidly becoming virtual, a "universal" brand can be effective and powerful. Libraries must take this advantage and work collectively to "rejuvenate" the brand. It is not simply about educating the information consumer about the current library. Trying to educate consumers whose habits and lifestyles are changing and have changed seldom works. It doesn't work for companies and it probably won't work for libraries. Rejuvenating the "Library" brand depends on the abilities of the members of the broad library community to redesign library services so that the rich resources—print and digital—they steward on behalf of their communities are available, accessible and used. Rejuvenating the brand depends on reconstructing the experience of using the library. While the need for localized points of distribution for content that is no longer available in just physical form is likely to become less relevant, the need for libraries to be gathering places within the community or university has not decreased. The data is clear. When prompted, information consumers see libraries' role in the community *as a place to learn, as a place to read, as a place to make information freely available, as a place to support literacy, as a place to provide research support, as a place to provide free computer/ Internet access* and more. These library services are relevant and differentiated.

Libraries will continue to share an expanding infosphere with an increasing number of content producers, providers and consumers. Information consumers will continue to self-serve from a growing information smorgasbord. The challenge for libraries is to clearly define and market their relevant place in that infosphere—their services and collections both physical and virtual.

It is time to rejuvenate the "Library" brand.

Subscribe to Rhapsody or iTunes or other music download services

45-year-old from the United States

Source: *Perceptions of Libraries and Information Resources,* OCLC, 2005, question 1240, "If you could provide one piece of advice for your library, what would it be?"

To provide **information on global issues** *from both past and present and offer usable information/ observations as to the* **possible future of all things.**

56-year-old from England

Source: *Perceptions of Libraries and Information Resources,* OCLC, 2005, question 810, "What do you feel is the main purpose of a library?"

Appendix A: Supporting Data Tables

All of the supporting data tables from the *Perceptions of Libraries and Information Sources* report are included in this Appendix A. The appendix is divided into Parts corresponding to the parts in the report.

Part 1.2

Usage Ratings for Information Sources—
by Region of Respondent
Please indicate if you have used any of the following sources/places
where you can obtain information, even if you have only used it once.

	Total Respondents	Australia Singapore India	Canada	United Kingdom	United States
Search engines	68%	71%	67%	67%	68%
Physical library	63%	65%	63%	56%	65%
Physical bookstore	61%	62%	64%	56%	62%
Online library	26%	32%	29%	11%	28%
Online bookstore	44%	38%	42%	41%	47%

Source: *Perceptions of Libraries and Information Resources,* OCLC, 2005, question 1305.

Usage Ratings for Information Sources—
by Age of U.S. Respondent
Please indicate if you have used any of the following sources/places
where you can obtain information, even if you have only used it once.

	Total U.S. Respondents	U.S. 14-17	U.S. 18-24	U.S. 25-64	U.S. 65+
Search engines	68%	78%	75%	70%	54%
Physical library	65%	73%	71%	65%	54%
Physical bookstore	62%	68%	68%	63%	51%
Online library	28%	31%	34%	29%	19%
Online bookstore	47%	37%	52%	51%	33%

Source: *Perceptions of Libraries and Information Resources,* OCLC, 2005, question 1305.

Usage Ratings for Information Sources—
by College Students across all Regions
Please indicate if you have used any of the following sources/places
where you can obtain information, even if you have only used it once.

	Total Respondents	College Students
Search engines	68%	75%
Physical library	63%	73%
Physical bookstore	61%	70%
Online library	26%	47%
Online bookstore	44%	55%

Source: *Perceptions of Libraries and Information Resources,* OCLC, 2005, question 1305.

Familiarity of Electronic Resources—
by Region of Respondent
Please indicate how familiar you are with each of the following electronic information sources.

	Total Respondents	Australia Singapore India	Canada	United Kingdom	United States
E-mail					
Extremely familiar	48%	51%	53%	45%	47%
Very familiar	10%	8%	9%	12%	10%
Somewhat familiar	3%	1%	2%	3%	3%
Not very familiar	1%	0%	0%	0%	1%
Just know the name	0%	0%	1%	0%	0%
Never heard of	0%	0%	1%	1%	0%
Search engine					
Extremely familiar	42%	46%	46%	41%	40%
Very familiar	13%	10%	12%	12%	14%
Somewhat familiar	6%	4%	5%	7%	7%
Not very familiar	1%	0%	1%	1%	2%
Just know the name	1%	0%	1%	1%	1%
Never heard of	1%	0%	1%	1%	1%
Instant messaging/online chat					
Extremely familiar	26%	26%	33%	21%	25%
Very familiar	13%	13%	15%	11%	13%
Somewhat familiar	15%	16%	11%	16%	15%
Not very familiar	10%	9%	7%	12%	10%
Just know the name	9%	6%	9%	14%	8%
Never heard of	2%	3%	1%	5%	2%
Online bookstore					
Extremely familiar	21%	17%	20%	22%	23%
Very familiar	19%	19%	19%	15%	20%
Somewhat familiar	17%	25%	21%	15%	14%
Not very familiar	8%	8%	10%	8%	7%
Just know the name	9%	8%	10%	11%	8%
Never heard of	3%	5%	6%	4%	2%

Source: *Perceptions of Libraries and Information Resources,* OCLC, 2005, question 505.

Familiarity of Electronic Resources—
by Region of Respondent (continued)

Please indicate how familiar you are with each of the following electronic information sources.

	Total Respondents	Australia Singapore India	Canada	United Kingdom	United States
Online news					
Extremely familiar	21%	20%	27%	15%	21%
Very familiar	16%	16%	16%	10%	18%
Somewhat familiar	21%	22%	21%	23%	21%
Not very familiar	8%	10%	4%	13%	8%
Just know the name	7%	6%	8%	10%	7%
Never heard of	3%	2%	4%	10%	2%
E-mail information subscriptions					
Extremely familiar	19%	19%	21%	14%	19%
Very familiar	16%	19%	17%	13%	15%
Somewhat familiar	21%	20%	22%	21%	21%
Not very familiar	9%	8%	5%	13%	10%
Just know the name	7%	7%	7%	10%	6%
Never heard of	6%	3%	7%	10%	6%
Topic-specific Web sites					
Extremely familiar	14%	10%	13%	5%	17%
Very familiar	12%	13%	13%	5%	13%
Somewhat familiar	18%	15%	20%	12%	20%
Not very familiar	12%	16%	12%	17%	10%
Just know the name	9%	13%	12%	12%	7%
Never heard of	15%	17%	15%	40%	8%
Electronic magazines/journals					
Extremely familiar	10%	13%	12%	7%	10%
Very familiar	11%	13%	16%	9%	10%
Somewhat familiar	22%	24%	19%	21%	22%
Not very familiar	19%	15%	18%	20%	21%
Just know the name	10%	6%	10%	12%	10%
Never heard of	15%	9%	10%	19%	17%
Library Web site					
Extremely familiar	10%	11%	13%	6%	10%
Very familiar	10%	14%	11%	5%	10%
Somewhat familiar	18%	19%	20%	12%	18%
Not very familiar	17%	14%	19%	18%	17%
Just know the name	10%	11%	9%	12%	9%
Never heard of	22%	16%	16%	37%	22%

Source: *Perceptions of Libraries and Information Resources*, OCLC, 2005, question 505.

Familiarity of Electronic Resources—
by Region of Respondent (continued)
Please indicate how familiar you are with each of the following electronic information sources.

	Total Respondents	Australia Singapore India	Canada	United Kingdom	United States
Blogs					
Extremely familiar	7%	7%	8%	2%	8%
Very familiar	7%	8%	8%	2%	7%
Somewhat familiar	16%	17%	15%	9%	17%
Not very familiar	14%	15%	13%	9%	16%
Just know the name	18%	18%	16%	17%	18%
Never heard of	31%	29%	34%	55%	25%
Online databases					
Extremely familiar	7%	8%	6%	4%	7%
Very familiar	6%	7%	6%	4%	6%
Somewhat familiar	17%	17%	17%	10%	18%
Not very familiar	19%	21%	18%	21%	19%
Just know the name	14%	9%	17%	16%	15%
Never heard of	30%	26%	30%	41%	28%
Ask an expert					
Extremely familiar	5%	5%	5%	4%	6%
Very familiar	8%	7%	11%	8%	7%
Somewhat familiar	18%	16%	17%	14%	19%
Not very familiar	19%	21%	18%	18%	19%
Just know the name	16%	15%	16%	18%	15%
Never heard of	28%	28%	27%	31%	27%
Audiobooks (downloadable/digital)					
Extremely familiar	4%	6%	5%	2%	4%
Very familiar	8%	12%	8%	4%	8%
Somewhat familiar	18%	19%	18%	14%	19%
Not very familiar	24%	19%	23%	26%	26%
Just know the name	20%	18%	25%	20%	19%
Never heard of	20%	17%	18%	27%	20%
Electronic books (digital)					
Extremely familiar	4%	9%	5%	4%	3%
Very familiar	8%	10%	11%	4%	7%
Somewhat familiar	20%	23%	21%	13%	21%
Not very familiar	22%	18%	23%	24%	22%
Just know the name	18%	14%	17%	20%	18%
Never heard of	21%	14%	17%	27%	22%

Source: *Perceptions of Libraries and Information Resources*, OCLC, 2005, question 505.

Familiarity of Electronic Resources—
by Region of Respondent (continued)
Please indicate how familiar you are with each of the following electronic information sources.

	Total Respondents	Australia Singapore India	Canada	United Kingdom	United States
Online librarian question service					
Extremely familiar	3%	3%	2%	2%	4%
Very familiar	4%	5%	3%	3%	4%
Somewhat familiar	12%	11%	13%	8%	13%
Not very familiar	19%	22%	22%	17%	17%
Just know the name	12%	11%	16%	10%	12%
Never heard of	47%	42%	40%	57%	48%
RSS feeds					
Extremely familiar	2%	2%	2%	1%	2%
Very familiar	2%	3%	3%	1%	2%
Somewhat familiar	5%	6%	3%	6%	5%
Not very familiar	8%	11%	6%	7%	7%
Just know the name	6%	9%	9%	6%	5%
Never heard of	75%	67%	75%	77%	77%

Source: *Perceptions of Libraries and Information Resources,* OCLC, 2005, question 505.

Familiarity of Electronic Resources—
by Age of U.S. Respondent
Please indicate how familiar you are with each of the following electronic information sources.

	Total U.S. Respondents	U.S. 14-17	U.S. 18-24	U.S. 25-64	U.S. 65+
E-mail					
Extremely familiar	47%	41%	49%	49%	42%
Very familiar	10%	5%	6%	10%	16%
Somewhat familiar	3%	4%	2%	3%	2%
Not very familiar	1%	0%	1%	1%	0%
Just know the name	0%	0%	0%	0%	0%
Never heard of	0%	4%	0%	0%	0%
Search engines					
Extremely familiar	40%	37%	51%	41%	27%
Very familiar	14%	6%	7%	14%	20%
Somewhat familiar	7%	3%	3%	7%	14%
Not very familiar	2%	1%	1%	2%	4%
Just know the name	1%	1%	1%	0%	2%
Never heard of	1%	5%	0%	0%	2%
Instant messaging/online chat					
Extremely familiar	25%	34%	40%	24%	13%
Very familiar	13%	7%	14%	14%	10%
Somewhat familiar	15%	7%	8%	16%	23%
Not very familiar	10%	1%	3%	12%	13%
Just know the name	8%	2%	0%	7%	21%
Never heard of	2%	6%	2%	1%	3%
Online bookstore					
Extremely familiar	23%	22%	33%	23%	15%
Very familiar	20%	17%	18%	22%	18%
Somewhat familiar	14%	18%	13%	13%	17%
Not very familiar	7%	7%	3%	8%	8%
Just know the name	8%	7%	7%	6%	17%
Never heard of	2%	9%	2%	1%	6%

Source: *Perceptions of Libraries and Information Resources*, OCLC, 2005, question 505.

Familiarity of Electronic Resources—
by Age of U.S. Respondent (continued)

Please indicate how familiar you are with each of the following electronic information sources.

	Total U.S. Respondents	U.S. 14-17	U.S. 18-24	U.S. 25-64	U.S. 65+
Online news					
Extremely familiar	21%	21%	27%	21%	12%
Very familiar	18%	15%	15%	18%	21%
Somewhat familiar	21%	20%	17%	21%	21%
Not very familiar	8%	6%	6%	8%	10%
Just know the name	7%	5%	3%	6%	10%
Never heard of	2%	7%	5%	1%	4%
E-mail information subscriptions					
Extremely familiar	19%	15%	23%	20%	13%
Very familiar	15%	16%	17%	15%	15%
Somewhat familiar	21%	20%	16%	22%	20%
Not very familiar	10%	6%	9%	9%	13%
Just know the name	6%	5%	7%	5%	8%
Never heard of	6%	9%	4%	5%	11%
Topic-specific Web sites					
Extremely familiar	17%	11%	18%	18%	14%
Very familiar	13%	10%	15%	13%	14%
Somewhat familiar	20%	18%	24%	21%	17%
Not very familiar	10%	8%	7%	10%	16%
Just know the name	7%	10%	10%	6%	8%
Never heard of	8%	24%	8%	6%	11%
Electronic magazines/journals					
Extremely familiar	10%	13%	13%	10%	3%
Very familiar	10%	9%	15%	10%	5%
Somewhat familiar	22%	19%	25%	23%	16%
Not very familiar	21%	18%	16%	22%	24%
Just know the name	10%	9%	9%	10%	13%
Never heard of	17%	15%	11%	15%	28%
Library Web site					
Extremely familiar	10%	10%	18%	10%	5%
Very familiar	10%	12%	17%	8%	10%
Somewhat familiar	18%	19%	19%	19%	12%
Not very familiar	17%	11%	6%	19%	20%
Just know the name	9%	11%	10%	9%	12%
Never heard of	22%	17%	13%	22%	32%

Source: *Perceptions of Libraries and Information Resources*, OCLC, 2005, question 505.

Familiarity of Electronic Resources—
by Age of U.S. Respondent (continued)
Please indicate how familiar you are with each of the following electronic information sources.

	Total U.S. Respondents	U.S. 14-17	U.S. 18-24	U.S. 25-64	U.S. 65+
Blogs					
Extremely familiar	8%	15%	16%	6%	2%
Very familiar	7%	8%	12%	6%	4%
Somewhat familiar	17%	16%	16%	19%	12%
Not very familiar	16%	9%	12%	15%	24%
Just know the name	18%	9%	14%	18%	27%
Never heard of	25%	22%	21%	26%	27%
Online databases					
Extremely familiar	7%	7%	11%	8%	2%
Very familiar	6%	4%	11%	6%	3%
Somewhat familiar	18%	15%	14%	20%	12%
Not very familiar	19%	15%	10%	21%	22%
Just know the name	15%	15%	16%	14%	22%
Never heard of	28%	34%	28%	26%	33%
Ask an expert					
Extremely familiar	6%	6%	7%	6%	3%
Very familiar	7%	8%	10%	7%	5%
Somewhat familiar	19%	21%	20%	20%	12%
Not very familiar	19%	15%	18%	21%	14%
Just know the name	15%	12%	20%	12%	23%
Never heard of	27%	25%	19%	25%	39%
Audiobooks (downloadable/digital)					
Extremely familiar	4%	4%	7%	4%	1%
Very familiar	8%	7%	11%	8%	7%
Somewhat familiar	19%	18%	24%	20%	9%
Not very familiar	26%	16%	21%	27%	26%
Just know the name	19%	22%	17%	17%	24%
Never heard of	20%	25%	19%	17%	30%
Online librarian question service					
Extremely familiar	4%	3%	9%	4%	2%
Very familiar	4%	7%	7%	3%	4%
Somewhat familiar	13%	12%	10%	14%	10%
Not very familiar	17%	15%	14%	17%	15%
Just know the name	12%	10%	14%	11%	14%
Never heard of	48%	46%	42%	48%	52%

Source: *Perceptions of Libraries and Information Resources*, OCLC, 2005, question 505.

Familiarity of Electronic Resources—
by Age of U.S. Respondent (continued)
Please indicate how familiar you are with each of the following electronic information sources.

	Total U.S. Respondents	U.S. 14-17	U.S. 18-24	U.S. 25-64	U.S. 65+
Electronic books (digital)					
Extremely familiar	3%	7%	7%	3%	2%
Very familiar	7%	5%	9%	8%	2%
Somewhat familiar	21%	18%	20%	24%	11%
Not very familiar	22%	17%	24%	20%	27%
Just know the name	18%	18%	18%	17%	27%
Never heard of	22%	24%	15%	21%	26%
RSS feeds					
Extremely familiar	2%	1%	4%	1%	0%
Very familiar	2%	2%	5%	2%	0%
Somewhat familiar	5%	5%	7%	5%	1%
Not very familiar	7%	6%	8%	8%	6%
Just know the name	5%	5%	5%	5%	7%
Never heard of	77%	77%	71%	76%	84%

Source: *Perceptions of Libraries and Information Resources,* OCLC, 2005, question 505.

*Where Electronic Information Searches Begin—*by Region of Respondent
Where do you typically begin your search for information on a particular topic?

	Total Respondents	Australia Singapore India	Canada	United Kingdom	United States
Search engine	84%	86%	86%	87%	82%
E-mail	6%	5%	2%	6%	7%
Topic-specific Web sites	2%	3%	1%	0%	3%
E-mail information subscriptions	2%	2%	2%	1%	2%
Online news	2%	0%	2%	1%	2%
Instant messaging/online chat	1%	1%	2%	1%	1%
Online bookstore	1%	1%	1%	2%	1%
Online database	1%	2%	1%	0%	1%
Library Web site	1%	0%	2%	1%	1%

Source: *Perceptions of Libraries and Information Resources,* OCLC, 2005, question 520.

*Where Electronic Information Searches Begin—*by Age of U.S. Respondent
Where do you typically begin your search for information on a particular topic?

	Total U.S. Respondents	U.S. 14-17	U.S. 18-24	U.S. 25-64	U.S. 65+
Search engine	82%	88%	84%	84%	67%
E-mail	7%	2%	6%	5%	16%
Topic-specific Web sites	3%	2%	3%	3%	7%
E-mail information subscriptions	2%	1%	1%	2%	2%
Online news	2%	1%	2%	1%	3%
Instant messaging/online chat	1%	1%	0%	1%	0%
Online bookstore	1%	0%	1%	1%	4%
Online database	1%	2%	1%	1%	0%
Library Web site	1%	1%	0%	1%	1%

Source: *Perceptions of Libraries and Information Resources,* OCLC, 2005, question 520.

Where Electronic Information Searches Begin— by College Students across all Regions
Where do you typically begin your search for information on a particular topic?

	Total Respondents	College Students
Search engine	84%	89%
E-mail	6%	1%
Topic-specific Web sites	2%	1%
E-mail information subscriptions	2%	1%
Online news	2%	1%
Instant messaging/online chat	1%	0%
Online bookstore	1%	1%
Online database	1%	2%
Library Web site	1%	2%

Source: *Perceptions of Libraries and Information Resources,* OCLC, 2005, question 520.

Where Electronic Information Searches Begin—
by Library Card Holders across all Regions
Where do you typically begin your search for information on a particular topic?

	Total Respondents	Library Card Holders	Non-Card Holders
Search engine	84%	85%	81%
E-mail	6%	4%	4%
Topic-specific Web sites	2%	3%	2%
E-mail information subscriptions	2%	1%	4%
Online news	2%	1%	2%
Instant messaging/online chat	1%	1%	0%
Online bookstore	1%	1%	1%
Online database	1%	1%	0%
Library Web site	1%	1%	0%

Source: *Perceptions of Libraries and Information Resources,* OCLC, 2005, question 520.

Part 1.3

Learning about Electronic Information Sources—
by Region of Respondent
Other than search engines, how do you learn about electronic information sources?
(Select all that apply.)

	Total Respondents	Australia Singapore India	Canada	United Kingdom	United States
Friend	61%	68%	67%	59%	58%
Links from electronic information sources or Web sites	59%	73%	66%	54%	55%
News media	52%	62%	53%	48%	50%
Promotions/advertising	39%	49%	43%	40%	34%
Online news	38%	40%	45%	23%	40%
Relative	37%	34%	41%	32%	38%
Coworker/professional colleague	35%	44%	46%	31%	30%
Instant messaging/online chat	22%	29%	33%	20%	18%
Reference from a library Web site	15%	19%	19%	11%	14%
Teacher	11%	11%	14%	5%	12%
Blogs	9%	8%	9%	2%	11%
Librarian	8%	9%	8%	5%	8%

Source: *Perceptions of Libraries and Information Resources,* OCLC, 2005, question 605.

Learning about Electronic Information Sources—
by Age of U.S. Respondent
Other than search engines, how do you learn about electronic information sources?
(Select all that apply.)

	Total U.S. Respondents	U.S. 14-17	U.S. 18-24	U.S. 25-64	U.S. 65+
Friend	58%	64%	69%	56%	57%
Links from electronic information sources or Web sites	55%	36%	43%	60%	51%
News media	50%	41%	38%	51%	59%
Promotions/advertising	34%	24%	21%	37%	35%
Online news	40%	31%	37%	43%	36%
Relative	38%	34%	33%	38%	46%
Coworker/professional colleague	30%	9%	28%	38%	11%
Instant messaging/online chat	18%	37%	27%	15%	14%
Reference from a library Web site	14%	17%	20%	12%	13%
Teacher	12%	46%	35%	6%	5%
Blogs	11%	12%	13%	12%	3%
Librarian	8%	17%	26%	5%	6%

Source: *Perceptions of Libraries and Information Resources,* OCLC, 2005, question 605.

Learning about Electronic Information Sources—
by College Students across all Regions
Other than search engines, how do you learn about electronic information sources?
(Select all that apply.)

	Total Respondents	College Students
Friend	61%	67%
Links from electronic information sources or Web sites	59%	61%
News media	52%	44%
Promotions/advertising	39%	26%
Online news	38%	42%
Relative	37%	26%
Coworker/professional colleague	35%	37%
Instant messaging/online chat	22%	26%
Reference from a library Web site	15%	36%
Teacher	11%	50%
Blogs	9%	13%
Librarian	8%	33%

Source: *Perceptions of Libraries and Information Resources,* OCLC, 2005, question 605.

Learning about Electronic Information Sources—
by Library Card Holders across all Regions
Other than search engines, how do you learn about electronic information sources?
(Select all that apply.)

	Total Respondents	Library Card Holders	Non-Card Holders
Friend	61%	62%	58%
Links from electronic information sources or Web sites	59%	61%	54%
News media	52%	55%	45%
Promotions/advertising	39%	37%	35%
Online news	38%	42%	41%
Relative	37%	38%	30%
Coworker/professional colleague	35%	36%	33%
Instant messaging/Online chat	22%	23%	21%
Reference from a library Web site	15%	20%	3%
Teacher	11%	13%	6%
Blogs	9%	10%	7%
Librarian	8%	11%	1%

Source: *Perceptions of Libraries and Information Resources,* OCLC, 2005, question 605.

Part 1.4

Information Sources Considered—by Region of Respondent

Next time you need a source/place for information, which source or sources would you consider?
(Select all that apply.)

	Total Respondents	Australia Singapore India	Canada	United Kingdom	United States
Search engines	91%	95%	91%	93%	89%
Library (physical)	55%	63%	61%	42%	55%
Online library	42%	48%	49%	34%	41%
Bookstore (physical)	37%	41%	44%	27%	37%
Online bookstore	30%	33%	31%	29%	30%

Source: *Perceptions of Libraries and Information Resources*, OCLC, 2005, question 1325.

Information Sources Considered—by Age of U.S. Respondent

Next time you need a source/place for information, which source or sources would you consider?
(Select all that apply.)

	Total U.S. Respondents	U.S. 14-17	U.S. 18-24	U.S. 25-64	U.S. 65+
Search engines	89%	86%	85%	90%	91%
Library (physical)	55%	62%	57%	53%	57%
Online library	41%	23%	37%	46%	35%
Bookstore (physical)	37%	32%	31%	40%	30%
Online bookstore	30%	13%	29%	32%	28%

Source: *Perceptions of Libraries and Information Resources*, OCLC, 2005, question 1325.

Information Sources Considered—
by College Students across all Regions

Next time you need a source/place for information, which source or sources would you consider?
(Select all that apply.)

	Total Respondents	College Students
Search engines	91%	90%
Library (physical)	55%	66%
Online library	42%	50%
Bookstore (physical)	37%	38%
Online bookstore	30%	34%

Source: *Perceptions of Libraries and Information Resources*, OCLC, 2005, question 1325.

Information Sources Considered—
by Library Card Holders across all Regions
Next time you need a source/place for information, which source or sources would you consider?
(Select all that apply.)

	Total Respondents	Library Card Holders	Non-Card Holders
Search engines	91%	92%	89%
Library (physical)	55%	64%	33%
Online library	42%	45%	36%
Bookstore (physical)	37%	40%	30%
Online bookstore	30%	31%	27%

Source: *Perceptions of Libraries and Information Resources,* OCLC, 2005, question 1325.

First Choice for Information—by Region of Respondent
Which source/place would be your first choice?

	Total Respondents	Australia Singapore India	Canada	United Kingdom	United States
Search engines	80%	85%	76%	85%	78%
Library (physical)	11%	6%	14%	7%	12%
Online library	6%	6%	6%	4%	6%
Bookstore (physical)	2%	2%	3%	1%	2%
Online bookstore	2%	1%	1%	3%	2%

Source: *Perceptions of Libraries and Information Resources,* OCLC, 2005, question 1335.

First Choice for Information—by Age of U.S. Respondent
Which source/place would be your first choice?

	Total U.S. Respondents	U.S. 14-17	U.S. 18-24	U.S. 25-64	U.S. 65+
Search engines	78%	77%	69%	81%	76%
Library (physical)	12%	14%	17%	10%	15%
Online library	6%	4%	8%	6%	8%
Bookstore (physical)	2%	4%	1%	2%	1%
Online bookstore	2%	2%	4%	1%	1%

Source: *Perceptions of Libraries and Information Resources,* OCLC, 2005, question 1335.

First Choice for Information—by College Students across all Regions
Which source/place would be your first choice?

	Total Respondents	College Students
Search engines	80%	72%
Library (physical)	11%	14%
Online library	6%	10%
Bookstore (physical)	2%	2%
Online bookstore	2%	2%

Source: *Perceptions of Libraries and Information Resources*, OCLC, 2005, question 1335.

First Choice for Information— by Library Card Holders across all Regions
Which source/place would be your first choice?

	Total Respondents	Library Card Holders	Non-Card Holders
Search engines	80%	78%	84%
Library (physical)	11%	12%	6%
Online library	6%	6%	6%
Bookstore (physical)	2%	2%	2%
Online bookstore	2%	2%	2%

Source: *Perceptions of Libraries and Information Resources*, OCLC, 2005, question 1335.

Information Brands with Worthwhile Information—by Region of Respondent

Please rate the degree to which you agree or disagree that each electronic information source provides worthwhile information. Base: Respondents who indicated usage of any of the list of 21 information brands

	Total Respondents	Australia Singapore India	Canada	United Kingdom	United States
Google.com					
Completely agree	55%	59%	56%	51%	54%
Agree	38%	35%	38%	44%	38%
Neither agree nor disagree	6%	6%	5%	4%	6%
Disagree	0%	0%	0%	1%	0%
Completely disagree	1%	0%	0%	0%	2%
Yahoo.com					
Completely agree	34%	36%	34%	29%	35%
Agree	51%	52%	53%	55%	50%
Neither agree nor disagree	12%	11%	8%	14%	12%
Disagree	1%	1%	3%	1%	1%
Completely disagree	1%	0%	1%	0%	2%
MSN Search					
Completely agree	29%	29%	35%	27%	27%
Agree	52%	49%	51%	54%	53%
Neither agree nor disagree	15%	18%	10%	15%	16%
Disagree	3%	4%	3%	2%	3%
Completely disagree	1%	1%	1%	1%	1%
Ask Jeeves.com					
Completely agree	25%	27%	20%	30%	25%
Agree	53%	53%	51%	51%	54%
Neither agree nor disagree	16%	17%	21%	12%	16%
Disagree	3%	1%	6%	5%	3%
Completely disagree	1%	2%	2%	2%	1%
Library Web site					
Completely agree	33%	33%	29%	29%	34%
Agree	45%	48%	38%	52%	45%
Neither agree nor disagree	19%	15%	32%	19%	17%
Disagree	3%	3%	1%	0%	4%
Completely disagree	0%	1%	0%	0%	0%
Netscape Search					
Completely agree	20%	13%	18%	6%	24%
Agree	52%	54%	55%	56%	50%
Neither agree nor disagree	25%	32%	19%	33%	24%
Disagree	2%	1%	7%	1%	1%
Completely disagree	1%	1%	1%	4%	1%
Online librarian question service					
Completely agree	23%	36%	9%	6%	24%
Agree	48%	48%	62%	39%	45%
Neither agree nor disagree	23%	15%	29%	56%	20%
Disagree	0%	0%	0%	0%	0%
Completely disagree	7%	0%	0%	0%	11%

Source: *Perceptions of Libraries and Information Resources*, OCLC, 2005, question 670.

Information Brands with Worthwhile Information— by Region of Respondent (continued)

Please rate the degree to which you agree or disagree that each electronic information source provides worthwhile information. Base: Respondents who indicated usage of any of the list of 21 information brands

	Total Respondents	Australia Singapore India	Canada	United Kingdom	United States
About.com					
Completely agree	29%	23%	15%	25%	32%
Agree	42%	53%	50%	43%	39%
Neither agree nor disagree	23%	23%	23%	9%	24%
Disagree	3%	0%	10%	22%	2%
Completely disagree	3%	1%	2%	0%	3%
AltaVista.com					
Completely agree	20%	23%	22%	12%	20%
Agree	51%	50%	44%	57%	53%
Neither agree nor disagree	26%	25%	32%	31%	24%
Disagree	2%	2%	2%	1%	3%
Completely disagree	0%	0%	0%	0%	0%
Lycos.com					
Completely agree	15%	9%	15%	13%	17%
Agree	51%	40%	51%	56%	52%
Neither agree nor disagree	32%	49%	29%	29%	29%
Disagree	3%	1%	5%	1%	3%
Completely disagree	0%	1%	0%	1%	0%
AOL Search					
Completely agree	19%	14%	12%	20%	21%
Agree	46%	48%	49%	57%	44%
Neither agree nor disagree	27%	34%	21%	20%	28%
Disagree	3%	1%	13%	0%	3%
Completely disagree	4%	2%	4%	3%	4%
Excite.com					
Completely agree	11%	12%	7%	7%	13%
Agree	51%	45%	53%	61%	51%
Neither agree nor disagree	35%	42%	39%	26%	33%
Disagree	2%	1%	1%	5%	3%
Completely disagree	0%	0%	0%	0%	0%
LookSmart.com					
Completely agree	12%	14%	16%	13%	8%
Agree	49%	53%	41%	42%	48%
Neither agree nor disagree	38%	32%	43%	37%	42%
Disagree	1%	1%	0%	7%	1%
Completely disagree	0%	1%	0%	0%	0%
Dogpile.com					
Completely agree	26%	29%	33%	25%	24%
Agree	37%	50%	33%	31%	37%
Neither agree nor disagree	33%	18%	32%	41%	34%
Disagree	2%	3%	2%	0%	2%
Completely disagree	2%	0%	0%	2%	3%

Source: *Perceptions of Libraries and Information Resources*, OCLC, 2005, question 670.

Information Brands with Worthwhile Information— by Region of Respondent (continued)

Please rate the degree to which you agree or disagree that each electronic information source provides worthwhile information. Base: Respondents who indicated usage of any of the list of 21 information brands

	Total Respondents	Australia Singapore India	Canada	United Kingdom	United States
Ask an Expert					
Completely agree	17%	17%	16%	18%	17%
Agree	38%	41%	43%	38%	47%
Neither agree nor disagree	30%	42%	38%	41%	33%
Disagree	2%	0%	3%	4%	3%
Completely disagree	0%	0%	0%	0%	0%
HotBot.com					
Completely agree	10%	10%	11%	2%	12%
Agree	39%	39%	57%	29%	36%
Neither agree nor disagree	46%	45%	30%	62%	49%
Disagree	4%	5%	2%	7%	3%
Completely disagree	0%	0%	0%	0%	0%
Teoma.com					
Completely agree	12%	12%	0%	0%	16%
Agree	32%	66%	0%	0%	32%
Neither agree nor disagree	33%	9%	0%	0%	52%
Disagree	2%	12%	0%	0%	0%
Completely disagree	0%	1%	0%	0%	0%
iWon.com					
Completely agree	14%	6%	11%	0%	16%
Agree	27%	19%	50%	0%	23%
Neither agree nor disagree	38%	66%	26%	0%	39%
Disagree	13%	9%	10%	0%	15%
Completely disagree	6%	0%	4%	0%	7%
AllTheWeb.com					
Completely agree	16%	27%	22%	7%	8%
Agree	28%	42%	27%	52%	20%
Neither agree nor disagree	32%	28%	51%	41%	42%
Disagree	3%	3%	0%	0%	4%
Completely disagree	11%	0%	0%	0%	26%
Gigablast.com					
Completely agree	3%	0%	0%	0%	5%
Agree	8%	0%	0%	0%	12%
Neither agree nor disagree	25%	0%	0%	0%	39%
Disagree	0%	0%	0%	0%	0%
Completely disagree	28%	0%	0%	0%	44%
Clusty.com					
Completely agree	0%	0%	0%	0%	3%
Agree	5%	0%	0%	0%	60%
Neither agree nor disagree	3%	0%	0%	0%	37%
Disagree	0%	0%	0%	0%	0%
Completely disagree	0%	0%	0%	0%	0%

Source: *Perceptions of Libraries and Information Resources,* OCLC, 2005, question 670.

Familiarity and Usage of Information Brands—by Region of Respondent
Please indicate how familiar you are with the following information sources
and if you have used each source, even if you have only used it once.

	Total Respondents	Australia Singapore India	Canada	United Kingdom	United States
Google.com - Have used	**71%**	**76%**	**72%**	**70%**	**70%**
Extremely familiar	40%	47%	46%	43%	35%
Very familiar	12%	10%	13%	8%	14%
Somewhat familiar	9%	6%	9%	11%	9%
Not very familiar	4%	2%	2%	2%	5%
Just know the name	3%	2%	2%	2%	3%
Never heard of	1%	0%	0%	0%	1%
Yahoo.com - Have used	**64%**	**70%**	**65%**	**51%**	**66%**
Extremely familiar	26%	29%	24%	20%	28%
Very familiar	17%	17%	21%	14%	16%
Somewhat familiar	17%	16%	22%	23%	15%
Not very familiar	5%	3%	4%	9%	4%
Just know the name	4%	2%	3%	8%	3%
Never heard of	1%	0%	1%	0%	1%
MSN Search - Have used	**48%**	**58%**	**53%**	**45%**	**45%**
Extremely familiar	16%	17%	20%	16%	14%
Very familiar	15%	14%	15%	14%	15%
Somewhat familiar	20%	22%	22%	18%	20%
Not very familiar	10%	10%	10%	12%	10%
Just know the name	12%	7%	10%	14%	14%
Never heard of	4%	2%	2%	4%	6%
Ask Jeeves.com - Have used	**46%**	**34%**	**45%**	**59%**	**46%**
Extremely familiar	11%	7%	11%	15%	11%
Very familiar	12%	10%	10%	14%	13%
Somewhat familiar	22%	20%	24%	25%	22%
Not very familiar	10%	10%	11%	8%	11%
Just know the name	14%	15%	16%	8%	15%
Never heard of	10%	24%	13%	1%	7%
AOL Search - Have used	**26%**	**17%**	**18%**	**20%**	**33%**
Extremely familiar	9%	6%	7%	10%	10%
Very familiar	9%	7%	7%	6%	11%
Somewhat familiar	20%	18%	22%	21%	19%
Not very familiar	14%	17%	11%	13%	14%
Just know the name	28%	34%	35%	29%	24%
Never heard of	7%	9%	10%	10%	5%
Netscape Search - Have used	**26%**	**24%**	**38%**	**10%**	**27%**
Extremely familiar	7%	7%	9%	3%	7%
Very familiar	10%	8%	12%	3%	12%
Somewhat familiar	18%	23%	23%	13%	17%
Not very familiar	14%	15%	14%	14%	14%
Just know the name	25%	24%	15%	31%	26%
Never heard of	14%	13%	13%	30%	11%

Source: *Perceptions of Libraries and Information Resources*, OCLC, 2005, question 665.

Familiarity and Usage of Information Brands—by Region of Respondent (continued)
Please indicate how familiar you are with the following information sources
and if you have used each source, even if you have only used it once.

	Total Respondents	Australia Singapore India	Canada	United Kingdom	United States
Lycos.com - Have used	**28%**	**30%**	**27%**	**32%**	**27%**
Extremely familiar	5%	6%	4%	7%	5%
Very familiar	8%	9%	8%	10%	7%
Somewhat familiar	19%	19%	23%	19%	18%
Not very familiar	14%	15%	13%	12%	14%
Just know the name	22%	17%	24%	20%	24%
Never heard of	18%	24%	19%	17%	17%
AltaVista.com - Have used	**28%**	**42%**	**29%**	**20%**	**26%**
Extremely familiar	6%	10%	6%	4%	5%
Very familiar	7%	11%	7%	4%	6%
Somewhat familiar	17%	23%	21%	18%	14%
Not very familiar	12%	14%	12%	9%	12%
Just know the name	21%	15%	26%	23%	20%
Never heard of	27%	13%	18%	35%	31%
Library Web site - Have used	**21%**	**22%**	**28%**	**8%**	**22%**
Extremely familiar	7%	7%	9%	2%	7%
Very familiar	6%	6%	4%	2%	8%
Somewhat familiar	12%	11%	18%	9%	12%
Not very familiar	11%	14%	11%	7%	11%
Just know the name	12%	12%	11%	10%	12%
Never heard of	45%	42%	39%	66%	42%
Excite.com - Have used	**21%**	**24%**	**26%**	**12%**	**21%**
Extremely familiar	4%	7%	4%	2%	4%
Very familiar	6%	5%	9%	5%	6%
Somewhat familiar	15%	20%	17%	9%	14%
Not very familiar	12%	14%	12%	8%	12%
Just know the name	22%	16%	18%	24%	24%
Never heard of	32%	28%	31%	46%	29%
iWon.com - Have used	**13%**	**4%**	**9%**	**1%**	**20%**
Extremely familiar	4%	1%	2%	1%	7%
Very familiar	4%	2%	4%	0%	6%
Somewhat familiar	8%	5%	7%	2%	11%
Not very familiar	7%	7%	6%	3%	9%
Just know the name	14%	15%	11%	6%	16%
Never heard of	57%	68%	66%	89%	44%
About.com - Have used	**15%**	**11%**	**15%**	**5%**	**19%**
Extremely familiar	3%	2%	4%	1%	4%
Very familiar	5%	3%	5%	1%	6%
Somewhat familiar	10%	11%	13%	5%	11%
Not very familiar	7%	10%	10%	6%	6%
Just know the name	13%	17%	12%	10%	12%
Never heard of	55%	53%	52%	74%	51%

Source: *Perceptions of Libraries and Information Resources,* OCLC, 2005, question 665.

Familiarity and Usage of Information Brands—by Region of Respondent (continued)
Please indicate how familiar you are with the following information sources
and if you have used each source, even if you have only used it once.

	Total Respondents	Australia Singapore India	Canada	United Kingdom	United States
Dogpile.com - Have used	**14%**	**10%**	**16%**	**9%**	**16%**
Extremely familiar	3%	4%	4%	2%	2%
Very familiar	3%	3%	4%	1%	4%
Somewhat familiar	7%	6%	9%	5%	7%
Not very familiar	7%	7%	9%	4%	8%
Just know the name	13%	11%	12%	8%	16%
Never heard of	58%	65%	55%	76%	53%
HotBot.com - Have used	**10%**	**13%**	**12%**	**7%**	**10%**
Extremely familiar	2%	3%	2%	0%	2%
Very familiar	3%	3%	5%	2%	3%
Somewhat familiar	9%	9%	13%	5%	9%
Not very familiar	10%	13%	10%	7%	9%
Just know the name	19%	21%	20%	17%	18%
Never heard of	54%	45%	46%	66%	55%
Ask an expert - Have used	**8%**	**9%**	**8%**	**4%**	**8%**
Extremely familiar	2%	3%	1%	1%	2%
Very familiar	3%	2%	2%	1%	4%
Somewhat familiar	10%	10%	8%	8%	11%
Not very familiar	13%	14%	16%	8%	13%
Just know the name	19%	18%	22%	20%	18%
Never heard of	49%	49%	45%	60%	48%
LookSmart.com - Have used	**7%**	**15%**	**7%**	**3%**	**5%**
Extremely familiar	2%	3%	1%	1%	2%
Very familiar	3%	6%	3%	1%	2%
Somewhat familiar	7%	14%	5%	5%	6%
Not very familiar	6%	11%	7%	4%	5%
Just know the name	14%	17%	17%	9%	13%
Never heard of	67%	45%	64%	79%	71%
Online librarian question service - Have used	**5%**	**7%**	**7%**	**2%**	**4%**
Extremely familiar	2%	3%	1%	2%	2%
Very familiar	2%	1%	2%	1%	3%
Somewhat familiar	9%	9%	11%	4%	9%
Not very familiar	11%	13%	13%	9%	11%
Just know the name	15%	17%	17%	12%	15%
Never heard of	58%	52%	55%	70%	57%
AllTheWeb.com - Have used	**4%**	**7%**	**5%**	**4%**	**3%**
Extremely familiar	1%	2%	2%	1%	1%
Very familiar	1%	2%	1%	0%	1%
Somewhat familiar	3%	6%	3%	4%	2%
Not very familiar	6%	9%	6%	3%	6%
Just know the name	8%	9%	8%	7%	8%
Never heard of	78%	68%	78%	81%	81%

Source: *Perceptions of Libraries and Information Resources,* OCLC, 2005, question 665.

Familiarity and Usage of Information Brands—by Region of Respondent (continued)
Please indicate how familiar you are with the following information sources
and if you have used each source, even if you have only used it once.

	Total Respondents	Australia Singapore India	Canada	United Kingdom	United States
Teoma.com - Have used	**2%**	**2%**	**1%**	**1%**	**2%**
Extremely familiar	1%	0%	0%	0%	1%
Very familiar	1%	1%	0%	0%	1%
Somewhat familiar	2%	3%	1%	1%	2%
Not very familiar	3%	5%	4%	2%	3%
Just know the name	3%	5%	3%	2%	2%
Never heard of	90%	85%	91%	94%	91%
Gigablast.com - Have used	**1%**	**1%**	**1%**	**0%**	**1%**
Extremely familiar	0%	1%	0%	0%	0%
Very familiar	1%	0%	1%	1%	1%
Somewhat familiar	2%	4%	2%	2%	2%
Not very familiar	5%	8%	4%	1%	5%
Just know the name	6%	6%	5%	7%	6%
Never heard of	86%	81%	87%	89%	86%
Clusty.com - Have used	**1%**	**0%**	**1%**	**0%**	**1%**
Extremely familiar	0%	0%	0%	0%	0%
Very familiar	1%	0%	0%	0%	1%
Somewhat familiar	1%	3%	1%	1%	1%
Not very familiar	4%	6%	5%	2%	3%
Just know the name	2%	3%	2%	2%	2%
Never heard of	92%	87%	92%	95%	92%

Source: *Perceptions of Libraries and Information Resources*, OCLC, 2005, question 665.

Part 2.1

Activities at the Library—by Region of Respondent
How frequently do you use your primary library for the following reasons?

	Total Respondents	Australia Singapore India	Canada	United Kingdom	United States
Borrow print books - Daily	**1%**	**1%**	**1%**	**0%**	**1%**
Weekly	12%	15%	15%	9%	11%
Monthly	13%	19%	14%	14%	11%
Several times a year	20%	19%	23%	20%	20%
At least once a year	9%	7%	7%	8%	10%
Not even once a year	10%	7%	12%	7%	11%
Never have used	17%	13%	14%	19%	18%
Used to use, but no longer do	19%	19%	14%	22%	19%
Leisure reading - Daily	**2%**	**1%**	**1%**	**1%**	**2%**
Weekly	9%	14%	9%	6%	9%
Monthly	10%	14%	14%	12%	8%
Several times a year	16%	16%	21%	17%	15%
At least once a year	10%	12%	9%	6%	10%
Not even once a year	10%	6%	12%	5%	11%
Never have used	23%	22%	14%	29%	25%
Used to use, but no longer do	20%	16%	19%	24%	20%
Read/borrow best-seller - Daily	**0%**	**0%**	**1%**	**0%**	**0%**
Weekly	6%	8%	7%	5%	6%
Monthly	10%	11%	9%	11%	10%
Several times a year	13%	16%	14%	12%	13%
At least once a year	10%	12%	11%	10%	10%
Not even once a year	11%	9%	12%	7%	12%
Never have used	31%	28%	30%	34%	32%
Used to use, but no longer do	17%	16%	15%	21%	17%
Use online databases - Daily	**2%**	**4%**	**3%**	**1%**	**2%**
Weekly	7%	10%	9%	4%	6%
Monthly	6%	7%	7%	4%	6%
Several times a year	11%	10%	12%	6%	12%
At least once a year	7%	7%	8%	4%	7%
Not even once a year	9%	8%	7%	6%	10%
Never have used	46%	39%	42%	61%	45%
Used to use, but no longer do	13%	15%	12%	14%	12%
Borrow DVDs/videos - Daily	**1%**	**0%**	**0%**	**0%**	**1%**
Weekly	4%	7%	4%	2%	4%
Monthly	7%	9%	6%	3%	8%
Several times a year	11%	10%	14%	8%	11%
At least once a year	8%	7%	9%	10%	7%
Not even once a year	9%	9%	11%	6%	9%
Never have used	48%	46%	45%	54%	48%
Used to use, but no longer do	13%	12%	11%	17%	12%

Source: *Perceptions of Libraries and Information Resources*, OCLC, 2005, question 840.

Activities at the Library—by Region of Respondent (continued)
How frequently do you use your primary library for the following reasons?

	Total Respondents	Australia Singapore India	Canada	United Kingdom	United States
Use the computer/Internet - Daily	**3%**	**6%**	**3%**	**3%**	**3%**
Weekly	5%	5%	6%	4%	5%
Monthly	5%	6%	5%	3%	5%
Several times a year	9%	11%	11%	4%	9%
At least once a year	7%	6%	8%	7%	7%
Not even once a year	9%	8%	12%	6%	10%
Never have used	42%	36%	33%	54%	44%
Used to use, but no longer do	18%	21%	22%	19%	16%
Research specific reference books - Daily	**2%**	**3%**	**3%**	**1%**	**1%**
Weekly	5%	9%	5%	4%	4%
Monthly	8%	10%	9%	9%	7%
Several times a year	21%	23%	23%	18%	20%
At least once a year	15%	16%	13%	13%	16%
Not even once a year	12%	8%	11%	10%	14%
Never have used	15%	9%	16%	15%	16%
Used to use, but no longer do	23%	22%	20%	29%	22%
Do homework/study - Daily	**2%**	**3%**	**3%**	**2%**	**2%**
Weekly	6%	9%	4%	4%	6%
Monthly	4%	4%	6%	3%	3%
Several times a year	10%	13%	10%	7%	9%
At least once a year	5%	6%	8%	4%	5%
Not even once a year	8%	7%	6%	6%	10%
Never have used	27%	23%	22%	34%	27%
Used to use, but no longer do	39%	35%	40%	40%	39%
Read magazines - Daily	**1%**	**1%**	**0%**	**0%**	**1%**
Weekly	5%	8%	7%	3%	4%
Monthly	6%	11%	7%	4%	5%
Several times a year	11%	12%	14%	7%	11%
At least once a year	7%	7%	7%	4%	8%
Not even once a year	10%	7%	10%	6%	12%
Never have used	42%	38%	39%	59%	40%
Used to use, but no longer do	17%	16%	16%	17%	18%
Socialize with friends - Daily	**2%**	**1%**	**1%**	**2%**	**2%**
Weekly	3%	5%	3%	2%	3%
Monthly	4%	3%	5%	2%	4%
Several times a year	5%	7%	8%	1%	4%
At least once a year	4%	5%	2%	4%	4%
Not even once a year	8%	5%	8%	6%	9%
Never have used	60%	57%	57%	71%	59%
Used to use, but no longer do	16%	17%	16%	14%	16%

Source: *Perceptions of Libraries and Information Resources,* OCLC, 2005, question 840.

Activities at the Library—by Region of Respondent (continued)
How frequently do you use your primary library for the following reasons?

	Total Respondents	Australia Singapore India	Canada	United Kingdom	United States
Get assistance with research - Daily	**1%**	**2%**	**2%**	**1%**	**1%**
Weekly	4%	7%	7%	4%	3%
Monthly	6%	8%	6%	5%	5%
Several times a year	15%	21%	15%	11%	14%
At least once a year	15%	13%	12%	14%	16%
Not even once a year	13%	9%	15%	9%	15%
Never have used	23%	20%	22%	30%	22%
Used to use, but no longer do	23%	21%	21%	25%	24%
Read daily newspapers - Daily	**2%**	**5%**	**1%**	**2%**	**2%**
Weekly	4%	7%	3%	3%	3%
Monthly	2%	3%	4%	2%	2%
Several times a year	6%	9%	10%	5%	5%
At least once a year	4%	4%	4%	3%	4%
Not even once a year	10%	9%	11%	5%	11%
Never have used	57%	50%	52%	63%	58%
Used to use, but no longer do	15%	13%	15%	17%	15%
Make photocopies - Daily	**1%**	**1%**	**1%**	**1%**	**1%**
Weekly	3%	4%	5%	2%	3%
Monthly	4%	8%	4%	5%	3%
Several times a year	10%	14%	14%	9%	8%
At least once a year	11%	8%	8%	5%	14%
Not even once a year	11%	8%	13%	7%	13%
Never have used	34%	24%	32%	42%	36%
Used to use, but no longer do	25%	32%	23%	28%	22%
Get copies of articles/journals - Daily	**1%**	**2%**	**0%**	**1%**	**1%**
Weekly	4%	7%	7%	3%	3%
Monthly	4%	9%	5%	4%	3%
Several times a year	15%	19%	15%	11%	14%
At least once a year	10%	8%	10%	7%	11%
Not even once a year	12%	11%	13%	8%	13%
Never have used	33%	25%	34%	44%	33%
Used to use, but no longer do	21%	19%	16%	23%	22%
Borrow music - Daily	**1%**	**0%**	**0%**	**0%**	**1%**
Weekly	2%	4%	2%	2%	2%
Monthly	3%	7%	5%	3%	2%
Several times a year	9%	7%	11%	8%	10%
At least once a year	5%	7%	7%	5%	4%
Not even once a year	9%	10%	9%	7%	9%
Never have used	56%	50%	53%	56%	58%
Used to use, but no longer do	14%	15%	12%	20%	13%

Source: *Perceptions of Libraries and Information Resources*, OCLC, 2005, question 840.

Activities at the Library—by Region of Respondent (continued)

How frequently do you use your primary library for the following reasons?

	Total Respondents	Australia Singapore India	Canada	United Kingdom	United States
Use audiobooks - Daily	**0%**	**1%**	**0%**	**0%**	**0%**
Weekly	1%	1%	3%	1%	1%
Monthly	3%	2%	3%	1%	3%
Several times a year	5%	8%	5%	3%	5%
At least once a year	4%	3%	6%	4%	4%
Not even once a year	7%	8%	8%	4%	8%
Never have used	70%	66%	67%	77%	70%
Used to use, but no longer do	9%	10%	8%	11%	8%
Attend an event - Daily	**0%**	**0%**	**1%**	**0%**	**0%**
Weekly	1%	2%	1%	1%	1%
Monthly	3%	3%	2%	2%	3%
Several times a year	7%	9%	9%	4%	6%
At least once a year	8%	7%	9%	7%	8%
Not even once a year	9%	8%	12%	5%	10%
Never have used	54%	54%	51%	62%	52%
Used to use, but no longer do	19%	17%	15%	18%	20%
Use electronic books - Daily	**0%**	**1%**	**0%**	**0%**	**0%**
Weekly	2%	4%	2%	2%	2%
Monthly	2%	4%	5%	2%	1%
Several times a year	4%	6%	4%	3%	4%
At least once a year	4%	5%	6%	4%	3%
Not even once a year	7%	7%	6%	7%	8%
Never have used	73%	67%	72%	74%	74%
Used to use, but no longer do	7%	7%	5%	9%	7%
Voter registration - Daily	**0%**	**0%**	**0%**	**0%**	**0%**
Weekly	1%	0%	1%	0%	1%
Monthly	0%	0%	1%	1%	0%
Several times a year	1%	1%	0%	1%	1%
At least once a year	3%	3%	3%	4%	3%
Not even once a year	6%	5%	4%	4%	7%
Never have used	79%	80%	86%	80%	77%
Used to use, but no longer do	10%	10%	4%	11%	11%
Get tax forms - Daily	**0%**	**0%**	**0%**	**0%**	**0%**
Weekly	0%	0%	1%	0%	0%
Monthly	0%	0%	0%	1%	0%
Several times a year	1%	2%	1%	1%	1%
At least once a year	13%	5%	4%	2%	20%
Not even once a year	6%	4%	3%	2%	9%
Never have used	67%	81%	86%	85%	54%
Used to use, but no longer do	12%	7%	5%	8%	17%

Source: *Perceptions of Libraries and Information Resources,* OCLC, 2005, question 840.

Activities at the Library—by Age of U.S. Respondent

How frequently do you use your primary library for the following reasons?

	Total U.S. Respondents	U.S. 14-17	U.S. 18-24	U.S. 25-64	U.S. 65+
Borrow print books - Daily	**1%**	**3%**	**6%**	**0%**	**1%**
Weekly	11%	16%	10%	12%	7%
Monthly	11%	13%	12%	10%	11%
Several times a year	20%	22%	22%	19%	21%
At least once a year	10%	12%	5%	11%	9%
Not even once a year	11%	8%	6%	12%	10%
Never have used	18%	21%	25%	15%	24%
Used to use, but no longer do	19%	5%	14%	21%	18%
Leisure reading - Daily	**2%**	**5%**	**8%**	**1%**	**1%**
Weekly	9%	12%	7%	9%	6%
Monthly	8%	10%	7%	7%	12%
Several times a year	15%	17%	15%	16%	11%
At least once a year	10%	13%	11%	9%	11%
Not even once a year	11%	8%	7%	12%	13%
Never have used	25%	24%	32%	23%	24%
Used to use, but no longer do	20%	10%	12%	22%	22%
Read/borrow best-seller - Daily	**0%**	**3%**	**0%**	**0%**	**0%**
Weekly	6%	6%	6%	6%	5%
Monthly	10%	9%	9%	9%	12%
Several times a year	13%	15%	12%	13%	13%
At least once a year	10%	11%	6%	10%	11%
Not even once a year	12%	12%	13%	13%	11%
Never have used	32%	38%	45%	29%	30%
Used to use, but no longer do	17%	6%	9%	20%	16%
Use online databases - Daily	**2%**	**3%**	**7%**	**1%**	**2%**
Weekly	6%	8%	11%	6%	2%
Monthly	6%	10%	12%	5%	3%
Several times a year	12%	20%	20%	11%	3%
At least once a year	7%	12%	5%	6%	9%
Not even once a year	10%	10%	7%	12%	6%
Never have used	45%	31%	27%	45%	66%
Used to use, but no longer do	12%	6%	11%	14%	9%
Borrow DVDs/videos - Daily	**1%**	**3%**	**4%**	**0%**	**0%**
Weekly	4%	6%	6%	4%	2%
Monthly	8%	8%	7%	9%	3%
Several times a year	11%	9%	8%	12%	12%
At least once a year	7%	7%	6%	7%	5%
Not even once a year	9%	10%	8%	9%	9%
Never have used	48%	49%	50%	45%	60%
Used to use, but no longer do	12%	8%	11%	14%	9%

Source: *Perceptions of Libraries and Information Resources*, OCLC, 2005, question 840.

Activities at the Library —by Age of U.S. Respondent (continued)
How frequently do you use your primary library for the following reasons?

	Total U.S. Respondents	U.S. 14-17	U.S. 18-24	U.S. 25-64	U.S. 65+
Use the computer/Internet - Daily	**3%**	**9%**	**10%**	**2%**	**2%**
Weekly	5%	14%	14%	4%	1%
Monthly	5%	11%	11%	4%	2%
Several times a year	9%	17%	15%	8%	4%
At least once a year	7%	13%	9%	6%	8%
Not even once a year	10%	12%	4%	11%	8%
Never have used	44%	14%	19%	48%	62%
Used to use, but no longer do	16%	10%	18%	17%	13%
Research specific reference books - Daily	**1%**	**4%**	**3%**	**1%**	**0%**
Weekly	4%	7%	7%	4%	0%
Monthly	7%	16%	15%	5%	4%
Several times a year	20%	27%	25%	20%	15%
At least once a year	16%	14%	15%	16%	18%
Not even once a year	14%	11%	8%	14%	16%
Never have used	16%	16%	14%	15%	21%
Used to use, but no longer do	22%	6%	14%	25%	26%
Do homework/study - Daily	**2%**	**9%**	**7%**	**0%**	**0%**
Weekly	6%	11%	15%	5%	0%
Monthly	3%	13%	12%	1%	0%
Several times a year	9%	18%	19%	6%	9%
At least once a year	5%	14%	6%	4%	2%
Not even once a year	10%	11%	7%	11%	6%
Never have used	27%	16%	12%	28%	39%
Used to use, but no longer do	39%	7%	22%	44%	43%
Read magazines - Daily	**1%**	**3%**	**2%**	**0%**	**0%**
Weekly	4%	5%	7%	3%	3%
Monthly	5%	10%	7%	4%	4%
Several times a year	11%	14%	8%	12%	8%
At least once a year	8%	12%	12%	8%	7%
Not even once a year	12%	11%	11%	13%	10%
Never have used	40%	39%	42%	38%	48%
Used to use, but no longer do	18%	5%	11%	21%	19%
Socialize with friends - Daily	**2%**	**8%**	**7%**	**1%**	**0%**
Weekly	3%	8%	8%	2%	1%
Monthly	4%	7%	7%	3%	1%
Several times a year	4%	12%	8%	3%	2%
At least once a year	4%	7%	12%	2%	4%
Not even once a year	9%	9%	4%	9%	10%
Never have used	59%	41%	44%	61%	69%
Used to use, but no longer do	16%	8%	11%	18%	13%

Source: *Perceptions of Libraries and Information Resources,* OCLC, 2005, question 840.

Activities at the Library—by Age of U.S. Respondent (continued)
How frequently do you use your primary library for the following reasons?

	Total U.S. Respondents	U.S. 14-17	U.S. 18-24	U.S. 25-64	U.S. 65+
Get assistance with research - Daily	1%	3%	2%	0%	0%
Weekly	3%	7%	9%	2%	0%
Monthly	5%	13%	9%	5%	2%
Several times a year	14%	22%	21%	11%	12%
At least once a year	16%	13%	16%	17%	15%
Not even once a year	15%	10%	10%	16%	15%
Never have used	22%	28%	18%	22%	27%
Used to use, but no longer do	24%	6%	16%	27%	29%
Read daily newspapers - Daily	2%	5%	6%	0%	2%
Weekly	3%	5%	7%	3%	1%
Monthly	2%	4%	4%	2%	1%
Several times a year	5%	8%	8%	4%	5%
At least once a year	4%	7%	1%	5%	3%
Not even once a year	11%	8%	11%	12%	7%
Never have used	58%	59%	53%	56%	69%
Used to use, but no longer do	15%	5%	9%	18%	12%
Make photocopies - Daily	1%	3%	1%	1%	0%
Weekly	3%	5%	8%	3%	1%
Monthly	3%	9%	9%	2%	2%
Several times a year	8%	13%	18%	6%	6%
At least once a year	14%	15%	13%	14%	11%
Not even once a year	13%	14%	8%	14%	8%
Never have used	36%	30%	26%	35%	53%
Used to use, but no longer do	22%	11%	17%	25%	21%
Get copies of articles/journals - Daily	1%	2%	2%	0%	0%
Weekly	3%	5%	5%	3%	0%
Monthly	3%	9%	6%	3%	1%
Several times a year	14%	15%	16%	15%	9%
At least once a year	11%	14%	15%	11%	11%
Not even once a year	13%	11%	8%	14%	14%
Never have used	33%	40%	32%	29%	47%
Used to use, but no longer do	22%	5%	15%	25%	18%
Borrow music - Daily	1%	3%	3%	0%	0%
Weekly	2%	6%	3%	2%	0%
Monthly	2%	7%	4%	2%	1%
Several times a year	10%	7%	10%	11%	6%
At least once a year	4%	5%	4%	4%	3%
Not even once a year	9%	7%	4%	11%	8%
Never have used	58%	60%	66%	54%	73%
Used to use, but no longer do	13%	6%	6%	17%	9%

Source: *Perceptions of Libraries and Information Resources*, OCLC, 2005, question 840.

Activities at the Library—by Age of U.S. Respondent (continued)
How frequently do you use your primary library for the following reasons?

	Total U.S. Respondents	U.S. 14-17	U.S. 18-24	U.S. 25-64	U.S. 65+
Use audiobooks - Daily	0%	2%	0%	0%	0%
Weekly	1%	3%	4%	1%	0%
Monthly	3%	3%	6%	2%	4%
Several times a year	5%	4%	4%	5%	7%
At least once a year	4%	5%	4%	4%	3%
Not even once a year	8%	9%	5%	9%	5%
Never have used	70%	68%	71%	70%	73%
Used to use, but no longer do	8%	7%	6%	9%	8%
Attend an event - Daily	0%	2%	0%	0%	0%
Weekly	1%	1%	1%	1%	1%
Monthly	3%	3%	5%	2%	4%
Several times a year	6%	5%	3%	7%	4%
At least once a year	8%	7%	8%	8%	9%
Not even once a year	10%	10%	5%	12%	7%
Never have used	52%	60%	63%	49%	52%
Used to use, but no longer do	20%	12%	15%	22%	23%
Use electronic books - Daily	0%	2%	0%	0%	1%
Weekly	2%	1%	5%	2%	0%
Monthly	1%	3%	4%	1%	1%
Several times a year	4%	5%	7%	3%	4%
At least once a year	3%	7%	5%	3%	1%
Not even once a year	8%	6%	4%	10%	7%
Never have used	74%	69%	67%	75%	80%
Used to use, but no longer do	7%	8%	7%	7%	7%
Voter registration - Daily	0%	2%	0%	0%	0%
Weekly	1%	2%	2%	0%	0%
Monthly	0%	0%	1%	0%	0%
Several times a year	1%	1%	5%	0%	0%
At least once a year	3%	3%	4%	4%	2%
Not even once a year	7%	2%	6%	8%	5%
Never have used	77%	84%	74%	75%	84%
Used to use, but no longer do	11%	5%	8%	12%	9%
Get tax forms - Daily	0%	1%	0%	0%	0%
Weekly	0%	1%	0%	0%	0%
Monthly	0%	1%	1%	0%	0%
Several times a year	1%	1%	3%	0%	1%
At least once a year	20%	5%	13%	22%	22%
Not even once a year	9%	5%	5%	10%	8%
Never have used	54%	81%	69%	47%	55%
Used to use, but no longer do	17%	4%	9%	20%	14%

Source: *Perceptions of Libraries and Information Resources,* OCLC, 2005, question 840.

Activities at the Library—by College Students across all Regions
How frequently do you use your primary library for the following reasons?

	Total Respondents	College Students
Borrow print books - Daily	**1%**	**3%**
Weekly	12%	24%
Monthly	13%	12%
Several times a year	20%	24%
At least once a year	9%	6%
Not even once a year	10%	9%
Never have used	17%	19%
Used to use, but no longer do	19%	2%
Leisure reading - Daily	**2%**	**4%**
Weekly	9%	17%
Monthly	10%	7%
Several times a year	16%	10%
At least once a year	10%	14%
Not even once a year	10%	5%
Never have used	23%	36%
Used to use, but no longer do	20%	7%
Read/borrow best-seller - Daily	**0%**	**1%**
Weekly	6%	6%
Monthly	10%	5%
Several times a year	13%	13%
At least once a year	10%	6%
Not even once a year	11%	8%
Never have used	31%	58%
Used to use, but no longer do	17%	3%
Use online databases - Daily	**2%**	**7%**
Weekly	7%	22%
Monthly	6%	15%
Several times a year	11%	19%
At least once a year	7%	7%
Not even once a year	9%	5%
Never have used	46%	22%
Used to use, but no longer do	13%	3%
Borrow DVDs/videos - Daily	**1%**	**0%**
Weekly	4%	9%
Monthly	7%	12%
Several times a year	11%	8%
At least once a year	8%	6%
Not even once a year	9%	6%
Never have used	48%	53%
Used to use, but no longer do	13%	4%

Source: *Perceptions of Libraries and Information Resources*, OCLC, 2005, question 840.

Activities at the Library—by College Students across all Regions (continued)

How frequently do you use your primary library for the following reasons?

	Total Respondents	College Students
Use the computer/Internet - Daily	**3%**	**15%**
Weekly	5%	18%
Monthly	5%	12%
Several times a year	9%	16%
At least once a year	7%	8%
Not even once a year	9%	4%
Never have used	42%	20%
Used to use, but no longer do	18%	8%
Research specific reference books - Daily	**2%**	**5%**
Weekly	5%	20%
Monthly	8%	17%
Several times a year	21%	29%
At least once a year	15%	12%
Not even once a year	12%	5%
Never have used	15%	8%
Used to use, but no longer do	23%	4%
Do homework/study - Daily	**2%**	**10%**
Weekly	6%	24%
Monthly	4%	14%
Several times a year	10%	22%
At least once a year	5%	7%
Not even once a year	8%	6%
Never have used	27%	9%
Used to use, but no longer do	39%	7%
Read magazines - Daily	**1%**	**1%**
Weekly	5%	12%
Monthly	6%	15%
Several times a year	11%	11%
At least once a year	7%	9%
Not even once a year	10%	5%
Never have used	42%	43%
Used to use, but no longer do	17%	3%
Socialize with friends - Daily	**2%**	**9%**
Weekly	3%	10%
Monthly	4%	5%
Several times a year	5%	10%
At least once a year	4%	9%
Not even once a year	8%	5%
Never have used	60%	46%
Used to use, but no longer do	16%	6%

Source: *Perceptions of Libraries and Information Resources,* OCLC, 2005, question 840.

Activities at the Library—by College Students across all Regions (continued)

How frequently do you use your primary library for the following reasons?

	Total Respondents	College Students
Get assistance with research - Daily	**1%**	**4%**
Weekly	4%	13%
Monthly	6%	16%
Several times a year	15%	24%
At least once a year	15%	11%
Not even once a year	13%	9%
Never have used	23%	19%
Used to use, but no longer do	23%	4%
Read daily newspapers - Daily	**2%**	**4%**
Weekly	4%	8%
Monthly	2%	9%
Several times a year	6%	9%
At least once a year	4%	4%
Not even once a year	10%	11%
Never have used	57%	49%
Used to use, but no longer do	15%	6%
Make photocopies - Daily	**1%**	**2%**
Weekly	3%	17%
Monthly	4%	17%
Several times a year	10%	16%
At least once a year	11%	10%
Not even once a year	11%	4%
Never have used	34%	24%
Used to use, but no longer do	25%	8%
Get copies of articles/journals - Daily	**1%**	**4%**
Weekly	4%	16%
Monthly	4%	12%
Several times a year	15%	26%
At least once a year	10%	11%
Not even once a year	12%	6%
Never have used	33%	19%
Used to use, but no longer do	21%	7%
Borrow music - Daily	**1%**	**0%**
Weekly	2%	8%
Monthly	3%	6%
Several times a year	9%	8%
At least once a year	5%	6%
Not even once a year	9%	5%
Never have used	56%	62%
Used to use, but no longer do	14%	4%

Source: *Perceptions of Libraries and Information Resources*, OCLC, 2005, question 840.

Activities at the Library—by College Students across all Regions (continued)
How frequently do you use your primary library for the following reasons?

	Total Respondents	College Students
Use audiobooks - Daily	**0%**	**0%**
Weekly	1%	5%
Monthly	3%	5%
Several times a year	5%	11%
At least once a year	4%	3%
Not even once a year	7%	10%
Never have used	70%	64%
Used to use, but no longer do	9%	2%
Attend an event - Daily	**0%**	**0%**
Weekly	1%	1%
Monthly	3%	4%
Several times a year	7%	11%
At least once a year	8%	6%
Not even once a year	9%	10%
Never have used	54%	58%
Used to use, but no longer do	19%	11%
Use electronic books - Daily	**0%**	**1%**
Weekly	2%	8%
Monthly	2%	9%
Several times a year	4%	11%
At least once a year	4%	8%
Not even once a year	7%	5%
Never have used	73%	54%
Used to use, but no longer do	7%	3%
Voter registration - Daily	**0%**	**0%**
Weekly	1%	2%
Monthly	0%	1%
Several times a year	1%	3%
At least once a year	3%	3%
Not even once a year	6%	3%
Never have used	79%	82%
Used to use, but no longer do	10%	6%
Get tax forms - Daily	**0%**	**0%**
Weekly	0%	1%
Monthly	0%	1%
Several times a year	1%	2%
At least once a year	13%	10%
Not even once a year	6%	6%
Never have used	67%	75%
Used to use, but no longer do	12%	5%

Source: *Perceptions of Libraries and Information Resources,* OCLC, 2005, question 840.

Suitability of the Library and the Bookstore for Specific Activities— by Region of Respondent

Comparing the library to your local bookstore, which do you feel provides a more suitable environment for activities/materials in regard to the following?

	Total Respondents	Australia Singapore India	Canada	United Kingdom	United States
Library is more suitable for...					
Free materials	95%	96%	96%	96%	94%
Free access to the Internet	95%	95%	97%	96%	95%
Special programs	89%	94%	91%	91%	87%
Access to free entertainment	86%	86%	90%	86%	85%
Book club/story hour	77%	82%	74%	84%	74%
Comfortable seating/meeting area	71%	86%	70%	78%	65%
Friendly environment	64%	72%	70%	69%	58%
Access to music	62%	67%	71%	75%	55%
It's where my friends are	43%	51%	47%	55%	37%
Find more current materials	40%	46%	33%	46%	39%
Coffee/snack shop	17%	28%	15%	35%	9%
Local bookstore is more suitable for...					
Coffee/snack shop	83%	72%	85%	65%	91%
Find more current materials	60%	54%	67%	54%	61%
It's where my friends are	57%	49%	53%	45%	63%
Access to music	38%	33%	29%	25%	45%
Friendly environment	36%	28%	30%	31%	42%
Comfortable seating/meeting area	29%	14%	30%	22%	35%
Book club/story hour	23%	18%	26%	16%	26%
Access to free entertainment	14%	14%	10%	14%	15%
Special programs	11%	6%	9%	9%	13%
Free materials	5%	4%	4%	4%	6%
Free access to the Internet	5%	5%	3%	4%	5%

Source: *Perceptions of Libraries and Information Resources,* OCLC, 2005, question 1230.

Suitability of the Library and the Bookstore for Specific Activities—
by Age of U.S. Respondent
Comparing the library to your local bookstore, which do you feel provides
a more suitable environment for activities/materials in regard to the following?

	Total U.S. Respondents	U.S. 14-17	U.S. 18-24	U.S. 25-64	U.S. 65+
Library is more suitable for...					
Access to music	55%	41%	45%	56%	64%
Find more current materials	39%	27%	29%	38%	59%
Free materials	94%	91%	92%	95%	97%
Free access to the Internet	95%	93%	91%	95%	98%
Book club/story hour	74%	67%	62%	75%	86%
Comfortable seating/meeting area	65%	57%	59%	65%	76%
Access to free entertainment	85%	72%	82%	86%	89%
Special programs	87%	75%	81%	87%	95%
Coffee/snack shop	9%	15%	11%	8%	11%
It's where my friends are	37%	46%	39%	32%	56%
Friendly environment	58%	59%	50%	57%	69%
Local bookstore is more suitable for...					
Access to music	45%	59%	55%	44%	36%
Find more current materials	61%	73%	71%	62%	41%
Free materials	6%	9%	8%	5%	3%
Free access to the Internet	5%	7%	9%	5%	2%
Book club/story hour	26%	33%	38%	25%	14%
Comfortable seating/meeting area	35%	43%	41%	35%	24%
Access to free entertainment	15%	28%	18%	14%	11%
Special programs	13%	25%	19%	13%	5%
Coffee/snack shop	91%	85%	89%	92%	89%
It's where my friends are	63%	54%	61%	68%	44%
Friendly environment	42%	41%	50%	43%	31%

Source: *Perceptions of Libraries and Information Resources,* OCLC, 2005, question 1230.

Suitability of the Library and the Bookstore for Specific Activities— by College Students across all Regions

Comparing the library to your local bookstore, which do you feel provides a more suitable environment for activities/materials in regard to the following?

	Total Respondents	College students
Library is more suitable for...		
Free access to the Internet	95%	94%
Free materials	95%	93%
Special programs	89%	78%
Access to free entertainment	86%	85%
Book club/story hour	77%	58%
Comfortable seating/meeting area	71%	65%
Friendly environment	64%	62%
Access to music	62%	56%
Find more current materials	43%	34%
It's where my friends are	40%	45%
Coffee/snack shop	17%	14%
Local bookstore is more suitable for...		
Coffee/snack shop	83%	86%
It's where my friends are	60%	55%
Find more current materials	57%	66%
Access to music	38%	44%
Friendly environment	36%	38%
Comfortable seating/meeting area	29%	35%
Book club/story hour	23%	42%
Access to free entertainment	14%	15%
Special programs	11%	22%
Free materials	5%	7%
Free access to the Internet	5%	6%

Source: *Perceptions of Libraries and Information Resources*, OCLC, 2005, question 1230.

Suitability of the Library and the Bookstore for Specific Activities— by Library Card Holders across all Regions

Comparing the library to your local bookstore, which do you feel provides a more suitable environment for activities/materials in regard to the following?

	Total Respondents	Library Card Holders	Non-Card Holders
Library is more suitable for...			
Free materials	95%	96%	94%
Free access to the Internet	95%	96%	94%
Special programs	89%	89%	88%
Access to free entertainment	86%	87%	83%
Book club/story hour	77%	78%	74%
Comfortable seating/meeting area	71%	72%	69%
Friendly environment	64%	67%	54%
Access to music	62%	63%	59%
It's where my friends are	43%	45%	39%
Find more current materials	40%	41%	40%
Coffee/snack shop	17%	15%	22%
Local bookstore more suitable for...			
Coffee/snack shop	83%	85%	78%
Find more current materials	60%	59%	60%
It's where my friends are	57%	55%	61%
Access to music	38%	37%	41%
Friendly environment	36%	33%	46%
Comfortable seating/meeting area	29%	28%	31%
Book club/story hour	23%	22%	26%
Access to free entertainment	14%	13%	17%
Special programs	11%	11%	12%
Free materials	5%	4%	6%
Free access to the Internet	5%	4%	6%

Source: *Perceptions of Libraries and Information Resources,* OCLC, 2005, question 1230.

Part 2.6

Satisfaction with the Information Provided by Librarian and Search Engine—
by Region of Respondent

Based on the most recent search you conducted through
(librarian/search engine), how satisfied were you with...?

Total Respondents	Librarian	Search Engine
Very satisfied	53%	54%
Satisfied	35%	35%
Neither satisfied nor dissatisfied	9%	5%
Dissatisfied	3%	4%
Very dissatisfied	0%	2%
Australia/Singapore/India		
Very satisfied	50%	51%
Satisfied	39%	39%
Neither satisfied nor dissatisfied	7%	5%
Dissatisfied	4%	4%
Very dissatisfied	0%	2%
Canada		
Very satisfied	56%	46%
Satisfied	34%	41%
Neither satisfied nor dissatisfied	7%	4%
Dissatisfied	4%	5%
Very dissatisfied	0%	4%
United Kingdom		
Very satisfied	46%	52%
Satisfied	35%	38%
Neither satisfied nor dissatisfied	9%	5%
Dissatisfied	9%	4%
Very dissatisfied	1%	1%
United States		
Very satisfied	54%	57%
Satisfied	34%	31%
Neither satisfied nor dissatisfied	11%	6%
Dissatisfied	1%	3%
Very dissatisfied	0%	2%

Source: *Perceptions of Libraries and Information Resources,* OCLC, 2005, questions 655 and 1050.

Satisfaction with the Information Provided by Librarian and Search Engine—
by Age of U.S. Respondent

Based on the most recent search you conducted through
(librarian/search engine), how satisfied were you with...?

Total U.S. Respondents	Librarian	Search Engine
Very satisfied	54%	57%
Satisfied	34%	31%
Neither satisfied nor dissatisfied	11%	6%
Dissatisfied	1%	3%
Very dissatisfied	0%	2%
U.S. 14-17		
Very satisfied	40%	60%
Satisfied	37%	32%
Neither satisfied nor dissatisfied	16%	3%
Dissatisfied	6%	4%
Very dissatisfied	1%	1%
U.S. 18-24		
Very satisfied	36%	63%
Satisfied	49%	28%
Neither satisfied nor dissatisfied	15%	5%
Dissatisfied	1%	2%
Very dissatisfied	0%	3%
U.S. 25-64		
Very satisfied	57%	57%
Satisfied	33%	32%
Neither satisfied nor dissatisfied	10%	7%
Dissatisfied	0%	3%
Very dissatisfied	0%	1%
U.S. 65+		
Very satisfied	62%	53%
Satisfied	27%	32%
Neither satisfied nor dissatisfied	9%	5%
Dissatisfied	2%	5%
Very dissatisfied	0%	5%

Source: *Perceptions of Libraries and Information Resources*, OCLC, 2005, questions 655 and 1050.

Satisfaction with the Information Provided by Librarian and Search Engine— by College Students Across all Regions

Based on the most recent search you conducted through
(librarian/search engine), how satisfied were you with...?

Total Respondents	Librarian	Search Engine
Very satisfied	53%	54%
Satisfied	35%	35%
Neither satisfied nor dissatisfied	9%	5%
Dissatisfied	3%	4%
Very dissatisfied	0%	2%
College Students		
Very satisfied	45%	60%
Satisfied	43%	30%
Neither satisfied nor dissatisfied	6%	8%
Dissatisfied	6%	1%
Very dissatisfied	0%	2%

Source: *Perceptions of Libraries and Information Resources,* OCLC, 2005, questions 655 and 1050.

Satisfaction with the Information Provided by Librarian and Search Engine— by Library Card Holders across all Regions

Based on the most recent search you conducted through
(librarian/search engine), how satisfied were you with...?

Total Respondents	Librarian	Search Engine
Very satisfied	53%	54%
Satisfied	35%	35%
Neither satisfied nor dissatisfied	9%	5%
Dissatisfied	3%	4%
Very dissatisfied	0%	2%
Library Card Holders		
Very satisfied	57%	55%
Satisfied	34%	34%
Neither satisfied nor dissatisfied	6%	6%
Dissatisfied	3%	4%
Very dissatisfied	0%	2%

Source: *Perceptions of Libraries and Information Resources*, OCLC, 2005, questions 655 and 1050.

Satisfaction with the Quantity of Information provided by the Librarian and the Search Engine—by Region of Respondent

Based on the most recent search you conducted through (librarian/search engine), how satisfied were you with...?

Total Respondents	Librarian	Search Engine
Very satisfied	50%	58%
Satisfied	34%	31%
Neither satisfied nor dissatisfied	13%	6%
Dissatisfied	3%	3%
Very dissatisfied	0%	2%
Australia/Singapore/India		
Very satisfied	45%	56%
Satisfied	43%	31%
Neither satisfied nor dissatisfied	6%	7%
Dissatisfied	5%	3%
Very dissatisfied	0%	2%
Canada		
Very satisfied	56%	52%
Satisfied	33%	38%
Neither satisfied nor dissatisfied	8%	3%
Dissatisfied	3%	4%
Very dissatisfied	0%	4%
United Kingdom		
Very satisfied	45%	61%
Satisfied	27%	31%
Neither satisfied nor dissatisfied	18%	5%
Dissatisfied	9%	3%
Very dissatisfied	1%	1%
United States		
Very satisfied	51%	60%
Satisfied	32%	29%
Neither satisfied nor dissatisfied	15%	7%
Dissatisfied	2%	3%
Very dissatisfied	0%	2%

Source: *Perceptions of Libraries and Information Resources,* OCLC, 2005, questions 655 and 1050.

Satisfaction with the Quantity of Information provided by the Librarian and the Search Engine—by Age of U.S. Respondent

Based on the most recent search you conducted through (librarian/search engine), how satisfied were you with...?

Total U.S. Respondents	Librarian	Search Engine
Very satisfied	51%	60%
Satisfied	32%	29%
Neither satisfied nor dissatisfied	15%	7%
Dissatisfied	2%	3%
Very dissatisfied	0%	2%
U.S. 14-17		
Very satisfied	32%	65%
Satisfied	47%	25%
Neither satisfied nor dissatisfied	18%	6%
Dissatisfied	1%	2%
Very dissatisfied	2%	2%
U.S. 18-24		
Very satisfied	33%	65%
Satisfied	48%	23%
Neither satisfied nor dissatisfied	17%	8%
Dissatisfied	1%	2%
Very dissatisfied	0%	3%
U.S. 25-64		
Very satisfied	55%	60%
Satisfied	28%	30%
Neither satisfied nor dissatisfied	15%	6%
Dissatisfied	3%	3%
Very dissatisfied	0%	1%
U.S. 65+		
Very satisfied	59%	48%
Satisfied	27%	34%
Neither satisfied nor dissatisfied	10%	7%
Dissatisfied	2%	6%
Very dissatisfied	2%	5%

Source: *Perceptions of Libraries and Information Resources,* OCLC, 2005, questions 655 and 1050.

Satisfaction with the Quantity of Information provided by the Librarian and the Search Engine—by College Students across all Regions

Based on the most recent search you conducted through
(librarian/search engine), how satisfied were you with...?

Total Respondents	Librarian	Search Engine
Very satisfied	50%	58%
Satisfied	34%	31%
Neither satisfied nor dissatisfied	13%	6%
Dissatisfied	3%	3%
Very dissatisfied	0%	2%
College Students		
Very satisfied	44%	65%
Satisfied	43%	26%
Neither satisfied nor dissatisfied	9%	7%
Dissatisfied	3%	1%
Very dissatisfied	1%	2%

Source: *Perceptions of Libraries and Information Resources,* OCLC, 2005, questions 655 and 1050.

Satisfaction with the Quantity of Information provided by the Librarian and the Search Engine—by Library Card Holders across all Regions

Based on the most recent search you conducted through
(librarian/search engine), how satisfied were you with...?

Total Respondents	Librarian	Search Engine
Very satisfied	50%	58%
Satisfied	34%	31%
Neither satisfied nor dissatisfied	13%	6%
Dissatisfied	3%	3%
Very dissatisfied	0%	2%
Library Card Holders		
Very satisfied	54%	59%
Satisfied	31%	30%
Neither satisfied nor dissatisfied	10%	6%
Dissatisfied	4%	4%
Very dissatisfied	1%	2%

Source: *Perceptions of Libraries and Information Resources,* OCLC, 2005, questions 655 and 1050.

Satisfaction with the Speed of Conducting the Search by the Librarian and the Search Engine—by Region of Respondent

Based on the most recent search you conducted through (librarian/search engine), how satisfied were you with...?

Total Respondents	Librarian	Search Engine
Very satisfied	41%	72%
Satisfied	40%	20%
Neither satisfied nor dissatisfied	15%	5%
Dissatisfied	4%	2%
Very dissatisfied	0%	2%
Australia/Singapore/India		
Very satisfied	40%	68%
Satisfied	40%	23%
Neither satisfied nor dissatisfied	13%	5%
Dissatisfied	6%	2%
Very dissatisfied	0%	2%
Canada		
Very satisfied	41%	72%
Satisfied	46%	20%
Neither satisfied nor dissatisfied	9%	3%
Dissatisfied	3%	1%
Very dissatisfied	1%	4%
United Kingdom		
Very satisfied	38%	68%
Satisfied	32%	26%
Neither satisfied nor dissatisfied	17%	4%
Dissatisfied	12%	1%
Very dissatisfied	2%	2%
United States		
Very satisfied	42%	74%
Satisfied	39%	17%
Neither satisfied nor dissatisfied	17%	6%
Dissatisfied	2%	2%
Very dissatisfied	0%	1%

Source: *Perceptions of Libraries and Information Resources,* OCLC, 2005, questions 655 and 1050.

*Satisfaction with the Speed of Conducting the Search by the Librarian and the Search Engine—*by Age of U.S. Respondent

Based on the most recent search you conducted through (librarian/search engine), how satisfied were you with...?

Total U.S. Respondents	Librarian	Search Engine
Very satisfied	42%	74%
Satisfied	39%	17%
Neither satisfied nor dissatisfied	17%	6%
Dissatisfied	2%	2%
Very dissatisfied	0%	1%
U.S. 14-17		
Very satisfied	26%	77%
Satisfied	36%	16%
Neither satisfied nor dissatisfied	30%	4%
Dissatisfied	6%	2%
Very dissatisfied	2%	2%
U.S. 18-24		
Very satisfied	29%	78%
Satisfied	48%	15%
Neither satisfied nor dissatisfied	16%	2%
Dissatisfied	6%	3%
Very dissatisfied	0%	3%
U.S. 25-64		
Very satisfied	44%	74%
Satisfied	39%	17%
Neither satisfied nor dissatisfied	15%	7%
Dissatisfied	1%	1%
Very dissatisfied	0%	1%
U.S. 65+		
Very satisfied	49%	64%
Satisfied	34%	22%
Neither satisfied nor dissatisfied	14%	4%
Dissatisfied	2%	6%
Very dissatisfied	1%	4%

Source: *Perceptions of Libraries and Information Resources,* OCLC, 2005, questions 655 and 1050.

Satisfaction with the Speed of Conducting the Search by the Librarian and the Search Engine—by College Students across all Regions

Based on the most recent search you conducted through (librarian/search engine), how satisfied were you with...?

Total Respondents	Librarian	Search Engine
Very satisfied	41%	72%
Satisfied	40%	20%
Neither satisfied nor dissatisfied	15%	5%
Dissatisfied	4%	2%
Very dissatisfied	0%	2%
College Students		
Very satisfied	38%	78%
Satisfied	44%	16%
Neither satisfied nor dissatisfied	13%	3%
Dissatisfied	4%	0%
Very dissatisfied	1%	2%

Source: *Perceptions of Libraries and Information Resources*, OCLC, 2005, question 655 and 1050.

Satisfaction with the Speed of Conducting the Search by the Librarian and the Search Engine—by Library Card Holders across all Regions

Based on the most recent search you conducted through (librarian/search engine), how satisfied were you with...?

Total Respondents	Librarian	Search Engine
Very satisfied	41%	72%
Satisfied	40%	20%
Neither satisfied nor dissatisfied	15%	5%
Dissatisfied	4%	2%
Very dissatisfied	0%	2%
Library Card Holders		
Very satisfied	45%	72%
Satisfied	38%	19%
Neither satisfied nor dissatisfied	13%	5%
Dissatisfied	4%	2%
Very dissatisfied	1%	2%

Source: *Perceptions of Libraries and Information Resources*, OCLC, 2005, questions 655 and 1050.

Satisfaction with the Overall Experience of the Search by the Librarian and the Search Engine—by Region of Respondent

Based on the most recent search you conducted through (librarian/search engine), how satisfied were you with…?

Total Respondents	Librarian	Search Engine
Very satisfied	48%	60%
Satisfied	36%	30%
Neither satisfied nor dissatisfied	11%	7%
Dissatisfied	4%	1%
Very dissatisfied	1%	2%
Australia/Singapore/India		
Very satisfied	48%	58%
Satisfied	39%	32%
Neither satisfied nor dissatisfied	9%	6%
Dissatisfied	2%	2%
Very dissatisfied	2%	2%
Canada		
Very satisfied	53%	58%
Satisfied	35%	29%
Neither satisfied nor dissatisfied	9%	8%
Dissatisfied	2%	1%
Very dissatisfied	1%	4%
United Kingdom		
Very satisfied	44%	57%
Satisfied	32%	31%
Neither satisfied nor dissatisfied	14%	9%
Dissatisfied	8%	3%
Very dissatisfied	2%	1%
United States		
Very satisfied	48%	62%
Satisfied	36%	29%
Neither satisfied nor dissatisfied	12%	6%
Dissatisfied	4%	1%
Very dissatisfied	0%	2%

Source: *Perceptions of Libraries and Information Resources,* OCLC, 2005, questions 655 and 1050.

Satisfaction with the Overall Experience of the Search by the Librarian and the Search Engine—by Age of U.S. Respondent

Based on the most recent search you conducted through (librarian/search engine), how satisfied were you with...?

Total U.S. Respondents	Librarian	Search Engine
Very satisfied	48%	62%
Satisfied	36%	29%
Neither satisfied nor dissatisfied	12%	6%
Dissatisfied	4%	1%
Very dissatisfied	0%	2%
U.S. 14-17		
Very satisfied	33%	67%
Satisfied	41%	27%
Neither satisfied nor dissatisfied	21%	4%
Dissatisfied	4%	1%
Very dissatisfied	1%	1%
U.S. 18-24		
Very satisfied	31%	70%
Satisfied	50%	23%
Neither satisfied nor dissatisfied	14%	3%
Dissatisfied	5%	1%
Very dissatisfied	0%	2%
U.S. 25-64		
Very satisfied	51%	62%
Satisfied	33%	29%
Neither satisfied nor dissatisfied	12%	7%
Dissatisfied	3%	1%
Very dissatisfied	0%	1%
U.S. 65+		
Very satisfied	59%	53%
Satisfied	33%	32%
Neither satisfied nor dissatisfied	3%	5%
Dissatisfied	4%	3%
Very dissatisfied	0%	7%

Source: *Perceptions of Libraries and Information Resources,* OCLC, 2005, questions 655 and 1050.

Satisfaction with the Overall Experience of the Search by the Librarian and the Search Engine—by College Students across all Regions

Based on the most recent search you conducted through (librarian/search engine), how satisfied were you with...?

Total Respondents	Librarian	Search Engine
Very satisfied	48%	60%
Satisfied	36%	30%
Neither satisfied nor dissatisfied	11%	7%
Dissatisfied	4%	1%
Very dissatisfied	1%	2%
College Students		
Very satisfied	40%	64%
Satisfied	44%	29%
Neither satisfied nor dissatisfied	10%	5%
Dissatisfied	4%	0%
Very dissatisfied	2%	2%

Source: *Perceptions of Libraries and Information Resources,* OCLC, 2005, questions 655 and 1050.

Satisfaction with the Overall Experience of the Search by the Librarian and the Search Engine—by Library Card Holders across all Regions

Based on the most recent search you conducted through (librarian/search engine), how satisfied were you with...?

Total Respondents	Librarian	Search Engine
Very satisfied	48%	60%
Satisfied	36%	30%
Neither satisfied nor dissatisfied	11%	7%
Dissatisfied	4%	1%
Very dissatisfied	1%	2%
Library Card Holders		
Very satisfied	52%	61%
Satisfied	34%	29%
Neither satisfied nor dissatisfied	9%	6%
Dissatisfied	4%	2%
Very dissatisfied	1%	2%

Source: *Perceptions of Libraries and Information Resources,* OCLC, 2005, questions 655 and 1050.

Part 3.6

Positive and Negative Associations of Libraries
Please list two positive and two negative associations with the library.

Positive Associations		Negative Associations	
Products and Offerings			
Books (4.8%) • Free (4.4%) • Many (3.5%) • Variety (2.8%) • Borrow (1.3%) • Good (0.4%) • Available (0.2%) • Access (0.2%) • Browse (0.1%) • Current (0.1%)	18%	**Books** (0.4%) • Not available/wait (3.7%) • Not current (1.5%) • Difficult to access (1.3%) • Limited variety (1.3%) • Not what's needed (1.1%) • Not taken care of/dirty (0.7%) • Return to library (0.7%) • Too many (0.3%) • Carry/heavy (0.2%)	12.8%
Information (6.7%) • Lots (4.4%) • Free (0.9%) • Variety (0.6%) • Reliable (0.5%) • Trust (0.4%) • Access (0.2%) • Current (0.2%) • Accurate (0.2%) • Available (0.2%) • Comprehensive (0.1%)	14.3%	**Information** • Hard to access/find/use (3.7%) • Not current (0.9%) • Not available/wait (0.7%) • Not what's needed (0.7%) • Limited variety (0.5%) • Too much information (0.3%)	6.8%
Materials (0.2%) • Variety (7.8%) • Lots (0.5%) • Free (0.4%) • Available (0.2%) • Borrow (0.1%)	9.2%	**Materials** • Limited variety (2.0%) • Not available/wait (2.8%) • Hard to access/find/use (1.8%) • Not current (1.3%) • Not what's needed (1.0%) • Not taken care of/dirty (0.7%) • Not able to check out (0.1%)	9.8%
Computer • Access to computer (1.8%) • Internet access (1.4%)	3.2%	**Computer** (0.2%) • Not available (1.7%) • Internet filter (0.3%) • Outdated (0.2%)	2.4%
Easy to access/find • Easy access (2.8%) • Easy to find (0.5%)	3.3%	**Time-consuming**	2.9%
Resources (1.7%) • Many (1.2%) • Variety (0.2%) • Free (0.1%)	3.2%		
Free • Free (4.9%) • Free access (3.2%)	8.1%		

Source: *Perceptions of Libraries and Information Resources*, OCLC, 2005, question 812 a and b.

Positive Associations (continued)		Negative Associations (continued)	
Customer/user Service			

Service (0.4%)
Meets needs (0.9%)
  • Online catalog (0.7%)
  • Public (0.6%)
  • Interlibrary loan (0.4%)
  • Organize (0.4%)
  • Browse (0.4%)
  • Hours (0.1%)
  • Search (0.1%)
  • Self service (0.1%)
  • Cooperative (0.1%)
  • Borrow (0.1%)
	4.5%	**Service**
		  • Limited/poor hours (7.9%)
		  • Fees (6.0%)
		  • Return date (4.8%)
		  • Online catalog (0.9%)
		  • Rules (0.9%)
		  • Library card/membership (0.8%)
		  • Waiting (0.7%)
		  • Not private (0.4%)
		  • Bad service (0.1%)
		  • Limitations on check outs (0.1%)
			23.2%

Staff			

Staff (0.2%)
  • Helpful (7.3%)
  • Friendly (1.6%)
  • Knowledgeable (0.9%)
  • Available (0.2%)
	10.2%	**Staff** (0.7%)
		  • Unfriendly (2.5%)
		  • Not available (0.5%)
		  • Not knowledgeable (0.5%)
		  • Not helpful (0.4%)
			4.4%

Facility/Environment			

Environment (1.4%)
  • Quiet (7.9%)
  • Friendly (0.3%)
  • Comfortable (0.2%)
  • Work (0.2%)
	10.0%	**Environment** (2.0%)
		  • Too quiet (3.2%)
		  • Too noisy (2.0%)
		  • Too crowded (1.2%)
		  • Limited parking (1.0%)
		  • Too small (0.5%)
		  • Confusing layout (0.4%)
		  • Dirty (0.4%)
		  • Homeless people (0.4%)
		  • Not safe (0.2%)
			11.3%

		Travel there	7.6%
		Not convenient (3.5%) • Inconvenient location (1.5%)	5.0%
		Dull	2.2%
Miscellaneous			
Education	2.7%		
Research	2.2%		

Source: *Perceptions of Libraries and Information Resources,* OCLC, 2005, question 812 a and b.

Positive Associations with the Library—by College Students across all Regions

Please list two positive associations with the library.

	Total Respondents	College Students
Products and Offerings		
Books	18%	18%
Information	14%	16%
Materials	9%	8%
Free	8%	8%
Computers	3%	3%
Resources	3%	5%
Easy	3%	3%
Staff		
Staff	10%	9%
Facility/Environment		
Environment	10%	13%
Customer/User Service		
Service	4%	4%

Source: *Perceptions of Libraries and Information Resources*, OCLC, 2005, question 812a.

Positive Associations with the Library—by Library Card Holders across all Regions

Please list two positive associations with the library.

	Total Respondents	Library Card Holders	Non-Card Holders
Products and Offerings			
Books	18%	18%	16%
Information	14%	13%	17%
Materials	9%	10%	8%
Free	8%	8%	7%
Computers	3%	3%	3%
Resources	3%	3%	3%
Easy	3%	3%	3%
Staff			
Staff	10%	11%	8%
Facility/Environment			
Environment	10%	10%	9%
Customer/User Service			
Service	4%	5%	4%

Source: *Perceptions of Libraries and Information Resources*, OCLC, 2005, question 812a.

Negative Associations with the Library—by College Students across all Regions
Please list two negative associations with the library.

	Total Respondents	College Students
Products and Offerings		
Books	13%	13%
Materials	10%	12%
Information	7%	7%
Time-consuming	3%	4%
Computers	2%	3%
Facility/Environment		
Environment	11%	12%
Travel there	7%	6%
Not convenient	5%	2%
Dull	2%	4%
Customer/User Service		
Service	23%	23%
Staff		
Staff	4%	6%

Source: *Perceptions of Libraries and Information Resources,* OCLC, 2005, question 812b.

Negative Associations with the Library—by Library Card Holders across all Regions
Please list two negative associations with the library.

	Total Respondents	Library Card Holders	Non-Card Holders
Products and Offerings			
Books	13%	14%	10%
Materials	10%	10%	16%
Information	7%	6%	7%
Time-consuming	3%	3%	4%
Computers	2%	3%	4%
Facility/Environment			
Environment	11%	12%	13%
Travel there	7%	7%	10%
Not convenient	5%	4%	3%
Dull	2%	2%	3%
Customer/User Service			
Service	23%	24%	25%
Staff			
Staff	4%	5%	1%

Source: *Perceptions of Libraries and Information Resources,* OCLC, 2005, question 812b.

Part 3.7

Decreased Activities Due to Internet Use—
by Region of Respondent
What activities do you engage in less often since you began using the Internet?

	Total Respondents	Australia Singapore India	Canada	United Kingdom	United States
Watch television	39%	41%	45%	38%	37%
Use the library	33%	38%	34%	33%	32%
Read books	26%	30%	25%	24%	25%
Read the newspaper	26%	34%	30%	26%	22%
Read magazines	25%	29%	26%	27%	23%
Go to the mall/physical store	23%	19%	18%	17%	27%
I don't use any sources less often than before I began using the Internet	23%	18%	23%	27%	23%
Purchase music	21%	26%	22%	18%	20%
Listen to the radio	21%	29%	20%	24%	19%
Fax documents	20%	33%	24%	23%	15%
Visit with friends/family in person	14%	14%	16%	10%	14%

Source: *Perceptions of Libraries and Information Resources,* OCLC, 2005, question 415.

Decreased Activities Due to Internet Use—
by Age of U.S. Respondent
What activities do you engage in less often since you began using the Internet?

	Total U.S. Respondents	U.S. 14-17	U.S. 18-24	U.S. 25-64	U.S. 65+
Watch television	37%	34%	31%	41%	28%
Use the library	32%	42%	43%	31%	26%
Read books	25%	32%	23%	26%	21%
Read the newspaper	22%	23%	25%	22%	17%
Read magazines	23%	17%	17%	24%	28%
Go to the mall/physical store	27%	12%	26%	29%	28%
I don't use any sources less often than before I began using the Internet	23%	17%	23%	22%	32%
Purchase music	20%	24%	26%	18%	20%
Listen to the radio	19%	27%	22%	16%	25%
Fax documents	15%	13%	12%	16%	14%
Visit with friends/family in person	14%	17%	14%	12%	21%

Source: *Perceptions of Libraries and Information Resources,* OCLC, 2005, question 415.

Decreased Activities Due to Internet Use—by College Students across all Regions
What activities do you engage in less often since you began using the Internet?

	Total Respondents	College students
Watch television	39%	40%
Use the library	33%	39%
Read books	26%	26%
Read the newspaper	26%	24%
Read magazines	25%	25%
Go to the mall/physical store	23%	21%
I don't use any sources less often than before I began using the Internet	23%	17%
Purchase music	21%	25%
Listen to the radio	21%	19%
Fax documents	20%	20%
Visit with friends/family in person	14%	14%

Source: *Perceptions of Libraries and Information Resources,* OCLC, 2005, question 415.

Decreased Activities Due to the Internet—
by Library Card Holders across all Regions
What activities do you engage in less often since you began using the Internet?

	Total Respondents	Library Card Holders	Non-Card Holders
Watch television	39%	40%	38%
Use the library	33%	33%	36%
Go to the mall/physical store	23%	24%	21%
Read books	26%	25%	29%
Read magazines	25%	25%	24%
I don't use any sources less often than before I began using the Internet	23%	22%	25%
Read the newspaper	26%	26%	25%
Purchase music	21%	22%	18%
Listen to the radio	21%	21%	22%
Fax documents	20%	21%	20%
Visit with friends/family in person	14%	14%	13%

Source: *Perceptions of Libraries and Information Resources*, OCLC, 2005, question 415.

Part 3.8

First (Top-of-mind) Association with the Library—
by Region of Respondent

	Total Respondents	Australia Singapore India	Canada	United Kingdom	United States
Books	69%	66%	68%	72%	69%
Information	12%	18%	14%	6%	10%
Research	5%	4%	4%	2%	6%
Building (Environment)	9%	7%	9%	11%	9%
Materials	5%	3%	4%	4%	5%
Reference	3%	4%	3%	2%	3%
Entertainment	2%	2%	2%	2%	2%

Source: *Perceptions of Libraries and Information Resources*, OCLC, 2005, question 807.

First (Top-of-mind) Association with the Library—
by Age of U.S. Respondent

	Total U.S. Respondents	U.S. 14-17	U.S. 18-24	U.S. 25-64	U.S. 65+
Books	69%	76%	71%	75%	50%
Information	10%	6%	8%	16%	14%
Research	6%	6%	5%	6%	1%
Building (Environment)	9%	8%	14%	11%	5%
Materials	5%	2%	3%	6%	8%
Reference	3%	1%	1%	18%	4%
Entertainment	2%	1%	2%	2%	4%

Source: *Perceptions of Libraries and Information Resources*, OCLC, 2005, question 807.

First (Top-of-mind) Association with the Library—
by College Students across all Regions

	Total Respondents	College Students
Books	69%	69%
Information	12%	8%
Building (Environment)	9%	13%
Research	5%	6%
Materials	5%	3%
Reference	3%	1%
Entertainment	2%	3%

Source: *Perceptions of Libraries and Information Resources*, OCLC, 2005, question 807.

First (Top-of-mind) Association with the Library—
by Library Card Holders across all Regions

	Total Respondents	Card Holders	Non-Card Holders
Books	69%	70%	63%
Information	12%	11%	14%
Building (Environment)	9%	8%	11%
Research	5%	5%	4%
Materials	5%	5%	2%
Reference	3%	3%	1%
Entertainment	2%	3%	6%

Source: *Perceptions of Libraries and Information Resources*, OCLC, 2005, question 807.

Part 3.9

Main Purpose of the Library—
by Region of Respondent

	Total Respondents	Australia Singapore India	Canada	United Kingdom	United States
Information	53%	52%	60%	47%	52%
Books	31%	24%	27%	42%	32%
Research	14%	12%	14%	6%	16%
Materials	11%	12%	13%	11%	10%
Entertainment	10%	8%	12%	9%	11%
Reading	6%	5%	7%	7%	6%
Building (Environment)	4%	3%	3%	2%	4%

Source: *Perceptions of Libraries and Information Resources*, OCLC, 2005, question 810.

Main Purpose of the Library—
by Age of U.S. Respondent

	Total U.S. Respondents	U.S. 14-17	U.S. 18-24	U.S. 25-64	U.S. 65+
Information	52%	45%	49%	56%	62%
Books	32%	40%	32%	26%	27%
Research	16%	17%	20%	15%	13%
Entertainment	11%	11%	8%	10%	14%
Materials	10%	8%	9%	12%	13%
Reading	6%	7%	5%	7%	5%
Building (Environment)	4%	5%	7%	3%	2%

Source: *Perceptions of Libraries and Information Resources*, OCLC, 2005, question 810.

Main Purpose of the Library—
by College Students across all Regions

	Total Respondents	College Students
Information	53%	49%
Books	31%	33%
Research	14%	20%
Entertainment	10%	12%
Materials	11%	10%
Reading	6%	6%
Building (Environment)	4%	6%

Source: *Perceptions of Libraries and Information Resources*, OCLC, 2005, question 810.

Main Purpose of the Library—
by Library Card Holders across all Regions

	Total Respondents	Card Holders	Non-Card Holders
Information	53%	53%	51%
Books	31%	34%	29%
Research	14%	13%	17%
Entertainment	10%	11%	9%
Materials	11%	12%	8%
Reading	6%	6%	8%
Building (Environment)	4%	4%	3%

Source: *Perceptions of Libraries and Information Resources*, OCLC, 2005, question 810.

Part 4.3

Advice for the Library—by Region of Respondent

If you could provide one piece of advice to your library, what would it be?

	Total	Australia Singapore India	Canada	United Kingdom	United States
Products and Offerings					
Add to Collection	**13.4%**	**14.5%**	**13.9%**	**7.7%**	**14.1%**
Add - books	8.1%	9.0%	7.4%	7.2%	8.1%
Add - materials	3.7%	3.9%	4.6%	0.3%	4.2%
Add - resources	0.3%	0.4%	0.0%	0.0%	0.4%
Add - information	0.2%	0.4%	0.2%	0.0%	0.2%
Add - more copies of books	0.9%	0.8%	1.4%	0.3%	0.9%
Add - more copies of materials	0.2%	0.0%	0.2%	0.0%	0.3%
Computers	**4.9%**	**4.9%**	**2.8%**	**3.4%**	**5.7%**
Add - computers	3.2%	0.6%	0.3%	0.3%	1.9%
Update - computers	1.7%	0.2%	0.1%	0.1%	1.3%
Update Collection	**7.3%**	**8.6%**	**11.1%**	**5.7%**	**6.4%**
Update	0.8%	1.0%	1.4%	1.1%	0.5%
Update - books	3.9%	3.7%	6.2%	3.7%	3.4%
Update - materials	1.8%	2.7%	2.5%	0.0%	1.8%
Update - information	0.5%	1.2%	0.5%	0.6%	0.4%
Update - resources	0.3%	0.0%	0.1%	0.0%	0.2%
OPAC	**0.7%**	**1.0%**	**0.5%**	**0.6%**	**0.7%**
OPAC	0.1%	0.0%	0.0%	0.0%	0.1%
OPAC - searching	0.6%	1.0%	0.5%	0.6%	0.6%
Customer/User Service					
Access	**3.5%**	**4.3%**	**3.7%**	**3.4%**	**3.2%**
Access	0.5%	1.0%	0.7%	0.6%	0.4%
Access - disability	0.2%	0.2%	0.2%	0.3%	0.2%
Access - easier	0.7%	0.0%	0.9%	0.3%	1.0%
Access - online	1.8%	2.0%	1.8%	2.0%	1.6%
Access - remote	0.3%	1.0%	0.0%	0.3%	0.1%
Service	**16.1%**	**12.9%**	**19.9%**	**17.8%**	**15.7%**
Service	0.2%	0.2%	0.0%	0.0%	0.2%
Service - check	0.3%	0.8%	0.0%	0.0%	0.4%
Service - classes	0.4%	0.2%	0.5%	0.3%	0.4%
Service - close library	0.2%	0.2%	0.0%	0.0%	0.2%
Service - don't close	0.3%	0.0%	0.5%	0.3%	0.3%
Service - extend hours	9.0%	6.5%	14.1%	12.0%	7.7%
Service - free internet	0.3%	0.6%	0.5%	0.3%	0.2%
Service - ILL	0.1%	0.2%	0.2%	0.0%	0.1%
Service - longer lending	0.9%	0.8%	0.9%	2.3%	0.6%
Service - more activities	1.3%	1.4%	0.9%	0.9%	1.5%
Service - no copy fee	0.4%	0.0%	0.0%	0.6%	0.5%
Service - no fees	0.4%	0.2%	0.7%	0.0%	0.4%

Source: *Perceptions of Libraries and Information Sources,* OCLC, 2005, question 1240.

Advice for the Library—by Region of Respondent (continued)

If you could provide one piece of advice to your library, what would it be?

	Total	Australia Singapore India	Canada	United Kingdom	United States
Customer/User Service (continued)					
Service - no fines	0.6%	0.6%	0.2%	0.3%	0.8%
Service - no more buildings	0.0%	0.0%	0.0%	0.0%	0.1%
Service - renew	0.5%	0.4%	0.0%	0.0%	0.8%
Service - reserve online	0.2%	0.0%	0.2%	0.3%	0.2%
Service - return books	0.3%	0.2%	0.2%	0.6%	0.2%
Service - rules	0.6%	0.4%	0.7%	0.0%	0.8%
Service - shelving	0.1%	0.0%	0.0%	0.0%	0.2%
Service - support	0.0%	0.0%	0.2%	0.0%	0.0%
Service - train staff	0.0%	0.0%	0.0%	0.0%	0.1%
Promote	**5.6%**	**6.3%**	**5.1%**	**8.6%**	**4.8%**
Promote	2.5%	3.1%	1.8%	3.4%	2.2%
Promote - activities	0.2%	0.2%	0.5%	0.6%	0.1%
Promote - fun	1.4%	2.0%	0.5%	2.0%	1.4%
Promote - hours	0.2%	0.2%	0.2%	0.6%	0.2%
Promote - materials	0.2%	0.2%	0.0%	0.0%	0.4%
Promote - resources	0.5%	0.2%	1.4%	0.6%	0.3%
Promote - services	0.5%	0.4%	0.7%	1.4%	0.2%
Facility/Environment					
Environment	**18.9%**	**21.4%**	**15.0%**	**31.8%**	**16.5%**
Environment	2.0%	0.6%	1.2%	3.2%	2.4%
Environment - café	1.4%	1.8%	1.2%	4.9%	0.7%
Environment - clean	0.4%	0.6%	0.2%	0.6%	0.3%
Environment - expand	2.2%	2.2%	1.2%	1.7%	2.6%
Environment - inviting	2.0%	2.0%	1.4%	4.9%	1.5%
Environment - light	0.7%	1.0%	0.9%	0.6%	0.5%
Environment - location	0.3%	0.4%	0.5%	0.3%	0.2%
Environment - maps	0.1%	0.0%	0.0%	0.0%	0.2%
Environment - more quiet	1.3%	2.0%	0.9%	1.4%	1.1%
Environment - organization	0.9%	0.2%	1.2%	1.1%	1.0%
Environment - parking	0.8%	1.0%	0.7%	1.7%	0.6%
Environment - seating	2.9%	5.1%	3.2%	2.9%	2.1%
Environment - shelving	0.9%	1.0%	0.5%	2.6%	0.6%
Environment - signage	0.4%	0.4%	0.5%	0.3%	0.5%
Environment - social rooms	0.3%	0.2%	0.0%	0.3%	0.4%
Environment - study areas	0.3%	0.4%	0.5%	0.3%	0.2%
Environment - temperature	0.2%	0.2%	0.0%	0.3%	0.2%
Environment - update	1.8%	2.0%	1.2%	4.9%	1.3%

Source: *Perceptions of Libraries and Information Resources,* OCLC, 2005, question 1240.

Advice for the Library—by Region of Respondent (continued)

If you could provide one piece of advice to your library, what would it be?

	Total	Australia Singapore India	Canada	United Kingdom	United States
Staff					
Staff	6.4%	7.3%	4.6%	5.2%	6.8%
Staff	0.1%	0.8%	0.0%	0.0%	0.0%
Staff - more friendly	4.5%	4.7%	2.5%	4.6%	5.0%
Staff - more helpful	0.3%	0.4%	0.0%	0.3%	0.3%
Staff - more knowledgeable	0.2%	0.2%	0.2%	0.0%	0.2%
Staff - need more	1.2%	1.2%	1.8%	0.3%	1.2%
Staff - need new	0.1%	0.0%	0.0%	0.0%	0.1%
Satisfaction					
Satisfied as is	6.1%	4.7%	6.0%	2.9%	7.3%
Miscellaneous					
Testimonials	0.9%	1.0%	1.4%	0.9%	0.8%
Nothing	10.2%	7.3%	8.8%	7.2%	12.1%
Other	3.3%	3.5%	4.2%	2.3%	3.2%
Don't know	3.4%	2.4%	4.4%	4.3%	3.2%
Funding	0.8%	1.2%	0.7%	0.3%	0.8%

Source: *Perceptions of Libraries and Information Resources*, OCLC, 2005, question 1240.

Advice for the Library—by Age of U.S. Respondent
If you could provide one piece of advice to your library, what would it be?

	Total U.S. Respondents	U.S. 14-17	U.S. 18-24	U.S. 25-64	U.S. 65+
Products and Offerings					
Add to Collection	**14.1%**	**19.8%**	**12.4%**	**12.0%**	**10.2%**
Add - books	8.1%	13.2%	7.7%	5.1%	4.0%
Add - materials	4.2%	5.0%	2.4%	5.1%	4.8%
Add - resources	0.4%	0.5%	0.5%	0.2%	0.0%
Add - information	0.2%	0.4%	0.3%	0.0%	0.0%
Add - more copies of books	0.9%	0.5%	1.6%	0.7%	1.1%
Add - more copies of materials	0.3%	0.2%	0.0%	0.7%	0.3%
Computers	**5.7%**	**6.5%**	**8.4%**	**5.1%**	**2.0%**
Add - computers	1.9%	2.9%	7.1%	2.7%	0.8%
Update - computers	1.3%	3.6%	1.3%	2.4%	2.0%
Update Collection	**6.4%**	**7.6%**	**7.9%**	**5.1%**	**4.0%**
Update	0.5%	0.5%	0.8%	0.7%	0.0%
Update - books	3.4%	4.1%	3.7%	2.2%	2.8%
Update - materials	1.8%	2.3%	2.4%	1.5%	0.6%
Update - information	0.4%	0.2%	0.8%	0.2%	0.3%
Update - resources	0.2%	0.4%	0.3%	0.5%	0.3%
OPAC	**0.7%**	**0.7%**	**0.8%**	**1.0%**	**0.3%**
OPAC	0.1%	0.0%	0.0%	0.5%	0.0%
OPAC - searching	0.6%	0.7%	0.8%	0.5%	0.3%
Customer/User Service					
Access	**3.2%**	**2.3%**	**4.5%**	**2.2%**	**4.5%**
Access	0.4%	0.2%	0.5%	0.5%	0.3%
Access - disability	0.2%	0.0%	0.0%	0.2%	0.6%
Access - easier	1.0%	1.4%	0.5%	0.2%	1.7%
Access - online	1.6%	0.7%	3.2%	1.0%	2.0%
Access - remote	0.1%	0.0%	0.3%	0.2%	0.0%
Service	**15.7%**	**12.6%**	**9.2%**	**23.0%**	**17.6%**
Service	0.2%	0.2%	0.0%	0.0%	0.3%
Service - check	0.4%	0.2%	0.3%	0.2%	0.6%
Service - classes	0.4%	0.0%	0.3%	0.7%	0.8%
Service - close library	0.2%	0.4%	0.0%	0.2%	0.3%
Service - don't close	0.3%	0.2%	0.3%	0.2%	0.6%
Service - extend hours	7.7%	3.4%	3.7%	15.4%	9.6%
Service - free internet	0.2%	0.4%	0.0%	0.2%	0.0%
Service - ILL	0.1%	0.0%	0.3%	0.0%	0.3%
Service - longer lending	0.6%	0.9%	0.0%	1.2%	0.0%
Service - more activities	1.5%	1.4%	1.1%	2.0%	1.4%
Service - no copy fee	0.5%	0.9%	0.8%	0.0%	0.0%
Service - no fees	0.4%	0.2%	0.0%	0.5%	0.8%
Service - no fines	0.8%	1.3%	1.3%	0.2%	0.3%
Service - no more buildings	0.1%	0.0%	0.0%	0.0%	0.3%
Service - renew	0.8%	1.1%	0.5%	0.5%	0.8%
Service - reserve online	0.2%	0.0%	0.3%	0.2%	0.6%

Source: *Perceptions of Libraries and Information Resources,* OCLC, 2005, question 1240.

Advice for the Library—by Age of U.S. Respondent (continued)
If you could provide one piece of advice to your library, what would it be?

	Total U.S. Respondents	U.S. 14-17	U.S. 18-24	U.S. 25-64	U.S. 65+
Customer/User Service (continued)					
Service (continued)					
Service - return books	0.2%	0.2%	0.0%	0.7%	0.0%
Service - rules	0.8%	2.0%	0.5%	0.0%	0.3%
Service - shelving	0.2%	0.0%	0.0%	0.2%	0.6%
Service - support	0.0%	0.0%	0.0%	0.0%	0.0%
Service - train staff	0.1%	0.0%	0.0%	0.2%	0.0%
Promote	**4.8%**	**3.4%**	**2.9%**	**6.8%**	**6.5%**
Promote	2.2%	1.3%	0.8%	3.2%	4.2%
Promote - activities	0.1%	0.0%	0.0%	0.2%	0.3%
Promote - fun	1.4%	2.0%	1.6%	1.5%	0.3%
Promote - hours	0.2%	0.0%	0.3%	0.2%	0.3%
Promote - materials	0.4%	0.2%	0.3%	0.2%	0.6%
Promote - resources	0.3%	0.0%	0.0%	0.5%	0.8%
Promote - services	0.2%	0.0%	0.0%	1.0%	0.0%
Facility/Environment					
Environment	**16.5%**	**16.4%**	**20.3%**	**14.4%**	**13.0%**
Environment	2.4%	2.7%	2.4%	1.7%	1.4%
Environment - café	0.7%	0.5%	0.5%	1.2%	0.6%
Environment - clean	0.3%	0.2%	0.5%	0.5%	0.0%
Environment - expand	2.6%	2.5%	1.6%	1.5%	4.5%
Environment - inviting	1.5%	1.8%	1.6%	1.5%	0.8%
Environment - light	0.5%	0.7%	1.1%	0.2%	0.0%
Environment - location	0.2%	0.0%	0.0%	0.2%	0.6%
Environment - maps	0.2%	0.4%	0.5%	0.0%	0.0%
Environment - more quiet	1.1%	0.2%	1.8%	1.0%	2.0%
Environment - organization	1.0%	0.9%	2.1%	1.0%	0.0%
Environment - parking	0.6%	0.0%	0.3%	1.0%	1.7%
Environment - seating	2.1%	2.5%	3.7%	1.5%	0.6%
Environment - shelving	0.6%	0.5%	0.5%	0.5%	0.6%
Environment - signage	0.5%	0.7%	0.5%	0.2%	0.3%
Environment - social rooms	0.4%	0.7%	0.0%	0.7%	0.0%
Environment - study areas	0.2%	0.4%	0.3%	0.2%	0.0%
Environment - temperature	0.2%	0.2%	0.5%	0.2%	0.0%
Environment - update	1.3%	1.4%	2.4%	1.2%	0.0%

Source: *Perceptions of Libraries and Information Resources*, OCLC, 2005, question 1240.

Advice for the Library—by Age of U.S. Respondent (continued)

If you could provide one piece of advice to your library, what would it be?

	Total U.S. Respondents	U.S. 14-17	U.S. 18-24	U.S. 25-64	U.S. 65+
Staff					
Staff	**6.8%**	**10.3%**	**8.7%**	**4.6%**	**1.4%**
Staff	0.0%	0.0%	0.0%	0.0%	0.0%
Staff - more friendly	5.0%	7.7%	6.3%	3.4%	1.1%
Staff - more helpful	0.3%	0.4%	0.5%	0.0%	0.0%
Staff - more knowledgeable	0.2%	0.4%	0.3%	0.0%	0.0%
Staff - need more	1.2%	1.4%	1.6%	1.2%	0.3%
Staff - need new	0.1%	0.4%	0.0%	0.0%	0.0%
Satisfaction					
Satisfied as is	**7.3%**	**4.0%**	**5.0%**	**8.3%**	**13.6%**
Miscellaneous					
Nothing	12.1%	7.7%	13.7%	13.0%	16.1%
Other	3.2%	4.3%	2.4%	1.7%	4.5%
Don't know	3.2%	2.9%	4.2%	13.2%	4.0%
Funding	0.8%	0.7%	0.0%	0.7%	1.7%
Testimonials	0.8%	1.3%	1.6%	2.7%	0.8%

Source: *Perceptions of Libraries and Information Resources,* OCLC, 2005, question 1240.

Appendix B: Sample Verbatim Comments

The following tables include a random 10 percent sample of the verbatim responses for these survey questions:

Q807: What is the first thing you think of when you think of a library?

Note: All verbatim comments are presented as entered by survey respondents, including spelling, grammatical and punctuation errors.

Q807: What is the first thing you think of when you think of a library?	Age	Geographic Region	Student Status
Lots of books to have to sort through to find what you want & lots of reading	17	Australia	High school
fees/ overdue books	17	Australia	High school
Work. Work and more work	18	Australia	College undergraduate
Books, and HOW you are going to find the one book you are after!	18	Australia	College undergraduate
Difficulties finding physical books using the Dewey Decimal system	19	Australia	College undergraduate
having to search throuh many books to find relevant information	19	Australia	College undergraduate
I LIKE READING BOOKS. HOWEVER IN SAYING THIS I WOULD RATHER SOMETHING IN MY HANDS THAN ON A COUMPUTER.	22	Australia	
Internet	22	Australia	
Time	25	Australia	
labourious	25	Australia	
Lovely, lovely books! The complete package!	26	Australia	College undergraduate
access to good information and resources	29	Australia	College undergraduate
Free information	30	Australia	
boring	30	Australia	
good references	31	Australia	
out of date books	32	Australia	
not quick enough	32	Australia	
The need to visit the library	32	Australia	
Well, I had a bad experience with a librarian, so I have issues there.... but aside from that, I think of knowledge being made available to everyone.	33	Australia	
great range of books	33	Australia	
Range of books	33	Australia	
books and a woman in glasses	34	Australia	
free resources	38	Australia	
Access to information for study and leisure.	38	Australia	College post graduate
Books, beautiful books, wonderful books, books, books, books, books	38	Australia	
books, looking looking	39	Australia	
brick & mortar	39	Australia	
Any information, general reading, research, basic knowledge is available to you.	40	Australia	
range of choice	41	Australia	
A variety of information sources - eg books, journals, data bases.	42	Australia	
the amount of books to be lent out, also the information the librian can assist people with	44	Australia	
That I should register again at the library	44	Australia	
Quietness	46	Australia	
beautiful olf building fillde with books and a great 'book' smell	46	Australia	
Borrow the books, useing internet	46	Australia	
endless supply of books.....mmmm,boookss...	47	Australia	

Q807: What is the first thing you think of when you think of a library?	Age	Geographic Region	Student Status
The catalogue.	47	Australia	
The joy of books(reading)	47	Australia	
rules	47	Australia	
I am a card holder but the local library doaes not cover many of my interests and the non foction books are 15 yrs old	48	Australia	
books	49	Australia	
EDUCATION	49	Australia	College post graduate
Having to look through rows of indexes & books.	50	Australia	
Hours of operation and hard to find books	50	Australia	
quiet place to read and have a coffee	51	Australia	
New books	51	Australia	
mouldy, old, out of date books	51	Australia	
research materials, newspaper and magazine back copies.	51	Australia	
Outdated reference material	52	Australia	
Peace and quiet, a time to browse	53	Australia	
Driving to the library	53	Australia	
cheap and useful information	54	Australia	
any information	54	Australia	
Good access, good selection	54	Australia	
A place to get a book or source information	55	Australia	
books	55	Australia	
DVD's	55	Australia	
Inconvenient to get to.	56	Australia	
The knowledge of the librarian, and the availability of services.	56	Australia	
Sitting for hours looking for an answer, as my time is limited.	57	Australia	
FREE	57	Australia	
wonderful array of dreams, imagination, gacts, fiction and fun	57	Australia	
At the moment music CDs.	57	Australia	
Using a computer when I am away from home Borrowing books when I am at home	58	Australia	
Quiet Please!	59	Australia	
getting information that i have not be able to find elsewere	60	Australia	
can it give me the info i need quickly	60	Australia	
stacks of musty books	62	Australia	
Borrowing music CDs and cassettes.	63	Australia	
a place where I can find information and get a credible good advise	64	Australia	
It used to be a major source of information for me , prior to the internet.	64	Australia	
Answers.	65	Australia	
Not useful tome as long as I can access the Internet	70	Australia	
I think of all the books and the computers in the library.	15	Canada	High school
The coffee shop attatched to it.	16	Canada	High school
books	17	Canada	High school
I despise searching the library for books and other sources. It takes a long time and rarely can you find sources needed. This difficult process is the first thing I think of when I think of using the library.	18	Canada	High school
Fiction	20	Canada	College undergraduate
research and studying	20	Canada	College undergraduate
Reference material.	20	Canada	College undergraduate
Study	20	Canada	
books	20	Canada	College post graduate
resourses relaxation	20	Canada	

Q807: What is the first thing you think of when you think of a library?	Age	Geographic Region	Student Status
Uncomfortable chairs	21	Canada	College undergraduate
books	21	Canada	College undergraduate
quiet, boring, The Library we have here doesn't even have a wide variety of books and never had, so i kind of gave up on libraries a long time ago	21	Canada	
books and research	22	Canada	College undergraduate
have not time to go	23	Canada	
A great location for finding information from thousands of books. The libraian is there to assist us in locating the information we are seeking.	23	Canada	
BOOKS - but I like books!	25	Canada	
old books	26	Canada	
quiet and relaxing	26	Canada	
bad hours	27	Canada	
Rows and rows of books.	28	Canada	
books	28	Canada	
borrowing books	28	Canada	College undergraduate
Books (I adore them) and then their website (access to journals etc) without going to the library.	29	Canada	College undergraduate
books	30	Canada	
Free book loans	31	Canada	
Books and Videos	31	Canada	
Free, easy access to knowledge.	32	Canada	
get books for my daughter to read only	32	Canada	
where to start	32	Canada	
Rows and rows of books	32	Canada	
I think of a place (building) where there are many books and references sources available to use.	32	Canada	
the books i want are always out, that's why i buy from chapters.	32	Canada	
Archival documents ie) periodicals	32	Canada	
Big building with books, often older books.	32	Canada	
doing an online search and request for material from the comfort of my home	33	Canada	
books	33	Canada	
wasting fuel[the drive]	34	Canada	
Deafening silence	35	Canada	
Free access to books.	35	Canada	
Books for reading pleasure and archives/information about the surrounding region.	35	Canada	
Hub of data - whether it's in electronic or print format, the library should have what I need.	35	Canada	
free info or books	35	Canada	
borrowing books	36	Canada	
Literature, books I like to read	37	Canada	
very helpful,friendly, knowledgeable, resourceful,easy to use, always available, free	37	Canada	
Books, boring, shhhhh.	37	Canada	
books, cds, movies	37	Canada	
Not open when needed. (rural)	37	Canada	
Books, and lots of them!	38	Canada	
happy i love the library and go there weekly.	38	Canada	
I can borrow what I can't afford	39	Canada	
Out of date information	40	Canada	
information	40	Canada	

Q807: What is the first thing you think of when you think of a library?	Age	Geographic Region	Student Status
books	40	Canada	
Finding books of interest to my reading preferences(Biographies,war history,and automotive)	40	Canada	
A facility that is mostly concerned with books.	42	Canada	
I seldom have to buy books anymore - almost anything I want is at the Library! Being able to reserve books online is the greatest!!	42	Canada	
being quiet	42	Canada	
checking out books	43	Canada	
busy place!	43	Canada	
returning books. I always buy books.	44	Canada	
historical hardcopy information storage	44	Canada	
a building with endless information and entertainment	44	Canada	
out dated information (I live in a small rural community)	44	Canada	
resources that are available in book form	45	Canada	
having to loan a book and making sure its back when it is supposed to be	45	Canada	
Librarians.	45	Canada	
don,t need it now	45	Canada	
help to search	45	Canada	
reference books	45	Canada	
Be prepared to search for your info.	45	Canada	
information	45	Canada	
Love Libraries, used to almost live there and have read hundreds of books but just don't have the time anymore	45	Canada	
Books on shelves	45	Canada	
recreational reading	46	Canada	
I love the smell of books in the library. I also know that the people who work there know their job and I have always found them to be more than willing to assist when I have questions.	46	Canada	
having to get the book back on time	46	Canada	
Getting the books I wish to read	46	Canada	
information	46	Canada	
out of date reading material.	47	Canada	
Will they have the book I am looking for?	47	Canada	
A place to borrow books, music, magazines etc., without running the risk of buying and then not liking them.	48	Canada	
Books of interest for offline use	48	Canada	
the use of bboks for 'free'	48	Canada	
Electronic journals	48	Canada	
BOOKs lots of books a place to escape to for quiet	48	Canada	
Best selling books	49	Canada	
adventure	49	Canada	
Passwords to get into the site. Hard to find items	49	Canada	
Clumsy	49	Canada	
find the web site	50	Canada	
books	50	Canada	
Books and info	50	Canada	
OLD paper archive, out of date.	50	Canada	
To be frank, boring.	50	Canada	
a building where you do research, read books or borrow books	51	Canada	
Lots of book not necessarily recent	51	Canada	
Old fashion.	52	Canada	
have lots of time to look.	53	Canada	
Limited hours, deadlines to return books	53	Canada	
The books I am looking to pick up to read are often not there	53	Canada	
a place where you find answers to your questions	53	Canada	

Q807: What is the first thing you think of when you think of a library?	Age	Geographic Region	Student Status
the smell of books, the excitment in discovering a good book,	53	Canada	
anything that I want to read	54	Canada	
Reference location	54	Canada	
everything on knowledge	54	Canada	
Unlimited information	54	Canada	
computers	54	Canada	
source of a variety of printed material for pleasure and information	55	Canada	
genealogy	55	Canada	
time	55	Canada	
information	55	Canada	
Books, though I know they have other media available	55	Canada	
Learning	56	Canada	College undergraduate
so many wonderful books, so little time	57	Canada	College post graduate
comfortable place with decent lighting	57	Canada	
books but i also know they have other services	58	Canada	
beautiful books and lots of them, on any subject you want	58	Canada	
Finding the books I really want to read, but cannot afford to buy.	60	Canada	
Lots of books & the time it would take to go there & search for what I want	60	Canada	
New Books	61	Canada	
Equality. Libraries more than any other institution make the access of information available to anyone who wants it. Libraries run literacy programs, have volunteers teach ESL courses, Give open access joyfully to all the literatue, art, and periodicals	61	Canada	
reference material	62	Canada	
rows of books	63	Canada	
pleasant place to be	64	Canada	
Having to search for something in a large data base.	65	Canada	
A DULL PLACE THAT I HAVE TO WALK TO; TO BE FAIR, I DO NOT READ MANY NON-FICTION BOOKS, OR BOOKS FOR THAT MATTER, I SUBSCRIBE TO TECHNICAL MAGAZINES I ENJOY TO KEEP UP WITH TECHNOLOGY, I LOOK UP THE REST OF THE INFORMATION ON COMPUTER AS NEED BE.	66	Canada	
Reference materials	67	Canada	
Borrowing books and videos looking for information	68	Canada	
How much reading material I have to choose from.	68	Canada	
Having a good selection of good reading!	68	Canada	
Too far to visit on a regular basis and would interfere with my time on the computer.	69	Canada	
books	69	Canada	
Computers are available. Also all types of research books and novels	71	Canada	
Local building with books and on-line service available (which I don't use).	75	Canada	
Storries	22	India	
Easy accessibility	24	India	
Knowledge	25	India	
Boring	26	India	
Well the first think that comes to my mind is that a library contains all the valuable information in the form of books,magazines and journals that can be of great use to enlighten oneself more precisely to make oneself more knowledgeable.	27	India	
silence	30	India	

Q807: What is the first thing you think of when you think of a library?	Age	Geographic Region	Student Status
Membership requirements	31	India	
peace	35	India	
Books!	35	India	College post graduate
colection of books	37	India	
a place where u find lots books, information and referels.	39	India	
i get information from various web holders where i delete which is not warant and hold which is relevant to my work. i save the entire data which is usable to my work.	39	India	
Books	43	India	
school	44	India	
plenty of books, quiet place to sit and read	48	India	
LIBRARY IS RESOURCE FOR KNOWLEDGE	51	India	
aplace where I can access all the info needed	51	India	
Authentic Info	51	India	
It is tedious to go to library,it is easy to trace the information on internet.	54	India	
a world of books	54	India	
information/ knowedge	54	India	
Can I get the latest books on the subject of my interest	55	India	
index	56	India	
no comment	58	India	
books and magazines	61	India	
A great collection of books.	62	India	
Service and wide source of information	66	India	
Catalog/index	71	India	
story books	18	Singapore	College undergraduate
Lots of ancient books.	20	Singapore	
I can find books that I want.	21	Singapore	
books	23	Singapore	
reference	27	Singapore	
quiet and cosy place to read	27	Singapore	
A place to relax and enjoy borrowing a good book.	28	Singapore	
Fast, accurate and quick response	29	Singapore	
Knowledge	31	Singapore	
Research and Reading	31	Singapore	
difficult to find what you really need without spending hours looking.	32	Singapore	College post graduate
to collect info	32	Singapore	
Distance from home :>	33	Singapore	
Having to visit the it personally to get reference material with ease of mind that there is always someone to help when you need them	33	Singapore	
reference books	33	Singapore	
Dull looking environment	34	Singapore	
A place you can borrow books and do research	34	Singapore	
have to take a train to the library	35	Singapore	
Good resource, but may not always have the resource available at that moment when we need it urgently.	35	Singapore	College post graduate
free info	37	Singapore	
BOOKS & many Outdated Informations.	37	Singapore	
RESEARCH READ NEWSPAPER	37	Singapore	
Borrowing books of reference and reading pleasure.	37	Singapore	
Free access to lots of books !	39	Singapore	
diligent people researching for materials	40	Singapore	
safety, fees	40	Singapore	College post graduate

Q807: What is the first thing you think of when you think of a library?	Age	Geographic Region	Student Status
librarians	42	Singapore	
books	46	Singapore	
Books and information/ references.	48	Singapore	
if professional data is required.	48	Singapore	
Borrow books & search for information & reading pleasure.	48	Singapore	
Quiet	17	U.K.	High school
too old	19	U.K.	College undergraduate
cosy place to read books	19	U.K.	
i just do - i only really use university library and wonder if the book is gonna be there	21	U.K.	College undergraduate
Its to far away	21	U.K.	
Books and e-mails	21	U.K.	
aisles full of books	22	U.K.	College undergraduate
Books / information	22	U.K.	College post graduate
Books.	22	U.K.	
quite	23	U.K.	College undergraduate
Its a hassle to go there	23	U.K.	
loads of new books to read	23	U.K.	
location	24	U.K.	
books and being told to be quiet	25	U.K.	
books for fun	26	U.K.	
silence	26	U.K.	
Have to make an effort to go there	26	U.K.	
reading	26	U.K.	
borrowing books for free	27	U.K.	
Silence.	27	U.K.	
books business information	27	U.K.	
easily accesing to informations on line, the availability of books, journals ect..	28	U.K.	College post graduate
paradise! lots of books about everything!	28	U.K.	
borrowing books/music	29	U.K.	
getting there and the closing times and so quiet and not very friendly	29	U.K.	
QUIET	29	U.K.	
Boring and quiet	30	U.K.	
great way to read books and rent films	30	U.K.	
quiet place with lot of information	31	U.K.	
free access	31	U.K.	
boring	31	U.K.	
good selection of books	32	U.K.	
getting reminders	33	U.K.	
Old dusty buildings i used to frequent as a child	33	U.K.	
books	33	U.K.	
Books. (The borrowing of)	33	U.K.	
Under resourced.	34	U.K.	
Boring	34	U.K.	
Books that I have to give back	34	U.K.	
novels	34	U.K.	
rows of books	35	U.K.	
a building with books	35	U.K.	
information books computers	37	U.K.	
Books, CDs, DVDs	37	U.K.	
BOOKS	38	U.K.	
books	38	U.K.	

Q807: What is the first thing you think of when you think of a library?	Age	Geographic Region	Student Status
homework-kids school projects	39	U.K.	
Borrowing books	39	U.K.	
Silence A very lonely atmosphere (some may like that, I don't!)	40	U.K.	
Overdue books and fines	41	U.K.	
old books	41	U.K.	
I don't like having to return books	41	U.K.	
books books and books,	41	U.K.	
Peace and quiet	41	U.K.	
reference books	42	U.K.	
Shelves of books	42	U.K.	
It's a walk up to the town and I have to take my children	43	U.K.	
i dont like library books	44	U.K.	
A place to borrow books	44	U.K.	
Several buildings that I use for hiring books looking up information	44	U.K.	
information+education sources	44	U.K.	
Wide chooice of books	44	U.K.	
quite place	45	U.K.	
Stuffy and old fashioned. Used one when I was a child to do my homework.	45	U.K.	
books,newspapers, dvds	46	U.K.	
pleasure	46	U.K.	
Books / CD / DVDs to borrow	47	U.K.	
peace and quiet!	49	U.K.	
books	49	U.K.	
building full of books	49	U.K.	
Inconvenience of getting there.	50	U.K.	
vidio and cd hire for a week at a time better than other places which has one day hire	50	U.K.	
BOOKS!!!!!!!!!!!!!!!!!	50	U.K.	
varied source of information & entertainment in the form of books, periodicals, computers, audio & visual sources in the form of CD's etc.	51	U.K.	College undergraduate
Books	51	U.K.	
Helpful Staff	51	U.K.	
My childhood.I read ALL the fiction in the Junior Library.	51	U.K.	
books	51	U.K.	
good books for free	52	U.K.	
have to travel	52	U.K.	
Not convenient Total silence	53	U.K.	
LOTS OF BOOKS TO CHOOSE FROM.	53	U.K.	
Old fashioned	53	U.K.	
enjoyment	54	U.K.	
TICKETS	54	U.K.	
Informative information on subjects that I would not necessarily get from computer searches ie pictorial guides	54	U.K.	
Books, Video's, reference library.	55	U.K.	
How are books classified so that I can find what I want	56	U.K.	
Free lending service boks cds etc	56	U.K.	
Silence - I recently retired from teaching so my resources where generally available in my institution where I did use the library. I have not used a public library for many years.	56	U.K.	
old outdated books	56	U.K.	
Books, reading and CDs	57	U.K.	
books	57	U.K.	
quiet	57	U.K.	
a queue	58	U.K.	
getting a book	59	U.K.	

Q807: What is the first thing you think of when you think of a library?	Age	Geographic Region	Student Status
Its in the centre of the town where I live and its difficult to get to, i.e., no nearby free parking. I think its an old fashioned way of getting information.	60	U.K.	
BOOKS and reading to relax	60	U.K.	
information relaxation	60	U.K.	
a library is a place to borrow books from for leisure and also for fact finding and reference material	60	U.K.	
lots of good free books to borrow.	60	U.K.	
Resources	60	U.K.	
reading books	60	U.K.	
Autobiographies	61	U.K.	
lots of books and I can't read them all. I get a warm feeling when I enter a library a bit like a warm bath.	61	U.K.	
Originally-books! Now Computers & courses.	66	U.K.	
books, usually out of date	70	U.K.	
Both reading and reference books, in particular cookery.	71	U.K.	
books	71	U.K.	
Books	71	U.K.	
nowadays, failure - one time it was the prime source - but now, the personnel are not up to the job.	73	U.K.	
New fiction	80	U.K.	
books	80	U.K.	
fast internet access	15	U.S.	
Books. Duh.	15	U.S.	High school
Quiet sometimes dont find what you need	15	U.S.	High school
Hundreds of thousands of books;magazinds;DVD or VHS;reference books; librarians.	15	U.S.	High school
Books. Happy. YES!!!	15	U.S.	
computers	15	U.S.	High school
I wish I had more time to read!	15	U.S.	
The first thing I think about when I think of a library... BOOKS! I love books, I love reading, it's so relaxing.	16	U.S.	High school
Computer how-to books	16	U.S.	High school
The stereotypical librarians and stiff atmosphere.	16	U.S.	High school
free movie rentals	16	U.S.	High school
books haha	16	U.S.	High school
i think its going to take longer cause i dont like reading through books and copying it out or wrting down the source because on the internat you can print it	16	U.S.	
research	16	U.S.	High school
Information	16	U.S.	High school
I think computers with the library catalog on it.	16	U.S.	High school
books and late fees	17	U.S.	High school
Due dates	17	U.S.	High school
When I think of the library, I think of an abundance of information on all topics. I would rather research from a library or print source than the Internet.	17	U.S.	College undergraduate
lots of reference books that I can use (like encyclopedias)	17	U.S.	High school
The librarian hushing everyone.	17	U.S.	High school
BORING!!!	17	U.S.	
the fines	17	U.S.	High school
books	17	U.S.	High school
Late fees, old stuff	17	U.S.	High school
That weird old book smell.	17	U.S.	High school
Books. What else?	18	U.S.	College undergraduate
A great place to relax, to read, to think, and to study.	18	U.S.	College undergraduate

Q807: What is the first thing you think of when you think of a library?	Age	Geographic Region	Student Status
Useful librarians	18	U.S.	College undergraduate
lots of books and the great smell of old books	18	U.S.	College undergraduate
outdated and lame	18	U.S.	College undergraduate
free books, and internet	19	U.S.	College undergraduate
old musty books	19	U.S.	College undergraduate
A big building filled with books, cds, and other types of ways of getting information.	19	U.S.	College undergraduate
I think of a large selection of books and magazines of all topics as well as having access to online journals and other online information sources	19	U.S.	College undergraduate
Silence and being bored.	20	U.S.	College undergraduate
quiet place to think/work	20	U.S.	
books internet	20	U.S.	
see what new movies are out	20	U.S.	College undergraduate
A place you can go to get information, stories, etc. and most libraries you can rent movies and use computers.	20	U.S.	
A wide selection of books, both used and new.	21	U.S.	College undergraduate
Using the computer and the internet.	21	U.S.	
overwhelmed	21	U.S.	
Yea! New books!	22	U.S.	
Free movies.	22	U.S.	
Peace and friendly envirnoment.	22	U.S.	
Free books!	22	U.S.	
Remembering how to use the decimal system, how to cite sources, and hoping that the material I require is present.	22	U.S.	College undergraduate
takes too long	22	U.S.	College undergraduate
Dirty old books that you can find from other sources	23	U.S.	
book smell	23	U.S.	College undergraduate
Everything I need if i have the time	23	U.S.	College undergraduate
books	23	U.S.	College undergraduate
old books, quiet, smelly, wait time to use computers, innefficiency in getting information	23	U.S.	
how i'm addicted to LEARNING	23	U.S.	College undergraduate
the orange card	23	U.S.	College undergraduate
Books	23	U.S.	College post graduate
doing research via books and/or microfilm	24	U.S.	
A wonderful resource filled to the brim with glorious books... such a wealth of knowledge!	24	U.S.	College undergraduate
Books, i love all the books. To pick up a book and hold it in my hand is still a really cool feeling.	27	U.S.	College undergraduate
I am able to have access to all kinds of materials that I can 'check out' and take home, obtain the information needed, return the materials and not have to pay for said materials.	33	U.S.	
Reference	35	U.S.	College post graduate

Q807: What is the first thing you think of when you think of a library?	Age	Geographic Region	Student Status
tons and tons of books	35	U.S.	
Being able to touch the information and sort through it.	35	U.S.	
Comfort	38	U.S.	
Happiness. Satisfaction of Curiosity.	41	U.S.	
That I can only check out five books maximum that must be returned within two weeks. Five books could be read very quickly and I don't have time to run to the library every two weeks.	43	U.S.	
no parking	43	U.S.	
A source of information	43	U.S.	
Boring.hahaha	43	U.S.	
Books, audio and video	43	U.S.	College post graduate
freedom	44	U.S.	College post graduate
Free access to everything	44	U.S.	
Hassle to go there to get the information when I can get it online at home.	45	U.S.	High school
reference desk	45	U.S.	
free internet	46	U.S.	High school
free internet	46	U.S.	
My love of reading.	46	U.S.	
internet, books, reference material, photocopy machine, magazines - in that order	51	U.S.	
driving there	51	U.S.	
favorite authors, craft or picture type how to books	52	U.S.	
Inconvenient.	52	U.S.	
a place where I can find free materials to learn more about many subjects and check out movies	53	U.S.	
Great place to spend time browsing through old books	54	U.S.	
Browsing	54	U.S.	
Relax, browse quickly, tons of info right away if needed	55	U.S.	
hours of reading pleasure	56	U.S.	
Book source. Distance to travel to get there. Sometimes frustrating search. Sometimes rewarding search. Time limits to read books and return. Overall libraries are good.	56	U.S.	
Wonderful!! Books on tape, books, movies, music, resource.	57	U.S.	
all the free info one would ever need	57	U.S.	
Out of date books	58	U.S.	
out of date	58	U.S.	
Meeting place	59	U.S.	
info source which is being replaced with the internet because on the net you can get access to current info. Even though libraries have net access I have been relieing on my home net connection.	60	U.S.	
book lovers and smart people, as I used to be, but physical pain these days in looking for what I need	60	U.S.	
Books, lots of lovely books to browse through. Back issues of magazines and journals.	61	U.S.	
Heaven.	62	U.S.	
Real books	64	U.S.	
Getting in the car.	65	U.S.	
checking out books to read	65	U.S.	
Native American resources	65	U.S.	
Parking problems	65	U.S.	
I have to go to town	66	U.S.	
I have to get in my car & drive there	66	U.S.	
school	66	U.S.	

Q807: What is the first thing you think of when you think of a library?	Age	Geographic Region	Student Status
trying to get there when they are open and hope they have book and not have to order it from larger library	67	U.S.	
Up to date information, help to find the information, quite place to research.	67	U.S.	
Lack of time to read books before due to be returned. When I want to read a book, I purchase it. I then swap with a friend or sister.	67	U.S.	
information of all kinds available.	67	U.S.	
reference books and reading for pleasure	67	U.S.	
Genealogical research	67	U.S.	
high taxes	68	U.S.	
last place I want to go for info	68	U.S.	
audio books, access thru internet	69	U.S.	
take out books for entertainment reading or for information	69	U.S.	
checking out books to read for pleasure	69	U.S.	
music cds.	70	U.S.	
It's a nice place to be.	72	U.S.	
audio books	72	U.S.	
Interesting Reading	72	U.S.	
Books. that are free to read	73	U.S.	
Checking their book list online.	74	U.S.	
Do I have the time necessary and is the trip/information worth it?	74	U.S.	
A quiet place to get some research done.	74	U.S.	
browsing	74	U.S.	
Difficulty in finding what you are looking for.	75	U.S.	
awonderful place to find almost any information or entertainment.	77	U.S.	
Free use of books and ref. materal GOD only knows we pay enough taxes to suppoet a public library	77	U.S.	
the latest information and newest books	78	U.S.	
knowledgable resource.	79	U.S.	
many books in a distant building	83	U.S.	

Q810: What do you feel is the main purpose of a library?

Note: All verbatim comments are presented as entered by survey respondents, including spelling, grammatical and punctuation errors.

Q810: What do you feel is the main purpose of a library?	Age	Geographic Region	Student Status
To supply people with reading materials whether for entertainment or for research.	17	Australia	High school
A place that holds published information. A place where people can go to search for and locate information of a particular subject.	18	Australia	College undergraduate
Research	18	Australia	College undergraduate
To be able to borrow free materials	18	Australia	College undergraduate
Eduacation	22	Australia	
a place to find any information you need	23	Australia	
Book loaning	25	Australia	
educate our youth and help with social literacy levels	25	Australia	
allow free access to reading and resource materials and access to computers	26	Australia	
allowing people to read interesting things, be it fiction or non-fiction	26	Australia	
education and to let all people have access to the written word	28	Australia	
good available information.	29	Australia	College undergraduate
To have the ability to relay information to the public in the form of hard or soft copies (books or electronic).	30	Australia	
to supply the community with unlimited resourse	30	Australia	
to provide written materials as a refence to students	32	Australia	
borrow children's book for my daughter	33	Australia	
Help with Reaserch	35	Australia	
Information	35	Australia	
information	36	Australia	
Information for those people that don't have money to buy books or can't afford to have the internet in thier homes.	36	Australia	
information/entertainment source	39	Australia	
a storehouse of printed information	39	Australia	
Community resource	40	Australia	
Reference material and good books for reading	40	Australia	
to provide a free community resource centre	40	Australia	
choice of what to read	41	Australia	
to be able to use the library, to get books out to read them, use the computers when needed.	41	Australia	
free access to information	42	Australia	
to provide resources to enable the public to 'learn'	42	Australia	
A libraries main purpose is to be a source of information on a range of topics that are of interest to the communityy at large.	43	Australia	
A place to borrow books, Cds and DVDs	43	Australia	
encouraging reading and a place of reference	43	Australia	
kids-mums	43	Australia	
To help educate people.	43	Australia	
information center	44	Australia	
It is many things to many people.It is to provide people with the means to either relax or to learn.	47	Australia	
quiet place to study	47	Australia	

Q810: What do you feel is the main purpose of a library?	Age	Geographic Region	Student Status
To be able to allow the community to access as much up to date information as possible and good quality leasure reading materials.	48	Australia	
learning	49	Australia	
RESEARCH	49	Australia	College post graduate
a central source for the genral public to be able to access many things, including the borrowing of books, reference material, computer access and daily/weekly newspapers/magazines. Also a great learning enviroment for children	50	Australia	
Availability fo books and other media formats on a larege range of subjects	50	Australia	
borrowing books to read or for source material	50	Australia	
stor reference material usually local in nature. View expensive books	50	Australia	
to allow people to experiance reading and possibly helping people to obtain the required book	50	Australia	
To provide resources free of cost	50	Australia	
research of information	51	Australia	
to learn and explore	52	Australia	
borrow books and source information	52	Australia	
easy access to print media	52	Australia	
lending of books/magazines/newspapers for recreational reading providing quality reference material and assistance with research	52	Australia	
For me personally it is the books, but I also see it as a central point in the community for meetings, education etc.	53	Australia	
Service to the public	53	Australia	
Availability of a as much knowledge, fiction and non-fiction, in a multi-media format, as possible, as cheaply as possible. Words for the people.	54	Australia	
borrow books need for a short term, service for children such as story time!	54	Australia	
being able to borrow something, without having to buy outright	55	Australia	
books	56	Australia	
make information and entertainment freely available	58	Australia	
souce information	58	Australia	
A source of information and recreation.	59	Australia	
able to borrow books and resource information	59	Australia	
helping folks who are not on the net	60	Australia	
obtaining information	61	Australia	
INFORMATION FOR YOUTH	62	Australia	
reference books & information gathering	62	Australia	
Allows you to borrow books and other items which you would not be able to afford to buy for yourself.	63	Australia	
Provide any and all guidance to books, titles, information, summaries on any and all topics.	63	Australia	
To provide everyone with a sourse for information both emjoymenet and work and especially for children to have access to many different print and electronic media	63	Australia	
To act as a storehouse of knowledge.	64	Australia	
A free service, providing good reference material, also reading books instead of purchasing them.	64	Australia	
Access to specialised information	64	Australia	
A social responsive Information source.	65	Australia	
Acess to Information for Everyone	65	Australia	
before internet it was mainly to get information on what you were looking for now days there is the internet and you nearly find everything on the net	66	Australia	

Q810: What do you feel is the main purpose of a library?	Age	Geographic Region	Student Status
Books. C.D's, tapes,discs borrowing & internet access	67	Australia	
Access to information or reference material	70	Australia	
Information.	72	Australia	
I use it mainly for fiction borrowing for entertainment purposes, but have also ovtained reference material and sometimes films -- eg Shakespeare productions	75	Australia	
Information and entertainment	17	Canada	High school
a place to go and read with your children, a family orientated invironment, somewhere to study gather information	20	Canada	
For reliable information to be easily accessed so we can expand our knowledge.	20	Canada	
To provide a hub for people to base their research out of, through the use of books, journals and the internet.	20	Canada	College undergraduate
educating / edutaining people	22	Canada	
knowledge	25	Canada	
Libraries store information - whether it's books, magazines, articles, films, CD ROMS, etc... Libraries are a resource for professionals and students, or anyone who wants to learn about something.	25	Canada	
I have up to date information and resources for all age groups. To provide research materials for schools and fun material as well for general entertainemnt	26	Canada	
Being a repository for books (archival material) so that the masses may have access to material that they otherwise would not.	27	Canada	
Borowing books without the need of purchasing them.	27	Canada	
to provide and give people access to informations.	28	Canada	
To provide every individual with the opportunity to have access to information even without the use of a computer.	28	Canada	
a library is still to me a place to get book, bring it home for a few days or weeks	29	Canada	
a place to hold all the books you need/would like to read or own, other than your own home -- that's a lot of books! :)	29	Canada	College undergraduate
learning	30	Canada	
A free source of educational material.	31	Canada	
learning	31	Canada	
a repository for printed material both CURRENT and historic for public reference.	32	Canada	
to provide people access to books and also i nformation(via computer, tapes, movies, etc.)that they may not otherwise have access to.	32	Canada	
borrowing books, making them available to all classes of people	35	Canada	
books	36	Canada	
To provide information.	37	Canada	
as a place to go to escape and visit faraway places	37	Canada	
To provide people reading material,videos, music,art etc all in one place and to help with projects, assignments and any investigating. It is an essential service to any town, or city	37	Canada	
books and lending	38	Canada	College post graduate
Reference information	38	Canada	
to be a filtered information resource	38	Canada	
To provide the public with free access to fiction and non-fiction literature.	38	Canada	
As stated, to retrieve information from a variety of sources, which allow you to decide for yourself which is sound information. Also a librarian is there to assist you when needed. Who I would assume would know what they are talking about.	39	Canada	
To provide people doing research with access to the recorded knowledge base in their field.	39	Canada	

Q810: What do you feel is the main purpose of a library?	Age	Geographic Region	Student Status
Archiving old information	40	Canada	
For resource information	40	Canada	
A library is a repository for books and information. It is a place where people of all ages and backgrounds and education levels can go and find whatever reading material they are interested in reading.	41	Canada	
broadening your horizons through reading	43	Canada	
knowledge	43	Canada	
A place to begin the search for information on any topic.	44	Canada	
BOOKS AND INFORMATION	44	Canada	
to be a place that you can get information	44	Canada	
assistance	45	Canada	
collect human knowledge	45	Canada	College undergraduate
easy affordable access to information	45	Canada	
Encouraging literacy in the whole population.	45	Canada	
For me it's the atmosphere and all it has to offer - books, resource info and music to check out	45	Canada	
My children spend most of their weekends at the library. They do their homework there, play on the computers or get homework help online and before they leave they usually bring home books that they would like to read.	45	Canada	
The main purpose of a library is to inform, entertain by loaning out and suppling material to do this.	45	Canada	
to provide resources to the public at little or no cost	45	Canada	
provide information and entertainment materials without having to buy them	46	Canada	
To provide reference materials to people who want to learn more about any given topic. To point people in the right direction, so that they can research what they need and to education themselves in the process.	46	Canada	
a conduit for information to the general public and a reliable, trustworthy source	47	Canada	College post graduate
community resource to lend books and related materials; provides reference materials; programs for public; technology like computers for use	47	Canada	
enjoy reading books and information when I need to find it	47	Canada	
research	47	Canada	
resource	47	Canada	
Data storage and retreival	49	Canada	
like university it is there to promote critical thinking and the pleasures of expanding one's mind/knowledge base	49	Canada	
A great community organization to provide to the people of a city/region, reading, audio, internet, historical data. (There is more with kids reading, homework sessions, I just don't know how to put it)	50	Canada	
educate	50	Canada	
stimulate the brain	50	Canada	
The library has no purpose in my life. I guess it is more of a historical archive of old paper documents. Who knows?	50	Canada	
to help one gain knowledge	50	Canada	
A source of information on past and present of actual events in life. A source of material in which we can escape reality and live the life we are reading about, instead of our own lives.	51	Canada	
Be your filter of accurate information sources	53	Canada	
being able to find and take home books of interest.	53	Canada	
Provide access to general public for books, reference material etc	53	Canada	
share books and information for free	53	Canada	

Q810: What do you feel is the main purpose of a library?	Age	Geographic Region	Student Status
to provide communities with knowledge and to assist the people who cannot afford to purchase	53	Canada	
disemination of information	54	Canada	
an accessable location for one of man's most treasured collection	55	Canada	
knowledge and information	55	Canada	
to get all of the correct information one needs knowledge	55	Canada	
A source for people to do research or take out novels to read for pleasure without having to spend a lot of money.	56	Canada	College undergraduate
help with school work and find information that you might need.	56	Canada	
To stimulate curiosity and creativity and to enhance knowledge and education by providing all kinds of information, especially books, to the public.	57	Canada	College post graduate
To give the general public free access to books for research or pleasure so they can enjoy them or complete their studies without a large outlay of cash to buy the books.	60	Canada	
Serving the community	61	Canada	
diseminate knowledge	62	Canada	
educate the populous, provide an atmosphere condusive to learning or recreational reading.	63	Canada	
An information base for the masses.	65	Canada	
I HAVE NOT A CLUE AS THEIR AGENDA, OR WHO DETERMINES WHATEVER IT MAY BE. MY FATHER-IN-LAW USES THE LIBRARY TO READ MAGAZINES RATHER THAN SUBSCRIBE TO THEM (FREE LOADING). IF I TRUELY WANT SOME INFORMATION, I USUALLY WANT A COPY OF IT WITHOUT ILLEGALLY PHOTO COPPYING IT, SO I BUY IT.	66	Canada	
to supply information . To make a variety of authors available to library members.	68	Canada	
to help and educate	72	Canada	
Information dispensing	75	Canada	
Give knowledge	22	India	
To be a repository of knowledge	25	India	
The main purpose of a library is to deliver information and knowledge to a great extent.	27	India	
education share	30	India	
It provides books on every subject which an individual can not manage.	35	India	
it stores the data, which is used for the next generation to feel the touch of my work.	39	India	
to provide educational information on virtually all and any subjects one can think of.	39	India	
books, reading material	44	India	
books freely available or at a minimal cost to those who need to read or refer, secondly a place where you can find rare books	48	India	
quick indexing of information and updated knowledge, yet affordable	51	India	
Access to books on any subject,especially tech and ref	55	India	
expansion of info	56	India	
As far as possible to give the information asked for if possible free.	66	India	
To provide means of disseminating information by compilation & dispersal.	71	India	
People to have a condusive environment for reading	20	Singapore	
To provide free information.	20	Singapore	
for borrowing of reference and leisure books	23	Singapore	
Books	24	Singapore	
for specific resources	24	Singapore	College undergraduate

Q810: What do you feel is the main purpose of a library?	Age	Geographic Region	Student Status
to be able to read books quietly.	26	Singapore	
Find info	27	Singapore	
knowledge	27	Singapore	
A library main purpose is to encourage reading.	28	Singapore	
a source of reference	28	Singapore	
store good library books.	28	Singapore	
a place where you can access information and knowledge	31	Singapore	
Complete information, and interesting reading books	31	Singapore	
For enriching knowledge	32	Singapore	
Information Treasure Vault	34	Singapore	
Central information resource, supposedly.	35	Singapore	College post graduate
enjoyment	35	Singapore	
FOR STUDENTS & FOR THOSE WHO DIDN'T KNOW HOW TO USE WEBS FOR INFO.	37	Singapore	
To be able to have any book that you might want to read, reference etc.	37	Singapore	
a resource place	40	Singapore	College post graduate
to help bring knowledge and wisdom to public.	40	Singapore	
encourage reading as a hobby	42	Singapore	
Provide a source of research for everyone.	46	Singapore	
community service	46	Singapore	
For people who are too tight-fisted to buy themselves books to borrow them at the taxpayer's (ie everyone else's) expense	17	U.K.	College undergraduate
Books	18	U.K.	College undergraduate
a place to borrow books from, a source of information	19	U.K.	
allow people to access information and to learn to enjoy reading	22	U.K.	College post graduate
books ...got the rest at home	22	U.K.	
To be able to read books for free.	22	U.K.	
choice	23	U.K.	
find information somewhere quiet to sit	23	U.K.	
learning	23	U.K.	College undergraduate
A place were you could go research topics with assistance available. Taking out books of interest.	24	U.K.	
reserch	25	U.K.	
information	25	U.K.	
books and business information	27	U.K.	
Giving free information and knowledge to everyone	28	U.K.	
INFORMATION	29	U.K.	
borrowing books, resources, computers	30	U.K.	
so you can try books without payin for them. good for helping people who can't read properly	30	U.K.	
access free to everyone and help when you need it	31	U.K.	
to provide eople with the loan of books who might not necessarily have funds to do so and to provide inofrmation to others to wider there knowlege	31	U.K.	
books	33	U.K.	
books	33	U.K.	
books accesable to all	33	U.K.	
i do not use it however it is a good place for research but think the internet is better for information & faster	33	U.K.	
books	33	U.K.	
A free resource for the community for research, learning, and culture.	34	U.K.	
Large print Catherine Cookson novels	34	U.K.	
last resort for info	34	U.K.	
to supply free information	35	U.K.	

Q810: What do you feel is the main purpose of a library?	Age	Geographic Region	Student Status
For children or old people	35	U.K.	
access a variety if written information, whether it be fact or fiction	35	U.K.	
reserch	36	U.K.	
to give information	36	U.K.	
borrowing	38	U.K.	
For Learning, enjoyment, interacting with people, obtaining latest releases, able to get other than books eg. DVD'S videos, Information, contact point.	40	U.K.	College undergraduate
easy access	41	U.K.	
for reference books, local knowledge, internet (not that i have ever used it) basically reading	41	U.K.	
Provide access to books both fiction and reference for those who do not have access to any other source also a good place for quiet reading and research	41	U.K.	
Accessibility to reading materials for all	42	U.K.	
to allow easy access to books for everyone	42	U.K.	
To supply books and sources of information.	42	U.K.	
to serve the community both by providing access to books for everyone and encouraging people to broaden their horizons through reading and/or electronicn sources and information provided	43	U.K.	
i dont like books	44	U.K.	
to provide free information	44	U.K.	
to provide info on commumity and world through all media to all people with minimal fuss+cost.	44	U.K.	
information and enjoyment	46	U.K.	
for leasure reading and as a source of information	46	U.K.	
information	46	U.K.	
Assist those who cannot purchase items still enjoys books etc	47	U.K.	
A PLACE TO GO FOR FREE INFO BUT MAINLY A FREE BOOKSTORE	49	U.K.	
to get information	49	U.K.	
Acces to books for those who cannot afford to buy	50	U.K.	
Culture	50	U.K.	
finding out all the information that is required	50	U.K.	
to provide worthwhile reading matter without having to pay at point of use	50	U.K.	
To aid people to have books they would not be able to afford to buy, therefore help education and pleasure.	51	U.K.	
A community place to access books which you probably couldn't afford to buy	52	U.K.	
help	52	U.K.	
Information gathering	54	U.K.	
to allow easy access to a wide variety of entertainment & information	54	U.K.	
USE OF BOOKS	54	U.K.	
Books available on all subjects to all	54	U.K.	
education for kids	55	U.K.	
To provide a comprehensive reading and research resource, free of charge.	55	U.K.	
knowledge	56	U.K.	
to give the public a way of gaining information	57	U.K.	
To have various levels of information available at a low cost.	57	U.K.	
information	57	U.K.	
books - and a quiet place to check out reference requirments - internet access for those without a PC	59	U.K.	
to give information	59	U.K.	
allowing the public free access to read books	60	U.K.	
To supply information	60	U.K.	

Q810: What do you feel is the main purpose of a library?	Age	Geographic Region	Student Status
To supply books to the public, who pay for this service through their taxes etc.	63	U.K.	
Books and computers	65	U.K.	
Access to books	65	U.K.	
An essential resource for community use - particularly an encouragement to read	66	U.K.	
TO STOCK A WIDE SELECTION OF READING MATTER INCLUDING FICTION, TECHNICAL, SCIENTIFIC,DIY, HOBBY,RELIGION [ALL] IF I WANTED VIDEO`S CD`S I WOULD GO ELSEWHERE.	68	U.K.	
personally, as a means of borrowing books which I would otherwise have to buy. However the real purpose I suppose is as a source of information	69	U.K.	
encourage the spread of knowlege	70	U.K.	
Information, Advice, To supply reading material of a wide variety, Education etc	71	U.K.	
Provide information and entertainment	71	U.K.	
information	80	U.K.	
a ploace to study and research and check out books	14	U.S.	High school
A library is a place to find information or entertainment in the form of books.	15	U.S.	High school
A resource for people to learn and expand their knowledge by reading or using the internet.	15	U.S.	High school
and inexpensive way to learn	15	U.S.	High school
checking out books	15	U.S.	High school
Knowledge	15	U.S.	High school
last resort	15	U.S.	High school
a place to gain informaton, both in print and digital	16	U.S.	High school
a place to go to read and do reseach	16	U.S.	High school
allow people to barrow books	16	U.S.	High school
find hard material instead of virtual	16	U.S.	High school
keep books on paper	16	U.S.	High school
rent books	16	U.S.	High school
to allow people the opportunity to read books, listen to music, research topics, and watch cinema for free and without having to buy the items, but instead share them with the community.	16	U.S.	High school
to give the public free easy access to a lot of information-specifically, literature	16	U.S.	High school
To provide the public with an opportunity. It gives the people a chance to draw away from reality just for a moment, and it helps them to enjoy life.	16	U.S.	High school
a central place for students to locate and work together on a research project.	17	U.S.	High school
A chance for people to discovery a different world inside each book	17	U.S.	High school
A cool place to retrieve information	17	U.S.	
a plce to get information.	17	U.S.	
access to books that I'd like to read but don't have the money to buy or that I'm only going to read once.	17	U.S.	High school
Accessibility to up-to-date information and a quiet means of research and reading leisure	17	U.S.	High school
being able for the public to acess multiple types of information.	17	U.S.	
Books and information for free.	17	U.S.	High school
Education of the masses	17	U.S.	College undergraduate
enjoyment	17	U.S.	High school
give people entertainment that wont rot the brain	17	U.S.	High school
Information.	17	U.S.	High school

Q810: What do you feel is the main purpose of a library?	Age	Geographic Region	Student Status
It provides a great service to the community, whether it's information for a paper, for a do-it-yourself project, just something for leisure reading, or even just a place to study.	17	U.S.	
knowledge	17	U.S.	
Large information center for those who can't find it in other locations or do not have access to it.	17	U.S.	High school
spreading intelligence	17	U.S.	High school
The main purpose is to provide all people with the opportunity to widen their mind's horizons and creativity.	17	U.S.	High school
to provide a community with the privilege of access to literature, information, and other commodities such as music, videos, and/or internet access for reference.	17	U.S.	High school
to provide people with a free access to books and sources of information	17	U.S.	High school
to provide resources not available regularly to the community	17	U.S.	High school
To provide the general public free access to literature and educational/reference materials. It is a basic function of any government to educate/socialize their citizens, and public libraries accomplish this in the U.S..	17	U.S.	College undergraduate
A library is vital in order to get information. I trust and love libraries. The web cannot take over because the library is sacred.	18	U.S.	College undergraduate
As a student, it's a place to find reliable, scholarly sources for research. Personally, it's there for when I'm too broke to buy a book I want to read.	18	U.S.	College undergraduate
enrich our education	18	U.S.	High school
To provide the general public with as much knowledge as possible.	18	U.S.	College undergraduate
assist you in finding information and finding the right books you are searching for.	19	U.S.	
For parents to bring there little kids to get books and for the parents to teach the kids how to read instead of a computer doing it.	19	U.S.	College undergraduate
to provide resources to students (and non-students) and aide in finding the correct resources	19	U.S.	College undergraduate
a deposit of information	20	U.S.	College undergraduate
A place to do research and studying	20	U.S.	College undergraduate
A place to gather information, for free.	20	U.S.	College undergraduate
To provide information to those who want it. To accurately and expertly, within their means, provide the books the public is looking for and to provide a good network with Internet access for those who want to use it and with an accurate catalog to look up books within the library system.	20	U.S.	College undergraduate
To provide useful information for research and knowledge.	21	U.S.	College undergraduate
accumulation of research resources	21	U.S.	College post graduate
archives, books, research help	21	U.S.	College undergraduate
Research purposes	21	U.S.	College undergraduate
To allow its members access to books, videos, music, the internet, different activities, and a safe place to be. Perhaps education. Also depends what type of library. City library is mostly for the first bunch of reasons, University library would be mostly for research/educational purposes.	21	U.S.	College undergraduate
To allow people like myself to go in a building and read free books. Or find out free information. A libray is one of the few places that you can go to for free these days.	21	U.S.	

Q810: What do you feel is the main purpose of a library?	Age	Geographic Region	Student Status
To be able to research and reading for pleasure	21	U.S.	College undergraduate
To provide resources (books, films, periodicals, computer/internet access) for the public, for research, educational, and recreational purposes.	21	U.S.	College undergraduate
Able to borrow books without paying	22	U.S.	College undergraduate
Enlightenment	22	U.S.	
enteratinment	22	U.S.	
for people who cannot afford things like computers and books to have free access to information. That is something that is necessary in a free and open society.	22	U.S.	
A source of information in different forms of media for people.	23	U.S.	
An institution that disseminates knowledge.	23	U.S.	College undergraduate
different sources of information located under one roof	23	U.S.	College undergraduate
For people to intrigue the interest of there minds in a positive matter.And to learn.	23	U.S.	
To gather as much literature and information as possible in one place, and to share that wealth of resources with that community. It is important to have a place where anyone can go to learn (be it news, research, films and music, fiction, or non-fiction--there is value in it all).	23	U.S.	
books, research information	24	U.S.	
Find knowledge that is best presented in books or paper format. Such as design schematics or knowledge collected before the 1990s (i.e. old books)	24	U.S.	
information	24	U.S.	
It provides free access to books, computers, and reference materials to everyone in every community.	24	U.S.	College undergraduate
Literature and research material of all types is made available for public benefit.	24	U.S.	
rent books	24	U.S.	
Dissemination of information in the interests of strengthening civil society, from children's reading hour to access to news about political candidates, historical documents, hoity-toity literature...every last bit of it.	27	U.S.	College post graduate
access to literature	28	U.S.	
exposing readers to information that they may not be able to find anywhere else	29	U.S.	
To provide citizens access to a wide range of information through books, magazines, journals, and periodicals.	30	U.S.	College undergraduate
Share all the information with everyone for free.	32	U.S.	College undergraduate
To be able to borrow books that I would like to read without having to go to a book sotre and buy them. Also, it is a quiet, calming place to relax and read.	33	U.S.	
borrowing books; doing research	35	U.S.	
reference material for people who need to research as well as a place to borrow books for reading enjoyment	36	U.S.	
lending reading material free of charge	38	U.S.	
FREE access to information and insiration FOR ALL. As in for EVERYONE in a society.	41	U.S.	
Storage and dissemination of information. Smae as the Internet.	41	U.S.	
A center that one can go to obtain information. But as more people own computers, librarys will have to adapt or face becoming a museum	43	U.S.	
A great reference resource	43	U.S.	College post graduate

Q810: What do you feel is the main purpose of a library?	Age	Geographic Region	Student Status
To be a part of it's community and be a place that has not only reading for pleasure material, but also a good place to do research. I think the material in library is more trustworthy then that on the internet. A library is a place for people of all income levels to have a chance to read the lastest novel/books etc.	43	U.S.	
knowledge	45	U.S.	
a store house of information and access to information {internet}.	46	U.S.	High school
to help educate the community	46	U.S.	
free exchange of info; also a resource for school children with less money	47	U.S.	
information for all	47	U.S.	
learning	47	U.S.	
help customers find the information they are seeking and second, for children and anyone really, help foster love of reading and learning	49	U.S.	
Mind-material, either for entertainment or education	49	U.S.	
First, as a source of reading material; second, as a source of information.	54	U.S.	
for research and free reading material	57	U.S.	
To be an 'information station'.	57	U.S.	
A public library is a resource for families to read and do research. Libraries also provide activities for children. Libraries are a quiet place to read and relax or to do research and get help. Oh also, a place to look for potential school scholarships	58	U.S.	
An easy access to books.	58	U.S.	
having the right books for the right job	60	U.S.	
Informed information for the public that does and does not have a computer. Expanding one's mind with unlimited resources, hard copy, video, audio and reference info as well as computer access.	62	U.S.	
A knowledge center for a community or activity which provides books, periodicals and electronic media for use by citizens, members, employees or students.	63	U.S.	
Hang out for losers.	63	U.S.	
feeding the mind.	64	U.S.	
Provide books	64	U.S.	
Access to knowledge and information.	65	U.S.	
Afford the population access to reading material that they may not be willing to purchase.	65	U.S.	
Give many people the opportunity to use computers, read good books and magazines without having to buy them, special programs.	65	U.S.	
research	65	U.S.	
Access to needed information and book rentals.	66	U.S.	
books & research for the masses	66	U.S.	
knowledge	66	U.S.	
Research	66	U.S.	
make books easily available	67	U.S.	
Reference and study for school work. My kids used it often when in school.	67	U.S.	
To supply books worth borrowing and a source of information	67	U.S.	
Reference and research for people that are seeking knowledge about a subject.	68	U.S.	
getting books, studying material for school or college, useing a computer if you don't own one	69	U.S.	
books for the general public to have access to for free	69	U.S.	
To be there to supply the community with information that they need, or for entertaining books, cd's, video's	69	U.S.	

Q810: What do you feel is the main purpose of a library?	Age	Geographic Region	Student Status
To store History & provide reading material, and refernce materials to the public.	70	U.S.	
A GOOD SOURCE FOR INFO, COMPUTER USE, AND PEOPLE'S PLEASURE OF READING WANTED MATERIAL	70	U.S.	
a repository of info., a place from which to borrow books for pleasure/info., etc.	70	U.S.	
To provide wide ranges of materials (video, CDs, film, microfisch, computers)and reference materials in addition to fiction, non-fiction books and periodicals. To provide assistance in searches, to have wide connections to borrow materials not available locally	70	U.S.	
Providing materials from which a person can search and learn subjects.	71	U.S.	
a gathering of information of all media open to the public free of charge thanks to Andrew Carnegie and that should tell you that I'm old	72	U.S.	
A resource for information and data, as well as recreation.	72	U.S.	
book rental	72	U.S.	
The lending of books to the neighborhood residents. A place for shool children to do research in a quiet atmosphere where help is available if needed.	72	U.S.	
to provide info to peopole	72	U.S.	
to provide information and literature for the public.	74	U.S.	
A central source for accessing printed materials - present and past.	74	U.S.	
A cultural link for the community and a central source of information for those without other available sources.	74	U.S.	
Additional education	75	U.S.	
The U.S. public library, within in the limits of its budget, protects our republic by providing citizens with a means for obtaining information representing a wide range of views and information...as I learned as an undergraduate 'learn to use the library and you are forever saved from the tyranny of ignorance and the bias of your professors'	75	U.S.	
To be a resource for knowledge and to provide information/ reading material. These days most useful to people who do not have a computer handy to give them instant information.	75	U.S.	
To provide wonderful material to read. They have been very helpful in locating my husband's preferred book, Westerns and he has a hard time finding one he hasn't read. But they come up with one almost every time so help is the second purpose of a library.	75	U.S.	
research	76	U.S.	
for avid readers. for people who do not have computers at home	77	U.S.	
To obtain free information when needed	77	U.S.	
A wonderful concept - in action! Truly the foundation of a great society could be measured in the quality, quantity and accessibility of its libraries. If it has a single 'main purpose' it would be to educate, I think. I don't know of a library which doesn't strive to do that.	78	U.S.	
main purpose is to loan books, tapes, etc.	78	U.S.	
A ready and large source for information gathering.	81	U.S.	
Literature	83	U.S.	
Continuing education	86	U.S.	

Q812a: Positive associations with the library

Note: All verbatim comments are presented as entered by survey respondents, including spelling, grammatical and punctuation errors.

Q812a: Positive associations with library.	Age	Geographic Region	Student Status
* Books which can be borrowed for free. * Usually people available to help you with whatever you need.	17	Australia	High school
Being at University allows you membership of a large and well respected library on campus. There are librarians and other staff who can help you if you need advice, whereas searching online you cant ask anyone for help.	18	Australia	College undergraduate
Provides many services and products for free or cheaper than they would for the individual. Provides a wide variety of resources for people who would otherwise not have access to them.	20	Australia	College post graduate
YOU HAVE SOMEBODY THERE TO HELP YOU TO FIND EXACTLY WHAT YOU ARE LOOKING FOR IF YOU DONT KNOW WHAT YOU ARE DOING.	22	Australia	
freedom to learn if you choose	24	Australia	
endless references assistance in finding accurate informaiton	25	Australia	
generally have a wide range of materials to look at staff are usually helpful and trained to attend to your requests	25	Australia	College post graduate
Heaps of lovely, lovely books to browse, choose from & Read... for free! A full spectrum of choice: a range of topics, genres, etc	26	Australia	College undergraduate
A variety of books and now have internet access.	29	Australia	
1. helpful staff 2. free services	30	Australia	
its an outting for the kids and I. Wide range of facilities	30	Australia	
that it is social place with real people that you can get access to very specific material no found elsewhere at no cost, eg books.	32	Australia	
Easy acces to books that may be too expensive or out of print. Easy acces to the internet.	33	Australia	
Single Location for Information Staff to assist in the location of information.	34	Australia	
It is a wealth of knowledge and relaxation	35	Australia	
resources in abundance great for children	37	Australia	
books transferred closer to home libraray librarian wonderfully helpfull	38	Australia	
The Amount of resources availble. Friendly Atmosphere.	38	Australia	
LOTS OF BOOKS LOTS OF INFORMATION	39	Australia	
1) Cheap loans of books 2) Fantastic range of publications to choose from	40	Australia	
Great service - on line reservations Flexible public service e.g., table at train station to collect reserved book on the way to work	40	Australia	
lots of choice helpful people	40	Australia	
GOING ON THE INTERNET,READING BOOKS	41	Australia	
volume of information help if required	42	Australia	
Lots of different materials/books to use. Advice given if required.	44	Australia	
Membership is free. Great reference source.	45	Australia	
Quiet, contemplative time So many books and so little time!	47	Australia	
When studying my uni library was great. Not only for relevant books but also journals and articles.	48	Australia	
FRIENDLY LIBRARIANS. GOOD READING.	49	Australia	
always happy to go to the library, never know who you will run into	51	Australia	
Sole source of much information accessible to the public. Information is available to all, regardless of age, gender, race, belief etc.	51	Australia	

Q812a: Positive associations with library.	Age	Geographic Region	Student Status
my library has online access for searches and ordering Quiet space for reading newspapers	52	Australia	
1. good source of books I wouldn't otherwise find 2. good source of knowledgeable people who can guide my search for information	52	Australia	
Can find what I want easliy using computer files Pleasant surroundings to browse book shelves	53	Australia	
Able to borrow books free Cater for children	54	Australia	
Can get almost any book you want can order books and they will get trhem for you	55	Australia	
its free Covers the whole range of paper amnd electronic information sources and general reading	56	Australia	
Dewey Numbers to locate books Range of titles	59	Australia	
when looking for material to relax with in a library - it is easier to come across something suitable accidentaly. A book that doesnt fit in with my normal criteria, for instance , and this expands my awarness. It is also a centre to get out of the house to that doesnt cost the earth to enjoy.	59	Australia	
availability of borrowing books and all other sources they provide and information provided by reference books/ actual handling of books and actually 'seeing' the books etc	61	Australia	
THE LIBRARIANS ARE EXPERTS. ALL THE INFORMATION IS THERE SOMEWHERE.	62	Australia	
I can usually find what I need A very diverse cross section	68	Australia	
The possible ability to aquire information that may not be available from other souces. the option of alternative medium types, ie cd, dvd, video, etc	71	Australia	
My library has a very friendly , co-operative staff I can access other specialist libraries through it	75	Australia	
lots of info and theres always someone to help if you need it	14	Canada	High school
1)Lots of books 2)good info	16	Canada	High school
Lots of material Helpful/knowledgeable staff	16	Canada	High school
Any book you want Easy to use	17	Canada	High school
technologically advanced very informative	19	Canada	College undergraduate
friendly envronment lots of sources	20	Canada	College undergraduate
Novels Movies you can take out	21	Canada	College undergraduate
getting to borrow books, that you probably wouldn't otherwise have access too. And checking them out for free.	24	Canada	
Helpful librarians Many different information sources	26	Canada	
Generally Free (Inter)National cooperation	27	Canada	
sharing books, CDs and DVDs Doesn't typically cost anything	28	Canada	
free access to books, computer, other information - a centre to meet people for meetings and events	29	Canada	
An incredible source of references (information) Access to computer and librarians	32	Canada	
Conducive environment to quiet study... Archival records dating back to any given publication's inception...	32	Canada	
many resources, free to join	32	Canada	
Variety of media Discovering something new	35	Canada	
1-Calm - a good place to focus. 2-Helpful staff	36	Canada	
Free No charge Quiet \/Regulated enviroment	36	Canada	
Usually more than one copy of book/magazine in question. Knowledgable staff	36	Canada	
children love being there to pick out their own material availability of almost any reading source or material	37	Canada	
1. Great place to instill a love of reading in children. 2. Great variety of books.	38	Canada	
Book Exchange Information Resource	38	Canada	

Q812a: Positive associations with library.	Age	Geographic Region	Student Status
1. Helpful librarians 2. Finding books I wouldn't have heard of otherwise	39	Canada	
1. Quiet and easier for concentration 2. Wealth of information	39	Canada	
Libraries are embracing computer technology and now offer library users the best of both worlds when they visit. They can borrow conventional books, magazines and newspapers and they can also log on to the computer system and find lots of information there. Teachers and school administrators still advocate the use of libraries and encourage their students to visit, so I think libraries will be here for a while yet.	41	Canada	
Spending hours in the library as a child, taking home stacks of books. Looking forward to reading the latest book by a favourite author - even if I have to wait a while for my turn!	42	Canada	
Nice, helpful and KNOWLEDGABLE staff Quiet atmosphere LOTS of information	44	Canada	
Able to borrow new released reading materials Access to books and refrence materials not available at home	45	Canada	
-lots of books ... I love books -free internet access	45	Canada	
You have alot of info options. You can get the help of a expert.	45	Canada	
Staff is always friendly the staff will search for the book I want and have it in a couple of days	46	Canada	
Books Periodicals	47	Canada	
Not too far from home Comfortable area to take the children too for a few hours = get familiar with the joy of reading	47	Canada	
the two positive things are availability,and resources of there computers when you need information and sources needed,	47	Canada	
Being able to borrow books I couldn't afford to buy Finding a quiet place to study ,either for school or for my own pleasure	48	Canada	
Free resources and books Free databases and Internet	48	Canada	College undergraduate
knowledge, information	48	Canada	
Easy access Being able to read the information in the comfort of your easy chair	49	Canada	
1. It is great to have a library within the city. A good meeting place. A good resource place.	50	Canada	
too many to list smell of books no charge many diferent types of resources professional help	50	Canada	
I have learned so much in libraries, I've spent the better part of my life doing research. 'The more I learn, the more I learn!'	52	Canada	
Librarians are expert researchers	53	Canada	
If I can't find a book in an institutional setting I will use a public library. If I can't find the information I need on the Internet I will go to the library to find it, or ask them where I can get a copy.	54	Canada	
Information is the main purpose Study in a quite envirement	54	Canada	
wide access to lots of materials, especially things you would never have thought of looking for. comfortable place to sit undisturbed and assess information	57	Canada	
Get good books to read Get help with research when I need them	61	Canada	
staff were very helpful and the amount of research material available was more than adequate	62	Canada	
The librarian is there to help find what I want. I can flip through the book to see if it has the information I want.	63	Canada	
Excellent service	71	Canada	
save buying expensive learning books some there to help you to find the articale you are looking for	72	Canada	
May have older information not available via internet. Perhaps a wider range of topics available for any given topic.	75	Canada	
sense of ownership and encouragement to use effective organization of materials to assist search	79	Canada	

Q812a: Positive associations with library.	Age	Geographic Region	Student Status
Increase Knowledge Good Databank	31	India	
1.Any one can get infromation about all subject in library generally. 2. Its the cheapist means to get knowledge.	35	India	
Access to books Choice of browsing without purchasing	43	India	
1. Vast database for knowledge. 2. All information available	51	India	
to come to know some new topic/thing that I was not aware of. the simple joy of reading books	54	India	
You get wide choice for reference and books are easy to locate, lots of information can be retrieved.	54	India	
Most of the are available or procured on demand	55	India	
the books a peaceful place to read and relax	61	India	
learn always & almost all references needed.	71	India	
Lots of information. Free.	20	Singapore	
More reliable More types of sources, e.g info can be found in books, magazines, cds and dvds	20	Singapore	
books cafe	25	Singapore	
1. variety of books. 2. air-conditioned.	26	Singapore	
one stop learning place resourceful	27	Singapore	
1. It's free! 2. Lots of information you can learn, even those that you may not at first realise that you'll like to know.	29	Singapore	
most of the information and reseach available are trustworthy	29	Singapore	
You get to know lots of things without buying any books.	29	Singapore	College post graduate
1)Resource rich (in terms of the variety of books, audio and information services) 2)Advance technology	31	Singapore	
free. easy to find the books by category.	35	Singapore	
1. Online checking for availability of books 2. Reserve the book for borrowing	37	Singapore	
(1) plenty information can be found (2) free access to the library	44	Singapore	
A form of entertainment. An acknowledgable place.	44	Singapore	
Reliable and accurate.	48	Singapore	
Wide variety of books to choose /borrow FOC. Children / adults can find most information without having to buy lots of books & keep unnecessarily at home as they outgrow the books & become irrelevant.	48	Singapore	
wide variety of books able to browse the books freely	51	Singapore	
1 good reading enviroment 2 all that is required to know is at hand	54	Singapore	
source of learning they have become more child friendly	33	U.K.	
PERSONAL TOUCH, HELPFUL STAFF	38	U.K.	
most services are free and easy to access.helpful staff.	44	U.K.	
lots of book choice quiet place to gather info from printed word	57	U.K.	
So many books... free borrowing	17	U.K.	
1) you can find any reading material you want 2) its more personal	29	U.K.	
Loads of books. Have really good memories of libraries back in Australia when I was a kid.	34	U.K.	
Free at point of use Information Service Provider	37	U.K.	
Varity of information sources Sources available free	42	U.K.	
Enjoy looking through reference materials in the library. Enjoy taking out books to read either for pleasure or research.	54	U.K.	
Free to join. Lot of choice.	55	U.K.	
choice of literature free access to computers	60	U.K.	
Friendly & helpful staff.	66	U.K.	
It is Free. Good for information.	69	U.K.	
Wide range of books Out-of-print books	17	U.K.	College undergraduate
Get to read before you rent Lots of information available	18	U.K.	College undergraduate

Q812a: Positive associations with library.	Age	Geographic Region	Student Status
free access to books, access to computers	21	U.K.	
Loan books for free Quiet environment to work/relax	23	U.K.	
Quiet place to go Lots of reading material	23	U.K.	
inexpensive assistance available	24	U.K.	
it supplies all information you want, it save your time.	28	U.K.	College post graduate
Many obscure titles kept Knowledge of staff	31	U.K.	
good quiet learning enviroment. a dry warm place on a cold day.	34	U.K.	
Local information for the community,lists of courses going on in the area.	34	U.K.	
knowledge freedom	35	U.K.	
Friendly staff, Wide Range of Materials	40	U.K.	College undergraduate
Newly published books Helpful librarians	42	U.K.	
access to books mgs and newpapers that i wouldn't normally buy or could afford. reference filing for ease of access to material	44	U.K.	
BOOKS!!! INFORMATION!	50	U.K.	
huge selection well looked after	50	U.K.	
Wide range of materials and information. Time spent just browsing!	52	U.K.	
PLENTY OF CHOICE BOOKS FOR CHILDREN	53	U.K.	
Vast array of leisure and information available as well as electronic, various media resources.	56	U.K.	
it is free to join and to borrow	60	U.K.	
Have used the local library pc which was broadband supported. Useful for current local information.	62	U.K.	
PEACEFUL PLACE TO FIND INFO COVERS MOST TOPICS	17	U.K.	
a wide range of information, people are avaliable to speak to if you needed help locating material.	20	U.K.	
lots of information available range of materials (books, persiodicals etc)	22	U.K.	College post graduate
It's free. You get help to find a book if needed.	22	U.K.	
Free, wide range of books Often has free internet, which is useful if you are visiting a town, and need to check e-mail etc.	24	U.K.	
biggest collection anywhere in the world nice place to study	25	U.K.	
Can access info in tangible form - ie can pick it up and look at it. can go there for peace and quiet if you need to study without distractions	26	U.K.	
central information reference variety and quantity of information	28	U.K.	
INFORMATION FREE	29	U.K.	
information computers	30	U.K.	
1.good source of information 2.good source of entertainment	31	U.K.	
Books are free There is someone there to help if you can't find something	32	U.K.	
Good for childrens introduction to reading and books	32	U.K.	
Great way to get kids interested in books, learning and using their imagination. Cheap source of information - particularly expensive reference & specialist books you couldn't afford yourself.	34	U.K.	
it's free you can look at or borrow a large number of books of your choice at one time	35	U.K.	
accessing reference books that would otherwise cost a lot of money to buy borrowing language courses which are also very expensive to buy	38	U.K.	
Variety of material Range of material	41	U.K.	
Access to large collections of reading material. Ability to order material if not available at time.	42	U.K.	
Huge variety of books to read Pleasant and helpful staff	43	U.K.	

Q812a: Positive associations with library.	Age	Geographic Region	Student Status
help , relaxation	46	U.K.	
Time out for myself dicovering a book I really want to read	46	U.K.	
large selection of reading material good place for local information	48	U.K.	
Able to browse books one would maybe not be drawn to in a bookshop. Diverse choice of subject fiction and non-fiction	50	U.K.	
Cheerful surroundings Friendly staff	50	U.K.	
Friendly Staff Meeting like minded readers	51	U.K.	College undergraduate
More books than a bookshop for reference It's free	52	U.K.	
Wide selection of up to date books, fiction and non-fiction. saves the cost of having to buy a book especially if the information is one small paragraph in a very expensive book.	53	U.K.	
Lots of information to hand and accessible from other organisations Lots of different types of media	55	U.K.	
it almost always has the information i need in some form or other the librarians will telephone other libraries if they dont have the book or information that you require	57	U.K.	
Nearness to residence Wide range of choice	58	U.K.	
excellent facilities. Good atmosphere.	59	U.K.	
Support from experts Access to a range of sources	60	U.K.	
interaction with people free information	61	U.K.	
Ease of access Books sorted by category	66	U.K.	
Good book service good IT access	71	U.K.	
Love browsing and always have library books at home. Have found medical information invaluable	71	U.K.	
easy access free services (important to a pensioner)	72	U.K.	
books . classics, in depth research .facility , the way to obtain hard to get information.	73	U.K.	
free books as many as you want quite studying place	14	U.S.	High school
Gives books.... has magazines...	14	U.S.	High school
gives information easily accessible	14	U.S.	High school
lots of information helpful staff	14	U.S.	High school
1.Books 2.Information	15	U.S.	High school
accurat information internet	15	U.S.	High school
Being able to read for free. Having a large source of information in one place.	15	U.S.	High school
easy access internet access	15	U.S.	High school
Free & offers a ton of research assistance	15	U.S.	
free research working computers	15	U.S.	High school
Free transfer of Knowlege Peace and quiet	15	U.S.	High school
Good books helpful librarians	15	U.S.	High school
Good Books. Internet Access.	15	U.S.	High school
Has new and classic books Better resources than internet	15	U.S.	High school
If you have questions, you can ask a librarian. Loads of information on thousands of topics all in one building.	15	U.S.	High school
Many resources (computers, books, audio tapes, video tapes, librarians) Classes (in school and out)	15	U.S.	High school
You can take out free books. You can find book titles, authors, and when books come out from the library catalog, and find good books to read.	15	U.S.	High school
1. Quiet 2. Lots of information stored in the building.	16	U.S.	High school
books are free; you can do research quietly	16	U.S.	High school
endless amounts of books, and friendly service	16	U.S.	High school
'Free' Accesible to public, and encourages reading	16	U.S.	High school
great books; snack machines	16	U.S.	High school
-Many community activities -Provides many people with things they wouldn't yhave otherwise	16	U.S.	High school
More trustworthy information Quiet place to study	16	U.S.	High school
Smart Peaceful	16	U.S.	

Q812a: Positive associations with library.	Age	Geographic Region	Student Status
There are many sources of information available through the library, and the people there are always very friendly. It is also a very community oriented thing.	16	U.S.	High school
The library is 100% free. The librians are very well informed on where things are, and what information is what.	16	U.S.	
1. It has many resources to access information when it is needed. 2. It is quiet.	17	U.S.	High school
1. The is a large amount a information avalible. 2. The librarians are there to help with any problems a person may have.	17	U.S.	High school
Accurate information and reliability (knowing that the is=nformation will still be there, accessable to you, later on)	17	U.S.	High school
Books are wonderful. Libraries provide great access to information and new worlds.	17	U.S.	High school
Finding good videos/DVD's to watch each week from my public library; and finding good books to read or books related to a subject of interest or complementary books to ones I'm studying in school.	17	U.S.	College undergraduate
I only read books once usually so I like that I can check out books for free so that I don't have to pay for them yet only use them once. They are also a good place to access reference materials.	17	U.S.	High school
Knowledge, artistic expression	17	U.S.	College undergraduate
Knowledgeable staff, up-to-date database connecting to other libraries, accessible information from sources, organized classification system	17	U.S.	High school
lots of books well organized (i.e. card catalogue)	17	U.S.	High school
Lots of Information Free (for the most part)	17	U.S.	College undergraduate
Lots of information, quiet study place	17	U.S.	College undergraduate
many books, people to talk to if you have any quesitons	17	U.S.	High school
Quiet. Loads of knowlegdge.	17	U.S.	High school
Reading. Learning.	17	U.S.	High school
Safe Place. Free Books.	17	U.S.	High school
social comfy chairs	17	U.S.	High school
The easiest and cheapest way to get books to read and to get information for research	17	U.S.	High school
You can read books without having to pay for them. They have computers and encyclopedias and books for research.	17	U.S.	High school
lots of information assistance is always available	18	U.S.	College undergraduate
Safe and reliable information Multitudes of information	18	U.S.	College undergraduate
1. Parents can interact with their kids. 2. Kids have fun with the toys provide in the kids section.	19	U.S.	College undergraduate
accurate information variety of information	19	U.S.	College undergraduate
books! books!	19	U.S.	College undergraduate
Helpful librarians, and it has everything and if it doesn't they can get it for you.	19	U.S.	College undergraduate
nice librarians, helpful good work environment	19	U.S.	College undergraduate
Possibility to find interesting books/magazines. Fast computers for help.	19	U.S.	College undergraduate
at your own pace reading self-paced learning	20	U.S.	College undergraduate
'free' literature, as long as its not returned late Quiet are to relax to do your work	20	U.S.	College undergraduate

Q812a: Positive associations with library.	Age	Geographic Region	Student Status
Good reading, studying atmosphere; depending on the library and the collection itself, an excellent source for older and rock-hard sources for research papers.	20	U.S.	College undergraduate
source of lots of information more than just getting books - also good for pc use and making copies	20	U.S.	College undergraduate
1. Free library cards to check out books 2. Free use of computers and internet access for people that don't have it (or can't afford it)	21	U.S.	
Free Books Typically resources are simple to find	21	U.S.	College post graduate
Helpful Librarians and Many great books	21	U.S.	College undergraduate
plenty of material at your fingertips if the subject you are looking for does not need to be current, then it is a lot faster to use the library to get exactly what you want	21	U.S.	College undergraduate
There is an abundance of computers. There are very helpful rescources in the library.	21	U.S.	College undergraduate
Vast expanse of sources. Ease of location on a university campus.	21	U.S.	College undergraduate
free (if it's not late) get to physically look at the book before deciding to check it out	22	U.S.	College post graduate
helpful people gobs of information, ideas	22	U.S.	
Librarians, as trained professionals, can help you locate materials anywhere in their system. Theoretically, things are where they are listed to be, and as long as you can learn to use the system for locating them, it is relatively simple.	22	U.S.	College undergraduate
quiet, full of novels	22	U.S.	College post graduate
They give people access to books that they could not afford to go to the store and buy. They allow people who can not afford a computer to use the one at the library.	22	U.S.	College undergraduate
1. I can find information 2. Librarians are helpful	23	U.S.	
Extensive variety of genres and types of literature. Knowledgeable librarians.	23	U.S.	
Free books Great Place to meet chicks	23	U.S.	High school
Lots of books to read free of charge Feeling educated	23	U.S.	
The smell The amount of information available	23	U.S.	
1. Free 2. Wide variety of information available	24	U.S.	College undergraduate
University related libraries are convienient	24	U.S.	
wonderful information, helpful librarians	24	U.S.	
Free information Librarians there to help	28	U.S.	
very helpfull staff use of public books at no cost	28	U.S.	
1. There are knowledgable people available to answer questions and guide your search. 2. Some information can only be accessed for free at the library	30	U.S.	College undergraduate
provides books without having to buy them centralizes a lot of information	30	U.S.	
Someone to help with finding information Lots of very old stuff you wont find on the net	30	U.S.	
1. It is free 2. It gives me access to a tremendous amount of information.	33	U.S.	
Have the books I want, trusted resources	35	U.S.	
free rental of books and videos.	36	U.S.	
Books for adults and children. Availability to use computers for online purposes	38	U.S.	
Free there are librarians	39	U.S.	
educational, family-oriented	40	U.S.	
large assortment of materials friendly and helpful personell	40	U.S.	
1) it provides many sources of information in one place 2) it is free	41	U.S.	

Q812a: Positive associations with library.	Age	Geographic Region	Student Status
Books improve your life, by inspiring, teaching, keeping you involved and interested, and FREE TO THINK. LITERACY and being informed raise the standard of living of individuals and societies.	41	U.S.	
real people support. the touch the smell the ability to open and close a book right at your hands	41	U.S.	
free access to information. qualified staff to help you.	42	U.S.	
It's nice to be able to get out of the house to do some of my research. Having a person to help find what I may be looking for.	42	U.S.	
Decent selection. No charge to borrow books so I'd be more likely to read something that I would not pay to read.	43	U.S.	
Free access, latest books	44	U.S.	
free books and videos can sit there and read magazines	45	U.S.	
Internet access for those who don't have a computer. Someone to help you go a certain direction with a topic or assignment	45	U.S.	
1) wandering the isles and finding a nugget of a book. Discovery. 2) Help from a live person if needed.	46	U.S.	
a place one can go to be alone, even in a crowd, a place one can challenge any belief system one may possess, or can support any system the same way.	46	U.S.	
Wonderful children's reading programs. Access to computers to those who do not have them.	46	U.S.	
1. information is 'pure'--no-one edits it--no point of view 2. calm, quiet place	47	U.S.	
Libraries have every book. Libraries are free.	47	U.S.	
finding the data I need. Staff willing to assit you.	49	U.S.	
People available Multitude of books on different subjects by different authors.	49	U.S.	
Surrounded by books Peaceful	49	U.S.	
almost always quiet, and usually have one or more books that I need on almost any subject.	50	U.S.	
1)Large volume of material physically at my fingertipes. 2)Less searching, because there is less information to 'wade through'.	51	U.S.	
convenient--I order books on-line from all over the system and pick them up weekly I have far more books available to me than if I could only use and read those I purchased myself	51	U.S.	
free loaner books quiet, uncrowded	52	U.S.	
there is a human being on premise to help you when you are unable to find what you are looking for the diversity of the books, videos, audios, that you find there	52	U.S.	
Help by librarians when doing research or making suggestions for reading subjects of interest. Providing current materials and technology for their users.	53	U.S.	
Free, Wealth if knowledge, 24/7 info	54	U.S.	
1. I like being surrounded by books 2. Libraries smell good. Especially the very old ones with lots of old books.	55	U.S.	
ease of locating what I'm looking for, and books on tape	56	U.S.	
QUIET TIME FREE LITERARY AND COMPUTER ACCESSABILITY	56	U.S.	
It's a comfortable place to sit and read. It's also a good place to find information you might not be aware of on your own.	57	U.S.	
1) Ease of locating books and periodicals 2) Pleasant environment in which to work.	60	U.S.	
They have what I need, or can get it. Wonderfully helpful librarians	60	U.S.	
EASILY ACCESSIBLE TO THE HANDICAPPED WIDE ASSORTMENT OF BOOKS, CDS, ETC.	61	U.S.	
Access to biographies that expands one's understanding of the human condition. Provides ability to access info available with no out of pocket financial investment.	62	U.S.	

Q812a: Positive associations with library.	Age	Geographic Region	Student Status
I use the library all the time for reading material. The people who work there are great at looking up information for you when you ask them to. The library is a wonderful asset to any community.	62	U.S.	
take out audio books use genealogy resources	62	U.S.	
It is free It is convient	63	U.S.	
Comfortable learning environment; Some place to go to get answers to a question I have.	65	U.S.	
Friendly place for information I still enjoy the feel of a book in my hands this I can do without having to buy	65	U.S.	
1. A person can use library resources to expand their mind. 2. A fun happy place to visit.	66	U.S.	
1. Comfortable accomodations. 2. Easy to locate materials.	66	U.S.	
GOOD PLACE FOR MY GRANDCHILDREN TO GET HELP WITH HOMEWORK ASSIGNMENTS GOOD SOURCE FOR INFORMATION	66	U.S.	
i can renew books over the phone they order books for me from other branches	66	U.S.	
Quiet area to do research. Ability to browse without flipping from website to website.	66	U.S.	
They really researched a project for me. They also have movies & CD's that you can check out,	66	U.S.	
all the free reading I want up to date computer access & assistance	67	U.S.	
Comfortable surroundings. librarian helps with problems.	67	U.S.	
Extensive genealogy department Knowledgeable personnel	67	U.S.	
Multiple ways to gather information. A person who can steer you to the section you need.	67	U.S.	
Good research Dept/ Able to check out DVD	68	U.S.	
polite and helpful	68	U.S.	
RELAXING, INFORMATIVE	68	U.S.	
The ease of using for the information I need and the helpfulness of those working to find what I need	68	U.S.	
When I was younger, and computers were not available, the library was the best source of knowledge, and leisure reading.	68	U.S.	
BASE OF KNOWLEDGE AND BOOKS TO INFORM OR ENTERTAIN	69	U.S.	
Free access to unlimited information and avbbillity to borrow novels, research material, magazines, tapes, DVD's and all sorts of media.	69	U.S.	
Good for children to be able to see all the books and information.	69	U.S.	
Lovely, peaceful atmosphere. Always someone there to help me personally.	69	U.S.	
A QUIET PLACE TO READ AND STUDY. A NICE PLACE TO MEET OTHERS WHO LIKE TO READ.	70	U.S.	
Online catalogs Audio books	70	U.S.	
There are materials you can use to learn an area of interest. People are available to help you find what you need.	71	U.S.	
My local library has a much better supply and selection of current CDs than the main library in town. Longer hours,in town, including open on sunday	71	U.S.	
The atmosphere is friendly, the librarians are helpful and I can read as much as I want	71	U.S.	
Amount of information available. Timliness of information on the one hand as well as historical data when needed.	72	U.S.	
Hundreds of books to choose from and enjoy for no cost. A reasonable length of time before the book is due back.	72	U.S.	
I used the library extensively when I was in college (before computers!) and doubt I could have gotten through without it. The availability of books & other materials which one would not otherwise have access to.	72	U.S.	
MUCH INFORMATION, COMPUTERS	72	U.S.	

Q812a: Positive associations with library.	Age	Geographic Region	Student Status
QUANTITY OF INFORMATION AND ORGANAZATION	72	U.S.	
courteous assistance when needed. Can count on finding what you are looking for.	73	U.S.	
Helpfullness, knowledge	73	U.S.	
Order online Renew online	73	U.S.	
There is a librarian available to help when we need help. Local library sells used books at very low prices.	73	U.S.	
I love books, audio books when I travel can rent them for a month, so I have enough time to read them, also to read to children at school	74	U.S.	
My first introduction to the wonders of reading (1936 -thanks to a wonderful teacher) and The availability of books to feed my hunger on long nights (1949-50 A.F. Comm.Cntr.).	74	U.S.	
1. Quiet 2. Self help is possible.	75	U.S.	
I remember saturday afternoons, when 2:00 p.m. was story hour. With other boys and girls, we sat on the hardwood floor in a semi circle and listened to stories read by Miss Dunn, who was our head librarian. This was many decades ago. No matter what the subject was, I could always get sufficient information on it at the local library.	75	U.S.	
an oasis for learning teaching children to love books	76	U.S.	
Goodly number of a book for borrowing Promptness getting new book ordered and on shelf	77	U.S.	
1. Encouraging the young to utilize the library via various programs geared to their ages & interests. 2. Active in community activities, providing a platform for social interests and encouraging participation.	78	U.S.	
AMUSEMENT ENTERTAINMENT	78	U.S.	
Wealth of information No cost to use	78	U.S.	
other than being shushed I loved it	79	U.S.	
Pleasant people to deal with Very helpful	80	U.S.	
Recreation for 75 years of my life Resource for education purposes	82	U.S.	

Q812b: Negative associations with the library

Note: All verbatim comments are presented as entered by survey respondents, including spelling, grammatical and punctuation errors.

Q812b: Negative associations with library.	Age	Geographic Region	Student Status
Being Quiet Really Bad search systems	16	Australia	High school
It closes Need more recent material	16	Australia	High school
overdue books/fees having to leave the house	17	Australia	High school
Some libraries have fees. Some libraries are very narrow minded in information available.	17	Australia	
crowding not enough cross-referencing	18	Australia	College undergraduate
The catalogs on the computer are sometimes hard to use to find the book/article/journal that you want. The library can be busy and the information sometimes is not available - sometimes the book you need is on loan.	18	Australia	College undergraduate
date of publications (out of date) time spent looking for specific information	19	Australia	College undergraduate
difficulty finding information, penalties for forgetting to return books	19	Australia	College undergraduate
Have to physically be at the library to use its resources. May not necessarily contain the needed resources.	20	Australia	College post graduate
late fees the term of loans	21	Australia	
Geeky/nerdy people old	22	Australia	College undergraduate
need to sign up to take out books must be quiet	23	Australia	College undergraduate
Physical distance from home/work Overcrowded	23	Australia	
geeky aura	24	Australia	
Hard to access as there isn't one in my home town. Fines.	24	Australia	
can be a little overwhelming	25	Australia	College post graduate
have to physically go there dony unerstand the filing system	25	Australia	
a bit of a hassle to get to, time limits	26	Australia	
boring slow	27	Australia	
Poor Service Poor Range of Books	27	Australia	
can't always get what you want some resources old/out of date	28	Australia	
not up to date information, sometimes har dto get to a library to borrow stuff	29	Australia	College post graduate
queues for conputer resources never wnough books	29	Australia	College post graduate
Not able to get my hands on the specific book I wanted Not able to use the computers readily	30	Australia	
Sometimes too much information Sometimes hard to navigate	31	Australia	
due to the internet, everything is much faster, getting help when needed,some staff are just not knowledgible enough	32	Australia	
A little outdated. A lot of information now is readily available at home via internet.	33	Australia	
old world technology impossible to find info quickly	35	Australia	
time delays, registration	35	Australia	
fees for late returns, waiting for a long time for the book you want	36	Australia	
Grumpy librarians. Dead quietness	36	Australia	
Lack of particular books I want, no food or drink.	37	Australia	
can be hard to find ref information quickly	38	Australia	
Borrowing restrictions. Lack of resources.	40	Australia	
If you are not familiar with the cataloguing system you may find it hard to locate what you may be searching for. It would possibly take you longer to search for information through a library rather than on the net.	40	Australia	

Q812b: Negative associations with library.	Age	Geographic Region	Student Status
Moody librarians! Insufficient books on certain topics	40	Australia	
books are old and not in good condition.	42	Australia	
library card computer glitches	42	Australia	
having to actually go there have to be a member	43	Australia	
kids slow	43	Australia	
Perceived as a hidebound and stuffy entity where silence is golden. Large institution which can be somewhat intimidating for poeple who are not confidant with learning or exploring.	43	Australia	
Time consuming Materials can sometimes be outdated	43	Australia	College undergraduate
books tend to be out of date or, if current, are checked out. not enough IT	44	Australia	
Library is not in my own home, I have to travel to it. Sometimes the books get tatty because of the number of readers. Have to remember how to find reference books.	44	Australia	
Austerity and inability to rapidly find information.	45	Australia	
rude attendants and slow service.	47	Australia	
dusty have to search for info	50	Australia	
Libaries want to realize that ther are a lot of adult readers out there and we wantto see more adult books (not porn) balance the children's setion and the adults section more evenly oldies like a good book too	50	Australia	
not enough disabled parking	50	Australia	
Cataloguing - where is the information? Is it all in one place or is it scattered? Parameters for determining scope - breadth and depth - of the collection.	51	Australia	
must physically attend,less comfortable than home	51	Australia	
You have to leave home to get your book without guarantees thet you will find what you want. why go to the library when you can get the Information from the comfort of your own home.	51	Australia	
1. not as accessible as the internet 2. holdings can be limited so, while they have many books I wouldn't otherwise find, they also miss many I would like to borrow.	52	Australia	
Don't know where anything is anymore. The staff are too busy to help.	53	Australia	
have to travel to library as apposed to searching the net	55	Australia	
Having to go there if it's a rainy day. Time consuming	55	Australia	
Having to return the books within a certain time frame; not finding what I am looking for when I don't have a lot of time to spare	55	Australia	
A librarian who does not know the libraries resources. The inability to keep resonably up to date with the latest information and resources.	56	Australia	
sometimes you need to re-borrow the book because lending time too short. Not enough care taken (sometimes) to keep books in top condition.	56	Australia	
FINES LACK OF VARIETY IN DVD	57	Australia	
only one - some staff are not as well informed as others	57	Australia	
Restrictions in hours online tends to be USA influenced	57	Australia	
snooty librarians difficulty finding books (out of order)	58	Australia	
No conversations allowed with companions.	59	Australia	
Difficulty in getting the reading matter you require. CLosed atfer hours.	61	Australia	
1.require help to find what i need	62	Australia	
ADULTS SHOULD BE PAYING TO USE. TOO HARD TO GET TO.	62	Australia	
musty underfunded	62	Australia	
Inflexibility of systems and staff. Physical difficulties of access.	65	Australia	
sometimes the way the staff speak to you not enought time if you need to use the computer in library	66	Australia	
Not sufficient internet connections. Online Authers should be split into sections for ease of access.	70	Australia	

Q812b: Negative associations with library.	Age	Geographic Region	Student Status
Accessibility and less need to visit because data more easily available electronically	81	Australia	
you have to drive to go get your books and you have to drive back to return your books	14	Canada	High school
Doesn't always have what I need Material can take a while to come in from another place	16	Canada	High school
books not being in. no access to needed resources	19	Canada	College undergraduate
you have to go there and sift through lots of books to possibly find what you are looking for. you have a deadline to return the books.	21	Canada	
book already signed out Bad hours	23	Canada	College undergraduate
There are so many books that I do not know where to start We do not know who had the book before and do not know weither or not the person was sick, sort of like handeling money	23	Canada	
just plain boring too much searhing for your information	26	Canada	College post graduate
Time consuming Don't always fid what you are looking for	26	Canada	
you are boring if you go there It's not a fast way to find what you need	26	Canada	
Bad hours lack of up to date info	27	Canada	
First i live in a small town, and the library don't get a lot of new a books esch month. Second: the only have 2 computer with internet acces. Sometimes when i got ther the computer are already taken so i have to wait 30 minutes to have a chance to use one	29	Canada	
not to much help, you feel like you should know how it all works and if you don't they sometimes don't seem to want to help you. To quiet, sometimes you have to work in groups and you always feel like you can't talk	30	Canada	
Don't always have the resources to acquire the most up to date material. Not always open when I need it.	31	Canada	
a lot of manual work to get specifically what you need overdue fines	32	Canada	
Stuffy Old books	32	Canada	
someone has my library card from a purse theft.	33	Canada	
Forgetting to bring back books on time. Having to be so quiet.	35	Canada	
Librarians not always aware of their own collections (mainly the electronic resources). Resources not always current.	35	Canada	
You have to make a special trip to go. You have to go out of your way. Sometimes books ar eout and reserved for long periods of time delaying access to materials.	35	Canada	
1-Limited hours 2-Distance to travel to get to it	36	Canada	
Government, late fees.	37	Canada	
low tech	38	Canada	
reference books are not accessible at home ie cannot be taken out of the library. too many people around with germs and handling of books and items (I have a weakened immune system so this is a major issue)	38	Canada	College post graduate
hours are not always convenient sometimes hard to find what you're looking for	39	Canada	
you have to go though alot of books to find the information	40	Canada	
Many people think that computers are replacing the need for libraries and books and that libraries are oldfashioned and people would rather read books and magazines and newspapers online. Only nerds, intellectuals and dull people go to libraries, according to some people. They think it is not cool to be seen there.	41	Canada	
Something about libraries, bookstores and video stores gives me vertigo. Can't think of anything else negative, sorry	42	Canada	

Q812b: Negative associations with library.	Age	Geographic Region	Student Status
making the trip to the library parking ease of use	43	Canada	
Fines Waiting lists	44	Canada	
slower access to information restricted hours of access	44	Canada	College post graduate
cost of transportation to get to the library return deadlines/over due fees	45	Canada	
having to wait till the book or movie is avalible having to have the items back by a certain date	46	Canada	
1--requires travel 2--short rental periods	47	Canada	
always busy.(computers not available,books already out etc). most of the books are old and out of date.	47	Canada	
Books not being there when you need them. People just sitting in there taking up valuable space and time.	47	Canada	
uptight librarians many rules	47	Canada	College post graduate
sometimes you don't have enough time to read the book. not accessible 24/7	48	Canada	
INFORMATION NOT ALWAYS AVAILABLE,BOOKS NOT UPDATED REGULARLY	49	Canada	College post graduate
overdue costs short due dates	49	Canada	College post graduate
crowded unsavory clientelle in some cases	50	Canada	
limited by funding	50	Canada	
Sometimes can be slow and tedious trying to find the information you need.	50	Canada	
Good libraries are never close enough. Trying to find the material available	51	Canada	
getting there returning books on time	52	Canada	
Sour people to deal with.	52	Canada	
do not know how to look up information	53	Canada	
complex hard to find inormation	54	Canada	
Where I live it cost a yearly fee to possess a library card and it is cumbersome to get there.	55	Canada	
ease of finding material in books relaxing	57	Canada	
I don't like to go out to get books I want I get overwhelmed by the coice	58	Canada	
Very often research type information is very outdated. There is not enough money to allow the libraries to have all the materials they need.	58	Canada	
paying fines not nough computers	61	Canada	
Waiting in line for computer use	66	Canada	
unable to remove some reference texts out of the library	69	Canada	
bias in selection of materials. political or cultural censorship	79	Canada	
Formal environment Time and distance to physically reach	25	India	
1)Card based rule 2)Might not contain all the latest information.	27	India	
books may not be available at all the times	30	India	
have to return the books on time you have look for information yourself	31	India	
1. lack of latest infromation. 2. Some books available in libraries are only provided to the members only for reading purpose instead of keeping records etc.	35	India	
Crowded often Materials wanted may not be available, necessitates weeks-long wait in some cases	35	India	College post graduate
diffocult to mainain needs professional to maintain	37	India	
time consumed on research & restrictions	39	India	
To have to go to the library Registration process	43	India	
too many books, discipline	44	India	
too crowded, poorly lit atmosphere	48	India	
1. Time consuming 2. Cumbersome to locate information	51	India	
at times too many people too much of talking	51	India	

Q812b: Negative associations with library.	Age	Geographic Region	Student Status
non-Availability on time ineffective library management	51	India	
One feels tired,boring,time consuming - if the information needed is not exhaustive. sometimes you do not get information that is required.	54	India	
sometimes not getting the books you want,if you have to search for an author	54	India	
to travel long distance not to get what i want	54	India	
At times you have to wait along time to get a book on particular subject. Its avialable for a short duration	55	India	
limited sources	56	India	
noisy fellow readers messy cupboards	61	India	
too crowded; not enough books /info available	66	India	
Sometimes out of date & too many users at a point of time	71	India	
a place to burn time	16	Singapore	High school
old and used books	23	Singapore	
really old old books.	24	Singapore	College undergraduate
a fee required to search for newspaper articles/elctronic journals in the net	27	Singapore	
Pay for late return of books Do not always have the book you want	28	Singapore	
difficult to search books often unavailable	30	Singapore	
1)The borrowing duration is too short 2)Limited 24 hours book drop service	31	Singapore	
response is slow	32	Singapore	
A geek Dull	34	Singapore	
If internet line is down can't source anything Slow retrieval	34	Singapore	
Too many people; need to physically go to the library.	34	Singapore	
location - must take train to library. out-of-stock / out-dated books	35	Singapore	
materials too old, out-of-date loan period too short	35	Singapore	
Not enough resource available for people to use Too many people contributing to the noise pollution	35	Singapore	College post graduate
1. Online checking sometimes not accurate. 2. Not enough resources	37	Singapore	
Troublesome to go to library to get info	37	Singapore	
difficult to find exact source difficult to go to the physical library	40	Singapore	
need to pay fees to gain access to books/articles/journals only extract of books are available	40	Singapore	College post graduate
looking for the right source of information time constraints	44	Singapore	
uncomfortable seats. hardly any cafe for a hot drink or refreshment.	44	Singapore	
boring,quiet	46	Singapore	
unable to get latest materials/books ie have to queue to get popular books/reference books are normally not well kept	46	Singapore	
TOO MANY HOURS SPENT IN FIND THE INFORMATION	47	Singapore	
we get to pay charges to renew the same book. Many books have the pages torn out, esp. the good recipes.	48	Singapore	
You arent allowed to talk haha You have to have a library card to be able to take the books out	16	U.K.	
Annoying librarians Out dated facilities	17	U.K.	High school
You cant eat, drink, or smoke in most libraries Overdue fines Having to return the book	17	U.K.	
Old, dirty, out-of-date books Attitude that THEY are doing YOU a favour by gracing you with their presence, when its YOUR tax pounds/dollars etc. that are paying THEIR wages	17	U.K.	College undergraduate
people regard it as a boring place too much of a chore to go there when you can get the book off the net	19	U.K.	
stuffy moody librarian	20	U.K.	

Q812b: Negative associations with library.	Age	Geographic Region	Student Status
you have to get up and go! Not always the information you need as books may be out on loan.	20	U.K.	
books tend to be shabby, librarians tend to be bad tempered	21	U.K.	
To far away, Hard to find things	21	U.K.	
crowds and noise- queues for using computers- dirty torn books- books out of stock already loaned	22	U.K.	College undergraduate
too far away .....and erm pass	22	U.K.	
The book you want is not always there. You have to pay to order a book in specially.	22	U.K.	
old-fashioned, not as accesible as the internet	23	U.K.	
Lots of info to go through Not located convieniently	23	U.K.	
never have the book you want unfriendly staff	23	U.K.	
the silence rule no libarys have toilets and you can guarentee that everytime I walk into the libary, i need to go!	25	U.K.	
too busy sense of elitism about being a member	25	U.K.	
too quiet	25	U.K.	
not 'cool' to go to the library its for old people	26	U.K.	
The book you want many not be in Condition of books may be poor	26	U.K.	
Boring Opening hours are not suited to my study style	26	U.K.	
forgetting to return books on time opening hours	26	U.K.	
paying fines for late books boring	27	U.K.	
Not many people to give advice	28	U.K.	College undergraduate
1) its not always possible to take books back by due date 2) because of hours of buisness its not always possible to browse at will	29	U.K.	
very hard to find the information you need or book looking for atmosphere is not very inviting very cold and quiet	29	U.K.	
OLD FASHIONED TOO QUIET	29	U.K.	
outdated/old books/that goes for my local library anyway//	30	U.K.	
time limits not a wide enough choice of books	30	U.K.	
not having enough computers	31	U.K.	
not easy to search old fashioned	31	U.K.	
reminders and fines books not being available	33	U.K.	
very boring and should be closed thus saving the tax payer	33	U.K.	
only 3 books at a time don,t get the books long enough the book you want is never there	33	U.K.	
Our local one is a bit small and dated. Sometime can't find or don't have what you're looking for.	33	U.K.	
Boring Quiet	34	U.K.	
Tatty old books. Creeping around in case you make a noise and annoy the regulars.	34	U.K.	
stuffy and boring envirement too quiet to learn in.	34	U.K.	
too quiet, not always able to find info you want	34	U.K.	
Poor selection of books Inconvenient opening hours	34	U.K.	
some sites have to pay	35	U.K.	
not welcoming slow to find info	35	U.K.	
a large number of books are outdated fees	35	U.K.	
going out to look for what you need books already being used by other people	35	U.K.	
i forget to return books on time not easy for me to get to	36	U.K.	
not very child freindly stuffy	36	U.K.	
limited choice of books not always uptodate books	37	U.K.	
Too much info	37	U.K.	
Can be perceived to be: 1) stuffy 2) Haughty	37	U.K.	
mingers in there wasting time sheltering from the weather	37	U.K.	
Old Fashioned Boring	37	U.K.	
finding time to visit fines!!!	38	U.K.	
NOT ENOUGH TIME WITH BOOKS, OPENNING HOURS	38	U.K.	

Q812b: Negative associations with library.	Age	Geographic Region	Student Status
doesn't have classics on shelves(tho are availabe in storage) sometimes lack of knowledge of staff	39	U.K.	
Unfriendly staff, having to wait a long time for a book or do not have it in any library and have to wait for them to get a loan from outside the area.	40	U.K.	College undergraduate
taking books back fines for late return	41	U.K.	
Opening times Having to book to use internet facilities	41	U.K.	
Customer service leaves a lot to be desired in my local library. Too many 'Local' libraries have been closed cutting down on accessibility.	42	U.K.	
oppressive rude staff	42	U.K.	
Boring Hard to find information	42	U.K.	
accessibility quiet	43	U.K.	
poor state it's kept in limited resources	43	U.K.	
unhelpful staff huge size	43	U.K.	
Opening Hours May not have book/s in stock that I would be looking for.	44	U.K.	
Not sure where to look or find what I was looking for	46	U.K.	
Hours of opening Finding what you want	47	U.K.	
not having item you want having to renew subscription	47	U.K.	
not the right materials	49	U.K.	
boring,oldfashined	49	U.K.	
Assistants not always helpful. Too short a time limit on borrowing.	50	U.K.	
Internet not always available Staff not up to date with technology	50	U.K.	
to quiet impolite staff	50	U.K.	
time constraint on computer use time to reach library	51	U.K.	
finding time to use it finding the right words to start search	51	U.K.	
Limited stock. Dated, i.e. not up to date.	51	U.K.	
sometimes have to order what i want not open late i.e. after work	52	U.K.	
used books could carry diseases ----	52	U.K.	
Difficulty in parking. Not always convenient opening times	52	U.K.	
Distance from home Not open long enough	52	U.K.	
Inconvenient if you want the information immediately Not a good atmosphere, too sombre	53	U.K.	
fines pages missing	54	U.K.	
HAVE TO TRAVEL HAVING TO SEARCH	54	U.K.	
Due dates -- hate having to feel rushed if I haven't had time to finish reading/researching.	54	U.K.	
Opening hours of library having to order in books from other branches when you need them now	54	U.K.	
Time you have to wait for specialist or more abstruse information Dumb librarians - they tend to be well-versed in 'Arty' subjects but know nothing about scientific topics	55	U.K.	
Costs money if late returning books. Also costs money for some services.	55	U.K.	
Opening hours, I sleep very little Accessibility - library some distance away	55	U.K.	
Too many books to look through. Not open at all the right times.	55	U.K.	
Boring dull	56	U.K.	
The silence was thick. Not necessarily conducive to welcoming atmosphere. It is a long time since I used a public library.	56	U.K.	
there is no toilet in my library so getting information must be quick there needs to be more seats for the disabled	57	U.K.	
not being able to find info required not always open when needed	57	U.K.	
Small libraries don't always have the books required. Opening hours for working people.	57	U.K.	

Q812b: Negative associations with library.	Age	Geographic Region	Student Status
fines queues	58	U.K.	
poor parking facilities at most libraries. quite a lot of books in poor condition	58	U.K.	
queues locating information needed	58	U.K.	
am disabled, and difficult to park	60	U.K.	
Can have a small selection of reference books May have to wait for books	60	U.K.	
HAVE TO LEAVE THE HOME TO GET THIS INFORMATION	60	U.K.	
sometimes find it hard to find something I am looking for red tape.	61	U.K.	
Usually situated in town centres - hence car parking charges. Limited opening hours	65	U.K.	
Lack of funds in our area to purchase new books.	66	U.K.	
Lack of proper funding leads to: failure to keep stock up to date and relevant to local need	66	U.K.	
No means of accessing high shelves if small in stature	67	U.K.	
1. required information not always easy to locate. 2. information etc not always up to date.	68	U.K.	
Too far from were I live.	69	U.K.	
none	71	U.K.	
Slow Remote	71	U.K.	
because of cost-cutting shorter opening hours and less stock	72	U.K.	
when information not available it can take a long time to obtain books from other sourses some staff very abrupt	80	U.K.	
boring complicated	14	U.S.	High school
Only for nerds. Bums go there to keep warm.	15	U.S.	High school
sometimes hard to find info and not as quick as the internet	15	U.S.	High school
-when the book you want has been checked out -librarians aren't always the most considerate people	15	U.S.	High school
you have to have a membership you have to have the books back in short periods of time	15	U.S.	High school
policy drivenness	16	U.S.	High school
Researching for school papers Broken down computers	16	U.S.	High school
sometimes too much information	16	U.S.	High school
the stereotypical librarian, the concept that books are unintresting	16	U.S.	High school
Uncool Nerdy	16	U.S.	High school
Unqualified libriarians. Complicated search services.	16	U.S.	High school
BORING!! No fun in library!	17	U.S.	
fines, impatient librarians	17	U.S.	High school
Musty Book Smell A Mean libranian	17	U.S.	High school
old people, old books, fines, outdated information, archaic research tool	17	U.S.	High school
Only losers go to libraries Going to a library for research is outdated	17	U.S.	High school
overdue fines homeless people like to stay there sometimes	17	U.S.	High school
Rude librarians Limited resources	17	U.S.	College undergraduate
Confusing arrangements (Library of Congress system of organization) Not being open 24 hours a day	18	U.S.	College undergraduate
You must be extremely quiet. A lot of people don't like librarians.	18	U.S.	College undergraduate
musty atmosphere overwhelming row upon row of books	19	U.S.	College undergraduate
too quiet, limited selection of books	19	U.S.	College undergraduate
when they are open late fees for books that most people do not check out or have not been checked out in years	19	U.S.	College undergraduate
Books not always available, sporadic and incomplete collections of series of books, often mistreated and therefore disgruntled staff members.	20	U.S.	College undergraduate

Q812b: Negative associations with library.	Age	Geographic Region	Student Status
clostrophobic, overwhelming number of places to look for information	20	U.S.	
computer technology might be outdated needed materials are not always on-hand	20	U.S.	
sometimes difficult to find information because there is so much of it, sometimes too quiet and that's more distracting than noise	20	U.S.	College undergraduate
Dull Time consuming (looking for books)	21	U.S.	College undergraduate
Fines Hassle of keeping card	21	U.S.	
May not have what you need, not open 24 hours	21	U.S.	
Overdue fees Having to wait for a librarian	21	U.S.	
Sometimes it is very hard to find the books. Sometimes it is difficult to find someone to help.	21	U.S.	College undergraduate
not enough internet control...anyone could go look at porn usually there aren't friendly people working in the library	22	U.S.	
Not enough librarians; Not enough instructions on how to find books/use resources	22	U.S.	College undergraduate
Our library is old and crappy. The workers are cranky	22	U.S.	
Slow reserve response. Limited selections.	22	U.S.	
antiquated, physical	23	U.S.	College undergraduate
Can be overwelming to find what you need in a big library, but small libraries may not have as wide a selection overdue fines	23	U.S.	
government offices homeless sleep in back aisles	23	U.S.	College undergraduate
My taxes keep going up. I think they make the buildings fancier than they need to be.	24	U.S.	
too quiet, maybe outdated	24	U.S.	
You have to pay if you do not live in the city	24	U.S.	
sometimes outdated materials what you want isn't always in stock	25	U.S.	
ridiculous fees for out-of-city-limits patrons rude library staff	28	U.S.	
You have to travel there You have to be quiet	28	U.S.	
dewey decimal system overdue fines	32	U.S.	College undergraduate
books aren't always available traffic	35	U.S.	
liberal bias unfriendly librarians	35	U.S.	
The online card catalogues are harder to use, they tend to be ambigious about what library actually has the book you are looking up - they do not make it clear whether it is the library you are standing in, or a sister library. The librarians are not tech-savy, in my recent experience, and are easily frustrated with questions.	35	U.S.	
Looking and reading an entire book takes too long when the specific information can be gained online in a matter of minutes. Cross referencing takes a lot of time and effort.	38	U.S.	
Out dated materials and limited number of materials	38	U.S.	
Libraries here will start charging for internet. CONSTANT CUTS OF OPEN HOURS and funding for new materials.	41	U.S.	
libraries shrinking due to lack of funding no money to update materials	41	U.S.	
homeless people bad bathrooms	43	U.S.	
Nothing negative about a library. It just can't compete with individuals using computers to get information. The trip to the computer is a few seconds, where the trip to the library is measured in minutes.	43	U.S.	
Not convenient for fast searches.	46	U.S.	
Libraries' books may be old and out-of-date. People who go there for free internet access tie up resources for others.	47	U.S.	

Q812b: Negative associations with library.	Age	Geographic Region	Student Status
homeland security monitoring library use government cuts in library funding	48	U.S.	
waiting line travel time	49	U.S.	
unfiltered sites for children unsupervised computer usage for children	56	U.S.	
HAVING TO LEAVE THE HOUSE NOT HAVING WHAT I NEED	61	U.S.	
Grumpy librarians lack of resourses	65	U.S.	
Looking for jobs on there web sites. Trying to write cover letters on there computers.	65	U.S.	
Dificult in getting a computer to use. Some reference books can't be checked out.	66	U.S.	
our library system has no money to buy new books or materials they need more computers for the public to use	66	U.S.	
high taxes buracracy	68	U.S.	
Now I would find it very difficult to have to travel to a library for information every time I wanted it. Being able to access information from my home with my computer, makes it possible for me to find information I want - whenever I want to without needing time away from my responsibilities at home. I am caregiver to my elderly, ill mother...and would not have the freedom of going to a library at this time.	68	U.S.	
Was given the site, for home use, and it crashed my computer, and I can no longer access it from home. Having to wait for items either from State information exchange, sometimes having to wait for months. By then I've forgotten about what I needed, or I found it elsewhere.	68	U.S.	
Waste money;they never have enough.The budget tripled in one year when the went on puplic money.	68	U.S.	
YUCK...WE HAVE TO PAY $25.OO A YEAR AS MILLIAGE WAS TURNED DOWN NOT ENOUGH COMPUTERS FOR EVERYONE	68	U.S.	
Average person is not informed enough to be able to research info through card files.	69	U.S.	
Was only allowed on their computer for 30 min. Ours needs more computers.	69	U.S.	
I am handicapped and access is very limited to our library. The ramp is too steep for me to wheel my chair up myself Books are too high up for me to reach	70	U.S.	
When they can't find a book If they don't have what I want	70	U.S.	
Dewey system can be hard to navigate. Also the internet has now put all the librarys of the world ay your fingertips	71	U.S.	
Not convenient as computer i/e hours, distance Unwillingness of staff to help with problems	73	U.S.	
1. Has become a haven for the homeless 2. Card/computer files not always up to date.	75	U.S.	
1. State funding always much less than needed so attempts to overcome the shortages of funds make them pander, at times (maybe) 2. Shortened hours and too few books by desirable writers (due to fundngs lack)	78	U.S.	
card system replaced by computers. not always someone there to help find books.	79	U.S.	
Poor quality of audiobooks.	79	U.S.	
I always have to ask information about where to look for the information I need. It is too difficult to find it by myself, because there is so much information....I could waste toomuch time looking for it.	80	U.S.	

Q1240: If you could provide one piece of advice to your library, what would it be?

Note: All verbatim comments are presented as entered by survey respondents, including spelling, grammatical and punctuation errors.

Q1240: If you could provide one piece of advice to your library, what would it be?	Age	Geographic Region	Student Status
Have less rules about restricting what you can/can't do - what times you are allowed to visit, not allowed to listen to music through MP3 player/computer, even if you are listening with headphones etc. They seem to be of the belief that having fun is bad.	17	Australia	High school
Needs a more broad range of things, such as Audio Books and Comic books. Also needs more up to date books, new releases.	17	Australia	
To stay as you are there is always someone there to help when its needed.	17	Australia	High school
don't charge for putting books on hold adn let the public request new books	18	Australia	College undergraduate
needs more computers	18	Australia	College undergraduate
Review the current search catalog system as it is hard to find material relevent to the topic you search for.	18	Australia	College undergraduate
classify databases according to faculty. improve the search function of databases. improve signage/layout. extend the size of the room for group meetings (quiet talking and food and drinks allowed)	19	Australia	College undergraduate
good work	19	Australia	College undergraduate
Provide more scientific and skeptical books.	20	Australia	College post graduate
ADVERTISE ON THE T.V OR HAVE ADDS ON THE INTERNET. I THINK SOMEPEOPLE ARE ABIT BUSY AND FORGET ABOUT LIBRARY'S SO IF YOU REMIND PPL BY DOING THIS THEN YOU WILL GET MORE PPL IN.	22	Australia	
more librARIANS WHO NOW WAT THEY R DOING	22	Australia	
Get better digital and audio/visual facilities.	24	Australia	
Give people a reason to go there, rather than use the internet at home.	25	Australia	
make library more accesssible online for off campus students	25	Australia	
transfer more paper based information into digital format. Everything current is, but stuff from 5 or so years ago isnt	25	Australia	
Keep keeping up! You are an invaluable resource/facility in the community. Without you, many people's opportunity/desire to learn & develop would be greatly diminished (think Billy Connelly & Michael Caine's love of libraries)	26	Australia	College undergraduate
A better selection of Audio Books (recent and older books)	27	Australia	
keep up the good job	27	Australia	College undergraduate
improve signage. just having a sign with dewy numbers hanging from the ceiling is not enough.	28	Australia	
easy to read maps available so if you know the section you need you can get there without asking for help	29	Australia	College post graduate
Electronic access for all journals would be very useful to part time students that can't neccessarily cone in during opening hours	29	Australia	College post graduate
Make it more inviting,especially to children.	29	Australia	

Q1240: If you could provide one piece of advice to your library, what would it be?	Age	Geographic Region	Student Status
open 24 hrs	29	Australia	College post graduate
friendlier staff	30	Australia	
Just keep meeting the publics needs	30	Australia	
get more computers so more people can be online	32	Australia	
a cafe would be nice	33	Australia	
Try to get more funding to upgrade and expand	33	Australia	
Provide more online help for your online borrowing procedure.	35	Australia	
make it fun!	36	Australia	
A quiet reading area perhaps an upstairs area or a closed in area, and the childrens area needs to be brightened up and picket fenced so to speak so it is just for them a happy place to be	37	Australia	
having enough staff to support kids when then are there for research, sometimes they have to wait and in some cases leave	37	Australia	
a more current dvd and video library	38	Australia	
Fewer crappy romance novels, less new age crystal, shakra, spiritual junk and more non-fiction.	38	Australia	
more personal interaction between staff and clients	39	Australia	
improve collection of dvds/videos	39	Australia	
in a perfect world with better funding, some research materials could be more up to date!	39	Australia	
lighten up, make it comfortable and inviting for people.	39	Australia	
liven up the place	39	Australia	
Remain open after people finish work.	39	Australia	
Separate the childrens area from the main area a little more to ensure that the childrens noise doesn't disturb the other users of the library	39	Australia	
Ditch the paper notification of book availability and replace with e-mail.	40	Australia	
Layout of the library should be more lifestyle based and user friendly. It should offer its patrons the wow factor from the instance you walk in the door that this is the place you want to be in and have the comfort and ease to locate what you are after and feel at home and want to spend time there, quality and quantity.	40	Australia	
Relocate to a shopping centre so people don't have to go out of there way to get to you....lazy society that we are	40	Australia	
To be more pro active in helping people research and gain information	40	Australia	
be more friendly	41	Australia	
close while you still have a last gasping breath	41	Australia	
identify peoples needs, instead of thinking of a solution to a problem when the problem has not yet been properly identified	41	Australia	
keep referance books upto date	41	Australia	
NOT SURE,JUST ITS A GOOD PLACE TO SIT AND RELAX AND READ BOOKS AND ALSO TO SIT AND CHAT TO FREINDS,WHILE READING BOOKS.	41	Australia	
Look after the local community and less fortunate a bit better - include them a bit to promote education and literacy in the community	42	Australia	
Make it a quiet place and get rid of places where discussions can take place- it's too hard to concentrate around talkers.	42	Australia	

Q1240: If you could provide one piece of advice to your library, what would it be?	Age	Geographic Region	Student Status
Books are the heart of a library, so don't cut down on their numbers please.	43	Australia	
Not to library but to those who fund it that we need more money put into purchasing more books	43	Australia	College undergraduate
keep smiling	44	Australia	
Please continue the great service and make internet free. Also; do not let local government close you down. Although sometimes usage may seem low it is still vital that libraries remain an available free source of information.	44	Australia	
Provide a more homey atmosphere. Comfortable chairs. Make the librarians more approachable/friendly	44	Australia	
easier checkout facilites	45	Australia	
happy with liabry	45	Australia	
Increase the appeal to middle aged customers ..	45	Australia	
Provide more sophisticated books.	45	Australia	
Every library should have 'Chinese Language' section.	46	Australia	
Keep up to date information and books	46	Australia	
be more promt with help to visitors,be more happier less rude.	47	Australia	
extend opening hours	47	Australia	
Keep doing what you are doing.	47	Australia	
modenise	47	Australia	
provide more staff	49	Australia	
Get more librarian help for the students	50	Australia	
have longer hours	50	Australia	
It could be a bit more accessible for independent use by mobility impaired users	50	Australia	College post graduate
Retain good customer service with qualified staff	52	Australia	
centralize and provide a wider selection at a larger more comfortable location big enough to support the demand	53	Australia	
Open longer hours to cater for people who would like to visit after 5pm	53	Australia	
redecorate	53	Australia	
should promote community access - most people don't know about it	53	Australia	
To have more top American fiction available	53	Australia	
when they collect authors make sure they have the whole series as it is very frustrating to start reading a series and find they are not all their in order..	54	Australia	
Maeket more to the socially disadvantaged.	55	Australia	
Smile more	56	Australia	
Wake up to what people have been telling them about some of their staff	56	Australia	
Get mor info on line	57	Australia	
lighten up! get some humour, create more interest/reason for people to come here.	57	Australia	
Have friendly staff who explain how the library works/is laid out to anyone who seems unfamiliar with libraries	58	Australia	
Provide an area for conversations	59	Australia	
Things are changing there is a new bank in our local communitee - Think about providing this small town wih its own resource Library AGAIN.	59	Australia	

Q1240: If you could provide one piece of advice to your library, what would it be?	Age	Geographic Region	Student Status
When requesting a book be held that the library phones when it is in	59	Australia	
ORDER XTRA COPIES OF POPULAR TOPICS	60	Australia	
Provide more powerful lighting	61	Australia	
CLEAN UP IT IS ALL TO MESSY	62	Australia	
catch up with modern times	63	Australia	
Continue to provide for the range of people in the community	63	Australia	
Provide parking area nearby with handicap space .	64	Australia	
Communicate constantly their features & benefits to help shape Australians and Australia.	65	Australia	
provide more parking spaces	66	Australia	
duplicate the more popular items	68	Australia	
I am happy as things are	68	Australia	
Expand existing computer facilities to suit the new electonic savy younger generation while encouraging elder citizens to become familier with simple electronic processing.	71	Australia	
Hire more young people	15	Canada	High school
Ask the librarian if you can't find a book.	16	Canada	High school
get books from this century!!!	16	Canada	High school
A smile goes a long way. The environment, including the friendliness of the staff, makes a difference for me.	18	Canada	High school
let us eat and drink in the library..or at least designated study areas.instead of no food or drink at all anywhere	19	Canada	College undergraduate
easier method to find material	20	Canada	
Get books that appeal more to a younger generation (20's-30's).	20	Canada	
Be easier to use	21	Canada	College undergraduate
BE FRIENDLIER!!	24	Canada	
be better organized	25	Canada	
better hours open, being closed on sunday afternoons is stupid since so many students doing research need that time to find information, and are turned away	25	Canada	
if thier doing events they need to adverize it more, ive never seen any program or poster in the community about the libary	25	Canada	
bring down the cost of library membership. $10 seems a bit high to the general public...	26	Canada	
Don't shut down for 6 months for renevations.	26	Canada	
allow people to borrow books longer	28	Canada	
library is a very good place to study and do research.	28	Canada	
To have the resources made easier for people to use. I find that it is extremely hard to find what you are looking for without the assistance of the librarian.	28	Canada	
Hire people who really want to be there and will be friendly and readily available to help students who ask for help.	29	Canada	College undergraduate
Allow coffee inside!	30	Canada	
don't let publishing companys tell you what to stock, listen to what your members want	30	Canada	
make it easier to find the information by yourself	30	Canada	
None, they are great	30	Canada	

Q1240: If you could provide one piece of advice to your library, what would it be?	Age	Geographic Region	Student Status
find out what your patrons are looking for and try to keep the items as up-to-date as possible.	31	Canada	
Extend your hours (especially on weekends)	32	Canada	
I am currently very satisfied with the services offered at my library.	32	Canada	
make yourself and your services known to the local commnity, make the community WANT to come to the library	33	Canada	
This is only a small library. They need newer books and more books.	34	Canada	
a card that doesn't expire, a plastic card	35	Canada	
Friendlier staff	35	Canada	
free access to the internet currently you have to pay $1 per half hr	37	Canada	
Attract readers (children and parents) through increasing number of best selling children books	38	Canada	
Be more available	38	Canada	
keep collections up to date	38	Canada	
stop charging for groups to come in and rent space. be more accepting of all age groups and ethnic groups, not just special interest groups who have money	38	Canada	College post graduate
I believe they do a great service to the community... so no advice needed...except to please keep up the great work.	39	Canada	
If it just provides internet services, I can get that at home. Needs to advertise/inform that it has access to all of the most up-to-date reliable research sources or can get them easily.	40	Canada	
To update their technology so that they are current!!	40	Canada	
Please keep more current books available and more foreign newspapers and magazines. Today's reading public come from all parts of the world. They would like to read news about their country in their own language and from their own newspapers and magazines.	41	Canada	
longer hours restrict computer time so that people other than the kids who have suddenly appeared can access them.	42	Canada	
Post the hours the library is open in the local newspaper.	42	Canada	
Arrange seating so students can NOT sit in clusters and socialize. Library is for studying, not socializing.	44	Canada	College post graduate
Be more VISIBLE! Make email lists apparent and available. There are always classes and thing i find interesting but i NEVER find out about them until they are full. Have a electronic bulletin board -- not for discussion -- but for anouncements.	44	Canada	
More comfortable seating. More attractions for adults, it is great for children!	44	Canada	
make a seperate are for kids because they make too much noice	45	Canada	
Need a more well-lit, sunny and bright environment. The library is too dark and cold.	45	Canada	
provide a coffe/snack shop so a person can read, relax and have a treat	45	Canada	
The library that I visited last year and is close to my home has now desided to exclude us from their usage, because of town boundaries. We would have to pay about 145.00 each to stay a member of it. Now the library that we can us is about 30 km away and is not convenient for us.	45	Canada	
Turf out the present city council. Political support is imperative.	45	Canada	

Q1240: If you could provide one piece of advice to your library, what would it be?	Age	Geographic Region	Student Status
Make access to the online search engines much easier. Much of the information I look for does not have enough of a description to really decide whether it is good information, especially if I have to do an interlibrary loan. Mostly the descriptions are too vague. I do research for History, and I find it hard to find 'primary' resources - I usually have to go online for these.	46	Canada	
The library in the town which I live in Ontario needs to provide more English version books	46	Canada	
brochures/pamphlets avaiable to let public know how much information is available at the library and how to access it.	47	Canada	
clean up a bit	47	Canada	
great job but provide better cleaning services	47	Canada	
have a more personnel touch besides a hum drum feeling. and more casual feel and colour to the room.	47	Canada	
Please keep the street people out in the winter months they just come in to keep warm they don't read they just sit in chairs by the window and look outside.	47	Canada	
To get more up to date books and resources and make it easier and faster to borrow from inter library loan	47	Canada	
to make it available to outlying communities and not penalize everyone in a certain community based on the actions of one or two individuals.	47	Canada	
Air filtration- its located above where the fire engines are housed and the gas fumes bother me	48	Canada	
Better signage to direct a new-comer	48	Canada	
Provide more computers for the use of those unable to have one of their own at home or the use of one at work or school	48	Canada	
change the type of lighting to be less hard on the eyes	49	Canada	
have more free computer classes	49	Canada	
keep the doors open	49	Canada	
be more pleasent to people.	50	Canada	
Be open holiday hours. Maybe get relief employees. I know your regular employees are probably union, and therefore would want to take them as Stat days. Maybe at least do a survey to se how many people would like to go to the library during those off days.	50	Canada	
carry on	50	Canada	
keep up good work	50	Canada	
Make it free access always.	50	Canada	
secure more funding	50	Canada	
Be more current	51	Canada	
Less complicated electronic access	51	Canada	
Have human/friendly librarians.	52	Canada	
longer hours	52	Canada	
i think that information on some subjects needs updating	53	Canada	
have a little coffee shop	53	Canada	
Purchase MORE Books. The population has grown so much and the library budget has not!	53	Canada	
relaxing atmosphere coupled with private setting.	53	Canada	
To be honest some of the appeal is still remaining from my childhood days. So try to keep some of the flavour from days gone by.	53	Canada	

Q1240: If you could provide one piece of advice to your library, what would it be?	Age	Geographic Region	Student Status
I really can't thing of anything,I think the public libraries provide a very good service to the public-- but with using the computer it makes it easier for me to find information I would need on the internet without having to leave my home.	54	Canada	
Knowlegeble Librarion, Easier to get the information required	54	Canada	
more interest in illiteracy.	54	Canada	
get more friendly employees	55	Canada	
more staff would be helpful	57	Canada	College post graduate
Ceep up the good work	58	Canada	
My public library is very good and the people there are caring and very knowledgeable. Unfortunately, they need more space and better resources as well as more books, dvds, etc. I suppose they need to keep working to try to get the money to support their initiatives.	58	Canada	
Aim to become the one-stop-shopping, authoritative and trustworthy source for infomation i.e the mother of all search engines.	59	Canada	
choose materials of broader interest	59	Canada	
Obtain more current reading material	59	Canada	
Smile and be more frendly	60	Canada	
better access to free on -line information	61	Canada	
Build a new more up to date building that is accessible to all	61	Canada	
Hang in there! If govrnment (municipal,provincial/state/federal) funding is cut back, take it to the people. Libraries are too important to be left to Governments!	61	Canada	
More computers and more up to date books in my areas of interest please	62	Canada	
They seem to be doing a good job.	62	Canada	
Lower the prices on library cards and up the late return charges.	63	Canada	
Have better access to printers when material is printed from computer	66	Canada	
keep curent on technical information and the latest books	67	Canada	
Easier access. Parking is difficult and the number of students using the Library has increased greatly.	71	Canada	
More informal enviroment is needed	25	India	
To bring out a library website with a whole lot of information. free access to the internet. Bring about new Technologies. Weekly career related programmes. Latest books, magazines and various journals. Bring about CD based approach. Intoduction of online systems	27	India	
provide more books for indepth computer knowledge	30	India	
Be Online and provide remote access from home	31	India	
Allow more inter-library or inter-branch borrowing, charging fees as required.	35	India	College post graduate
be professional	37	India	
there are certain educational materials for kids like ASK ME WHY? which are missing and needs to be added	39	India	
should be quieter, more serene, staff should be friendly	48	India	
make use of all the services available well	51	India	
increase the sitting space	54	India	
make available all you have, online	54	India	

Q1240: If you could provide one piece of advice to your library, what would it be?	Age	Geographic Region	Student Status
expand opening hours	56	India	
Maintenance and upkeep of the books to be improved.	62	India	
Keep abreast with latest publications and buy regularly	66	India	
You can still do better, there is always scope for improvement	66	India	
have more information found in college libraries available.	16	Singapore	High school
Change the computers, it's very slow in my opinion.	19	Singapore	
More reading spaces.	20	Singapore	
Get up to date	24	Singapore	
newer books and magazines	24	Singapore	College undergraduate
get more best sellers rather than keep concentrating on getting books that you think is fit for the library	26	Singapore	
Get better staff.	27	Singapore	
provide more lockers	27	Singapore	
Have more internet terminals	28	Singapore	
They should lower the reservation fee, for example rebates for every third reservation made, since they have made a tidy sum on fines.	28	Singapore	
Get more copies of current and classic bestsellers, then sell off the books to reduce inventory when they are no longer in as high demand.	29	Singapore	
internet access at the snacl corners	29	Singapore	
there is nothing really much.	29	Singapore	College post graduate
more resources	31	Singapore	
To extend the borrowing duration and to install more 24 hours book drop	31	Singapore	
to have more computers	31	Singapore	
more friendly user and interactive	32	Singapore	College post graduate
Beef up on knowledge about how to information and help customers	33	Singapore	
Lighten the place so that it won't give a dull feeling	34	Singapore	
More talks and activities for children	34	Singapore	
Organize more activities.	34	Singapore	
Setting up a physical library at major offices can be good.	35	Singapore	College post graduate
Focus on children	36	Singapore	
Better search engines for books available in the library by: 1. Alphabetical Name 2. Author Name 3. Book Name 4. Subject Name	37	Singapore	
OPENING TIMING SHOULD 24 HOURS OPERATION SO THAT CAN CATERS TO ALL USERS	37	Singapore	
Turn to be information provider over the net	37	Singapore	
Allow free internet access	39	Singapore	
Check the books in the children's section more frequently. They can get pretty roughed up, and it's not nice to borrow a book to find that it's torn inside.	39	Singapore	
environment should be conducive for visitors	40	Singapore	College post graduate
make reference books more available eg lending out and not simply restrict to in-house use.	40	Singapore	

Q1240: If you could provide one piece of advice to your library, what would it be?	Age	Geographic Region	Student Status
make the search for information more user friendly	42	Singapore	
provide more full range of recipe book	42	Singapore	
Extend hours.	46	Singapore	
more new books esp the popular ones	46	Singapore	
TO CREATE AN ENVIRONMENT WHERE THE YOUNG PEOPLE WILL FEEL COMPELLED TO VISIT.	47	Singapore	
free acess to internet	48	Singapore	
Increase with more technical & Advance Information.	48	Singapore	
Just find that some of the books I borrowed home msometimes have an awful toxic smell. Can the library not stock up such books? The good recipe books of local authors that are on sale in Spore are seldom available but werntern ones are plentiful, how about stocking up more of the local ones since we are after asians & no matter what would prefer more local dishes.	48	Singapore	
Keep it hip and modern	49	Singapore	
Make the librarian friendlier.	16	U.K.	High school
nothing really, i think that the library is good as long as you can find the time to go in there, which unfortunately i don't have as I work full time	16	U.K.	
become more modern and fresh	17	U.K.	
Get videos avaiable to hire	17	U.K.	High school
Make everything more user friendly and geared to a younger generation	17	U.K.	High school
cafe	17	U.K.	
keep up the good work	17	U.K.	
Better environment	18	U.K.	College undergraduate
try not to make the library seem like such an uptight space, people tend to stay away from places that seem like no fun, try brightening up the library with colour and try not to have such uptight staff	19	U.K.	
organise the books somehow - alphabetical, dewy desimal etc	19	U.K.	
be nicer	21	U.K.	
let students borrow books for more than 2 weeks	21	U.K.	College undergraduate
Not to treat young people a less of a person then them.	21	U.K.	
Get some realy comfortable, big armchairs chairs, so that people can relax while they read	22	U.K.	College undergraduate
Train librarians to be more friendly and helpful	22	U.K.	College post graduate
The library is meant to be a quite place at all times - including children!	22	U.K.	
arrange the books in a more practical order	23	U.K.	
be more patiencent and polite to people	23	U.K.	
get new books in	26	U.K.	
become more up to date - newer books and music	26	U.K.	
extend opening hours	26	U.K.	
open at more convenient times for people who work	26	U.K.	
less strict on enforcing social restrictions eg silence	28	U.K.	
make the atmosphere more inviting and not so clinical	29	U.K.	
TO BE A BIT MORE MODERN IN DECOR	29	U.K.	
could they be open at lunchtimes	30	U.K.	

Q1240: If you could provide one piece of advice to your library, what would it be?	Age	Geographic Region	Student Status
Keep doing what you are doing	30	U.K.	
get more computers	31	U.K.	
provide drinks machine or snack vender encouraging people to stay longer	31	U.K.	
Update your computers and technology	31	U.K.	
More of a cafe feel please	32	U.K.	
more accessible car parking	32	U.K.	
longer opening times	33	U.K.	
increase the time for loans	33	U.K.	
Promote yourselves in sholls and colleges to a higher degree	33	U.K.	
Modernise and publicise more.	33	U.K.	
Just keep young children interested in reading	34	U.K.	
Get the staff to show some respect to lecturers!	34	U.K.	
more up to date wider books available	35	U.K.	
get a coffee shop and meeting room	36	U.K.	
Oblige the council to provide bigger grants and interact more with the community you serve	37	U.K.	
don't charge fines....??!!	38	U.K.	
NONE I LIKE IT THE WAY IT IS	38	U.K.	
Please invest in more books and a better seating area	38	U.K.	
less stuffy	40	U.K.	
Keep up to date with information and services	41	U.K.	
Keep up the good work	41	U.K.	
don't chat behind the desk when i am waiting to hand books in or waiting to have them stamped to take home	42	U.K.	
be more up to date	43	U.K.	
Update the dreary exteriors, I believe this is why people still think they are quiet, old fashioned places to be.	43	U.K.	
They are the experts	44	U.K.	
advertise more to the public in the local papers	46	U.K.	
Provide Parking for mums with todllers to encourage early reading and literacy	46	U.K.	
Advertise what is available to the public	46	U.K.	
Push facilities better.Make people more aware	47	U.K.	
Stop making it feel like a church	47	U.K.	
better organisation, less clutter, at the moment everything is in disorder	48	U.K.	
modernise	48	U.K.	
more new releases in fiction	49	U.K.	
let's have free photocopying	49	U.K.	
lighten up!	49	U.K.	
make it more accessible	49	U.K.	
advertise its services	50	U.K.	
Helpful Staff..I like to read best sellers give an oppinion to my readers club.....your staff cant provide the top ten list...I can find that on the internet..why should I use you?	50	U.K.	
lighten up	50	U.K.	
Continue to cater only for the cultural needs of native English people.	51	U.K.	
maybe get some books in braile	51	U.K.	

Q1240: If you could provide one piece of advice to your library, what would it be?	Age	Geographic Region	Student Status
To e-mail details of local events happening to any readers who may be interested especially events happening in association with the library	51	U.K.	College undergraduate
Have a quiet room with no children allowed for study purposes.	51	U.K.	
Have a beginers class for using the lbrary and computer systems. Better prepared at the begining ensures better usage.	51	U.K.	
Be more friendly and welcoming	52	U.K.	
Drag yourself into the present century!!!	52	U.K.	
Ask them to increase the access to electronic journals remotly	52	U.K.	
Please keep areas clean and tidy	52	U.K.	
Better opening times	53	U.K.	
ARRANGE A MORE FRIENDLY AREA TO SIT IN, RATHER THAN CHAIRS WHICH ARE TO LOW	53	U.K.	
Get online as a database and central major resource for downloading digital books to ipods and other portable equipment as this is way of the future like it or not.	54	U.K.	
more helpful signs	54	U.K.	
MORE SEATING	54	U.K.	
A more flexible lending programme, particularly allowing longer lending periods if the resource/book isn't being asked for by someone else. Perhaps a pre-booking/longer-term service might be helpful.	54	U.K.	
have a coffee shop in it	54	U.K.	
Get your reference collection onto the net	55	U.K.	
Smile more	55	U.K.	
become more accessible for people with visual impairment.	55	U.K.	
Expand physically and extend hours	55	U.K.	
To compete more with online technology.	55	U.K.	
Become more modern and attractive with friendly staff!!!	56	U.K.	
Keep up to date with current electronic developments.	56	U.K.	
Libraries need to diversify to keep up with all modern technologies. School libraries are inhibited by funding, very often. They should be warm and inviting places with colourful, useful displays, engaging young people.	56	U.K.	
increase floor space!	57	U.K.	
More late evening opening times	57	U.K.	
keep up with modern trends	58	U.K.	
Make it more welcoming	60	U.K.	
improve customer service	60	U.K.	
provide more in the way of internet access	60	U.K.	
Be more flexible with the rules	60	U.K.	
KEEP UP THE GOOD WORK	60	U.K.	
extend loan time	61	U.K.	
Initiate a genealogy section	62	U.K.	
better catalogue access	65	U.K.	
Increase the stock of books and recycle them more often.	66	U.K.	
Cannot fault our local library...no advice required!	66	U.K.	
Provide more help to access high shelves, do not have very low shelves either.	67	U.K.	

Q1240: If you could provide one piece of advice to your library, what would it be?	Age	Geographic Region	Student Status
Research users' interests more and keep lists of latest information (details , location, etc) so that if it does not have the required information, it can obtain it speedily from elsewhere.	68	U.K.	
My public library is excellent and I would hesitate to offer any advice, except perhaps to revert to the 'Dewey' system for ALL their books.	69	U.K.	
Our local library is excellent. Cannot think of any advice from me that would benefit them.	71	U.K.	
Make the library assistants more cheerful	71	U.K.	
Put all fiction on shelves in alphabetical order of author names	71	U.K.	
it needs more space, now too small for the incresed population in my area	72	U.K.	
Build a libary nearer to my home.	73	U.K.	
the public are there to be served	80	U.K.	
Advance the technology	15	U.S.	High school
better security	15	U.S.	High school
Don't require student ID's	15	U.S.	High school
Expand your collection and get rid of the outdated books...	15	U.S.	High school
Get even more books, and tell me wheather a website is creditable or not.	15	U.S.	High school
get your computer systems more up to date	15	U.S.	High school
help out more	15	U.S.	High school
Improve the web site more--I like the catalog, but if it could reference some sort of rating system it would be even better--I was looking at a new author today who has many books, and I had to go to an internet computer, check on amazon and see which books were most highly recommended, and go back to the catalog to see if they were available.	15	U.S.	High school
keep up the good work	15	U.S.	High school
That more funds need to be spent in the library than on the football team and that they need more books about things going on around us like romance novels and they even need more reference books.	15	U.S.	High school
To allow more activities involved with all different age groups to be involved with the library	15	U.S.	High school
update-make it look newer and hipper. also some of the books are musty so that makes it smell bad	15	U.S.	High school
YOU WERE STUPID FOR MOVING THE LIBRARY OUT OF MY TOWN!	15	U.S.	High school
Advocate teen literacy and literary appreciation, rather than focusing solely on young children and adults.	16	U.S.	High school
Alert visitors when their book is close to overdue. And automatically renew a book if there is no one else with that book on reservation.	16	U.S.	High school
be more attentive to other people.	16	U.S.	High school
Be more hip.	16	U.S.	High school
be more receptive to students looking for information	16	U.S.	High school
don't shut down	16	U.S.	High school
Encourage more funding, as best as you can.	16	U.S.	High school
get a librarian that does not talk on her cell phone when a student needs help	16	U.S.	
get more current entertainment media, and get more indepth/specialised books	16	U.S.	High school

Q1240: If you could provide one piece of advice to your library, what would it be?	Age	Geographic Region	Student Status
Get some people who know about the books they're lending out.	16	U.S.	High school
Help reduce fines to encourage previously frequent readers to read again at their libraries	16	U.S.	High school
Keep up the good work, the staff is great.	16	U.S.	High school
the librarian to lighten up and relax a little; i wish i could eat lunch in there, that way i could do work and eat at the same time.	16	U.S.	High school
to execpt people without attitude	16	U.S.	High school
to the librarians dont be so rude	16	U.S.	High school
Try to hire more than just one librarian. This will make helping the students faster and easier.	16	U.S.	High school
try to make librarian more outgoing	16	U.S.	High school
Update the computers and make more books accessible outside rather than the hidden attic.	16	U.S.	College undergraduate
update/new furniture	16	U.S.	High school
A more lively and modern atmosphere.	17	U.S.	High school
Acquire more diverse materials.	17	U.S.	College undergraduate
Assistance should be more readily available.	17	U.S.	College undergraduate
audio books on cd and educational dvds like documentarys are great!	17	U.S.	
automatic check-out	17	U.S.	High school
be friendlier	17	U.S.	High school
Be more open and supportive to members of the community you are in.	17	U.S.	High school
Don't get rid of older or more traditionally acceptable materials (books, movies, music) in favor of new best selling things which are often trashier and will not appeal to many people who go to a library as a source for finding relatively purer and more intellectual resources.	17	U.S.	College undergraduate
Don't require the library card if the person has an account.	17	U.S.	High school
escalators	17	U.S.	High school
faster computers	17	U.S.	High school
Get a place to watch DVD's and get some movies and cd's.	17	U.S.	High school
help your librarians look friendly and helpful instead of threatening and bored.	17	U.S.	College undergraduate
Hire more cheerful workers (honestly, it seems as if they're just waiting for five 'o clock to roll around so they can go home and kill themselves.)	17	U.S.	
I really think our library is well done. No complaints.	17	U.S.	High school
I would tell them that they need to higher employees with positive attitudes who want to help people.	17	U.S.	High school
It needs to improve with online notification of due dates	17	U.S.	High school
It would be to make sure librarians are more kind and more willing to help.	17	U.S.	High school
Keep truckin'.	17	U.S.	College undergraduate
Make even the large research books available to check out.	17	U.S.	College undergraduate
make it a cheerier place so people will want to come	17	U.S.	College undergraduate
more staff	17	U.S.	High school

Q1240: If you could provide one piece of advice to your library, what would it be?	Age	Geographic Region	Student Status
organize the books more like the manner of a book store, it is more familiar	17	U.S.	High school
Reach out to the non-readers.	17	U.S.	High school
relax a bit on the restrictions, provide a place for those working during their lunch to eat and work at the same time	17	U.S.	High school
stop charging customers to use certain services	17	U.S.	High school
They could set up a coffee shop to compete with the 'hipness' of big chain book store companies	17	U.S.	High school
They need to have friendlier people working there.	17	U.S.	High school
This is a hard question, being so involved with my library. I think that there are too many rules for the teens, though. There are around 20 rules posted in the Young Adult room, and that is just ridiculous, not to mention overwhelming for the younger teens that go in there. They have energy levels to the stars, and they are expected to be able to have the attention span to read and actually follow those rules? Yeah right.	17	U.S.	
To be more friendly in assisting in research.	17	U.S.	High school
To EXPAND!! The library is so small, and there aren't very many books. I am afraid of finishing every book in the library and then where would I go?	17	U.S.	High school
Try to appeal to kids more.	17	U.S.	High school
allow more equal opportunities for everyone to use the facilities - do not allow one group to use it for 80% of the time, while the other 20% of the time the other 80% of students are allowed to use it - especially computers	18	U.S.	High school
better lighting	18	U.S.	College undergraduate
Better organization.	18	U.S.	College undergraduate
Find a way to get more computers.	18	U.S.	College undergraduate
Redecorate! This whole sleek, modern look is just ugly. Libraries can keep up with technology without losing their charm.	18	U.S.	College undergraduate
They need to get their attitudes checked, and be friendly to people.	18	U.S.	
to be more nice to the age group of 13-16 year olds	18	U.S.	College undergraduate
bring back the older books	19	U.S.	
COntinue to support education and literacy among the community. When supporting the backbone of the community (education & literacy), don't be afraid to try new things and new methods.	19	U.S.	College undergraduate
do not charge for copies	19	U.S.	College undergraduate
e-mail reminders warning when books are due	19	U.S.	College undergraduate
keep it alive!	19	U.S.	College undergraduate
My public library needs to expand its horizons and add more books that appeal to more people.	19	U.S.	College undergraduate
Nothing. I think that my college library is very well kept. They have the latest information and technology and they have very helpful staff on hand.	19	U.S.	College undergraduate

Q1240: If you could provide one piece of advice to your library, what would it be?	Age	Geographic Region	Student Status
Don't let people use their cell phones so close to where people are studying.	20	U.S.	College undergraduate
Don't make the shelves so high, because it makes me only look at what is at my eye level.	20	U.S.	College undergraduate
I judge a store by how soon the employees greet me. If I can make it to the back of the store without a greeting, I leave. The last time I was at the library, I tore up my card and gave it to the employee. No one ever greeted me and I was treated rude. I bought a computer so I wouldn't have to go back. Be nice to people and greet them.	20	U.S.	
stop worrying about being politically correct and make more books that arnt politically correct available	20	U.S.	
add more article databases	21	U.S.	
Add more group study areas	21	U.S.	
don't direct everyone to the card catalog....get up and help them	21	U.S.	College undergraduate
Get more comfortable seating and get rid of the 'no food and drinks' policy so that people want to stay for longer periods of time at a stretch.	21	U.S.	College undergraduate
Have the workers more involoved with the students. For example, I went in the other night and had trouble finding a book. I went down and asked a group of workers, who were might I add, just standing around talking, about helping me find a book. They gave me a general direction on where to go. I still couldn't find it, so I asked another helper, who walked up with me. Ended up it was in a different section. She was great, so helpful and friendly. They should all be willing to help like that.	21	U.S.	College undergraduate
Just to keep up with technology, but they're doing the best they can in these tough times.	21	U.S.	College undergraduate
lower the fines	21	U.S.	College undergraduate
Make a way to search through all of the databases with one search engine, instead of having to search each database individually.	21	U.S.	College undergraduate
Make computers open to people who are studying by taking the people who just play games off when there is a limited number of computers.	21	U.S.	College undergraduate
Offer more children's activities during the school year!!	21	U.S.	
to allow the use of adult sites	21	U.S.	College undergraduate
be less formal	22	U.S.	
hire friendly people	22	U.S.	College undergraduate
keep up on technology (web based support)	22	U.S.	
Keep up the friendly and availble resources that they have.	22	U.S.	
fees are too expensive - i feel that universities as a whole take advantage of students who are already on a limited income. copy fees, late fees, rental fees, print cards, etc. should not be something which the library can profit off of, especially when many of those resources are manditory for one's class.	23	U.S.	College undergraduate
I love audio books, they are a great resource for new moms.	23	U.S.	
I was fully sastified with the library at my university.	23	U.S.	
Just keep on rolling with the times (staying up with what is hip, with new technologies) and keeping things accessible to all.	23	U.S.	
Nothing. Everything is cool like it is.	23	U.S.	

Q1240: If you could provide one piece of advice to your library, what would it be?	Age	Geographic Region	Student Status
stop using flourecent lighting, it gives people a headache if they have to stay in there for too long	23	U.S.	College undergraduate
The environment is the deterrent. The people who hang out in the library are typically not there for anything other than a warm place to spend the afternoon because they have no other place to go, which is fine except that the library is not a homeless shelter. I do not feel safe going to the library. The main branch is in the middle of downtown, which makes it inconveneient to access from both a parking and safety perspective (even though I only work a mile or so away). I used to enjoy hanging out at the library, especially as a child, as my mom is a librarian. But now that I am older and have access to a plethora of information on the Internet, I just don't see a need for it anymore, especially given the environment.	23	U.S.	
try to offer more programs for the children	23	U.S.	College undergraduate
advertise a bit more; until this survey I didn't really realize that a library might have music, movies, and audio books to borrow.	24	U.S.	
Be more helpful to students and to the locals who are not college students. Sometimes people are not very helpful to the local in the area.	24	U.S.	
Better signage	24	U.S.	
Find some way to help streamline the computer access....	24	U.S.	College undergraduate
I would suggest the library reach out to teens and 20 somethings. They are the group that uses the library least.	24	U.S.	College undergraduate
Update, update, update. Most books are out of date.	24	U.S.	
Get electronic access to older back issues of academic journals or take them out of the annex and put them back in the stacks.	27	U.S.	College post graduate
I'd advise them to hire younger and friendlier staff members in the ADULT section. They have great staff in the kids' section but in the main library (adult materials) it's a bunch of crusty old hags who don't want to help ANYONE.	28	U.S.	
better parking availability	30	U.S.	
Clearly mark areas of the library where specific types of information can be located. For instance, have a small sign at the end of each row indicating the types of information the books will contain, such as gardening, how-to, cooking, etc.	30	U.S.	College undergraduate
a class on how to use the library and to locate books	33	U.S.	
Add a cafe/coffee shop.	33	U.S.	
Do not get rid of the old library buildings. They are full of character and have the best little nooks and corners conducive to exploring thru reading. Not all new things are best!	38	U.S.	
Find a better system of catagorizing fiction books	38	U.S.	
don't let politics and rhetoric dictate your business	39	U.S.	
This is a great service that has been greatly expanded over the years that I have worked at the company -- keep up the good work!	39	U.S.	
advertise' available services and resources	40	U.S.	
Build a parking structure so people like myself who go to the library to do work don't have to pack up everything we have and run outside every hour or two to put money in a parking meter.	41	U.S.	
Stay as current as possible with technology	41	U.S.	

Q1240: If you could provide one piece of advice to your library, what would it be?	Age	Geographic Region	Student Status
stay open and keep the good old fashioned books to be held in your hand	41	U.S.	
they do a great job with what they have!	41	U.S.	
try to find funding to expand. The current facility is inadequate and the community has grown	41	U.S.	
Encourage employees to make more use of the library (not just the faculty). Offer programs to the staff community.	42	U.S.	
Create internet cafe type lounges to draw more traffic. Partner with Starbucks. That will bring in the patrons :)	43	U.S.	
Have an online service for selecting reading materials that can be delivered to my home or that I could pick up at a drive through window that was convenient and fast. I would agree to return the materials to a convenient drop box location to save costs.	43	U.S.	
move to a better location	43	U.S.	
allow personal wireless cards for use on library network	44	U.S.	College post graduate
Faster circulation of new books. It usually takes 4 weeks to put a new book onto the shelves.	44	U.S.	
increase hours	44	U.S.	
Offer longer check out periods for educators	45	U.S.	
Subscribe to Rhapsody or iTunes or other music download services.	45	U.S.	
Thanks, they do a pretty good job.	45	U.S.	
Resist U.S. Government intrusion	47	U.S.	
Update your system and inventory.	47	U.S.	
don't let homeland security bully you	48	U.S.	
Accessibility for the disabled.	49	U.S.	
Lose the attitude - librarians seem to think they are anointed keepers of information that is freely available elsewhere	49	U.S.	
MAKE ENVIRONMENT MORE FRIENDLY...ACCESSIBLE	50	U.S.	
Provide training on finding and using the databases which will work best for the individual researcher	50	U.S.	
To be abreast with the needs of the ppl in the area	50	U.S.	
Get a website so that I can see what materials are available in the library.	51	U.S.	College undergraduate
I think this survey is on the right track. The libraries should look at community spaces like Starbucks and Borders, and should also look at the value of online material like Google, and they should try to be more relevant in the current age.	51	U.S.	
Staff could be more courteous and helpful	51	U.S.	
Get a parking lot so people don't have to drive around to find a parking place in the middle of town	52	U.S.	
Try to find a way for materials to be returned on time so others could use them	52	U.S.	
Work to create a bookstore environment	52	U.S.	
Make finding something much easier and the staff more helpful and friendly	53	U.S.	
When there is a new book out, try to get it fast and get plenty of copies so that we don't have to wait months before we can read it, because in my case, I forget about it, or just lose interest in it.	53	U.S.	

Q1240: If you could provide one piece of advice to your library, what would it be?	Age	Geographic Region	Student Status
Become more welcoming to patrons. We still have librarians who act like they own the whole collection of books and don't want you to borrow them. We have librarians who act like it's a bother to help a patron. BE USER FRIENDLY!	55	U.S.	
Help the physically disadvantaged	55	U.S.	
realize people's time is as valuable as your own and try to help people a little quicker	55	U.S.	
Relax. Let kids enjoy themselves. Let them put their feet up and sprawl on the floor. Let them enjoy reading now so they'll enjoy it forever.	55	U.S.	
Run the library like a bookstore	55	U.S.	
Establish a Learning Commons like the one at University of Arizona, Tucson	56	U.S.	
A little more friendly, courteous workers	57	U.S.	
bring back the old card catalog	57	U.S.	
The public library has met or exceeded all my needs - the advice would be to keep up the good work	57	U.S.	
I like all the help I received when I needed it.	58	U.S.	
I think the biggest problem with public libraries is they're short on funding, which is sad. Maybe an auction like our local PBS stations to raise money. It's always about money isn't it?	59	U.S.	
Don't know. Our community college library is excellent. Perhaps a larger CD collection.	60	U.S.	
Keep the handicapped parking area and path to the door ice free. I know that's an almost impossible task here in MN.	60	U.S.	
Our library staff is very busy and help is difficult to get while there. I always ahve felt that I am an imposition if I ask a question. This needs to change to a more friendly environment to encourage more visits.	61	U.S.	
Do not charge for a library card	62	U.S.	
make everything free	62	U.S.	
Make information available as to what kinds of materials and services they have available to the public.	63	U.S.	
I'd have it set up more like Barnes & Noble with comfortable chairs and a coffee shop.	64	U.S.	
Put your resources into buying more books.	64	U.S.	
Don't let politics or politicians influence any of the activities that occur there.	65	U.S.	
Nothing - just don't have the time right now to use as I hope to in the future.	65	U.S.	
STAY OPEN LATER	65	U.S.	
You are doing a good job with the funds provided.	65	U.S.	
get faster computers-or connect to faster servers	66	U.S.	
I think there is a core element that uses the library over and over. They need to find ways to attract those who are not inclined to go to libraries. There is a large population that has probably never been to a library and has no idea what they offer.	66	U.S.	
replace outdated scientific and technical books	66	U.S.	
Stay friendly, and help those who need it to find things.	66	U.S.	
Update audio books -- Make newer books availiable.	66	U.S.	
you are doing a great job! keep it up!	66	U.S.	
Build a bigger building and update all electonic devices.	67	U.S.	

Q1240: If you could provide one piece of advice to your library, what would it be?	Age	Geographic Region	Student Status
keep it free	67	U.S.	
Nothing but to keep up the good work for people who need it	67	U.S.	
Open a branch closer to my home	67	U.S.	
Personnel could be more helpful, friendly	67	U.S.	
update checkout procedures	67	U.S.	
I think that the library is doing a good job in what it is doing. I have absolutely no advice for them. As far as I am concerned everything is great there.	68	U.S.	
keep u[the good work - maybe get more large print books for those with visual impairments	68	U.S.	
Don't let budget cuts cause you to have to close your doors.	69	U.S.	
Extended hours, particularly opening before 10:00 am.	69	U.S.	
LET PEOPLE KNOW WHAT YOU CAN PROVIDE IN MAILINGS TO RESIDENTS OF THE AREA. SOME OF U.S. TEND TO FORGET ABOUT THE RESOURCES OF THE LIBRARY	69	U.S.	
You're doing fine for the clientele that need you.	69	U.S.	
Entice the younger generation to read more	70	U.S.	
figure a way to sit books so that the titles are not on their sides. Kills my neck to try and read what is there. So no longer go.	70	U.S.	
keep growing	70	U.S.	
Library is small and old, county just purchased land to build a new facility. Hope they will keep the friendly and knowledgable attitude in their employees	70	U.S.	
Start up the library bus again.	70	U.S.	
Stay open and encourage children to read.	70	U.S.	
That library is a thousands miles away.. and is probably a hundred times bigger than when I went there 55 years ago !!!	70	U.S.	
Advertise more in local papers	71	U.S.	
Keep pushing for more funding	71	U.S.	
More and expanded diverse selection of books on cds- I use them while traveling, and have 'read' most of the ones in my library, now. I do trvel a lot. the library has a more expansive assortment of books on tape than CDs.	71	U.S.	
THANKS FOR BEING THERE.	71	U.S.	
Stop wasting money on building more branches when you don't have the money to buy the books for the shelves. You already had a library headquarters and built a new one duplicating the offices, the auditorium etc merely because it was in an are with political and financial pull. The shelves of the new library are only 20% filled. The exsisting library resources are inadequate, much of the books are mysteries, romances and general crap. Current non fiction is limited. Research materials are out of date and limited in scope.	73	U.S.	
Publicize their activities more and schedule more events that will attract more people.	74	U.S.	
Being able to order books to pick up from the web site at no charge.	74	U.S.	
make all materials available to all members of the county library system	74	U.S.	
aides are knowledgeable, could be friendlier	75	U.S.	
Build a branch closer than 5 miles away!	75	U.S.	
just keep on doing what you are doing	76	U.S.	

Q1240: If you could provide one piece of advice to your library, what would it be?	Age	Geographic Region	Student Status
keep on adding things which are available via the internet for those of us who depend on it.	77	U.S.	
Spend more money on books and less on surroundings	77	U.S.	
Add more genealogical materials	78	U.S.	
CONTINUE WITH WHAT YOU ARE DOING	78	U.S.	
To buy more books by an author who has produced more than one popular book, but library has only one of his works. Money is the problem; they can't help having to restrict their purchases.	78	U.S.	
Check quality of audiobooks.	79	U.S.	
Encourage citizens to support and press for a larger budget support for libraries.	79	U.S.	
Nothing. I just like it the way it is. It's great!	81	U.S.	
Take a bow	86	U.S.	

About OCLC

OCLC serves

54,000

libraries in

109

countries

OCLC Online Computer Library Center is a nonprofit membership organization that promotes cooperation among libraries worldwide. More than 54,000 libraries in 109 countries use OCLC services to locate, acquire, catalog, lend and preserve print and electronic library materials.

OCLC was established in Ohio in 1967 by a small group of libraries whose leaders believed that working together they could find practical solutions to some of the day's most challenging issues. What began as a way to automate the traditional library card catalog rapidly became a collaborative revolution that involved thousands of libraries around the world. Working together, OCLC and its member libraries cooperatively produce and maintain WorldCat—the OCLC Online Union Catalog—which now contains over 60 million bibliographic records and more than 1 billion library holdings.

Collaboration among librarians and OCLC solved the practical problem of automated cataloging. Ongoing collaboration led to additional OCLC services, including services that help libraries build e-content collections and provide online access to special library collections like maps, newspapers, photographs and local histories.

The OCLC membership jointly created the largest interlibrary loan system in the world. Recent expansions and new partnerships in Europe now enable the OCLC collaborative to exchange more than 9.5 million items annually to information consumers and scholars around the world.

The library content represented in WorldCat is now accessible to people using major search engines due to the Open WorldCat program that opens up the assets of the OCLC cooperative to the searchers of the world.

In addition to the many services offered, OCLC funds library research programs, library advocacy efforts, scholarships, market research and professional development opportunities.

OCLC Research incubates new technologies, sponsors the work of library scientists and represents libraries on a range of international standards bodies. OCLC Research is also actively engaged with the world's information community to further the science of librarianship.

OCLC library advocacy programs are part of a long-term initiative to champion libraries to increase their visibility and viability within their communities. Programs include advertising and marketing materials to reinforce the idea of the library as relevant, and market research reports that identify and communicate trends of importance to the library profession. Several of the reports are noted in the introduction to this report.

OCLC provides financial support for those beginning their library careers and for established professionals who excel in their endeavors through a series of annual awards and scholarships. Of note is the IFLA/OCLC Early Career Development Fellowship Program, jointly sponsored by the International Federation of Library Associations and Institutions (IFLA), OCLC Online Computer Library Center and the American Theological Library Association (ATLA). The program provides early career development and continuing education for library and information science professionals from countries with developing economies.

OCLC participates in WebJunction, which is an online community of libraries and other agencies that share knowledge and experience to provide the broadest public access to information technology. A service created by the Bill & Melinda Gates Foundation's U.S. Library Program, OCLC and other partners, WebJunction features articles, handouts, courses and forum discussions that are practical, down-to-earth and friendly. WebJunction addresses the real issues that librarians and library staff face every day.

OCLC's vision is to be the leading global library cooperative, helping libraries serve people by providing economical access to knowledge through innovation and collaboration. OCLC is headquartered in Dublin, Ohio, USA and has offices throughout the world.

OCLC Online Computer Library Center
6565 Frantz Road
Dublin, Ohio 43017 USA
www.oclc.org

OCLC Asia Pacific
6565 Frantz Road
Dublin, OH 43017-3395 USA
www.oclc.org/asiapacific/en/

OCLC Canada
701, rue Salaberry
Chambly, Québec J3L 1R2 Canada
www.oclc.org/ca/

OCLC Latin America and the Caribbean
6565 Frantz Road
Dublin, OH 43017-3395 USA
www.oclc.org/americalatina/en/

OCLC Mexico
Ave. Amores 707 desp.401, Col. Del Valle
03100 Mexico, D.F. Mexico
www.oclc.org/americalatina/en/

OCLC Middle East and India
6565 Frantz Road
Dublin, Ohio 43017 USA
www.oclc.org/middleeast/en/

OCLC PICA Netherlands
Head office and Service Centre for Netherlands, Belgium, Luxembourg
Schipholweg 99
P.O. Box 876
2300 AW Leiden, The Netherlands
www.oclcpica.org

OCLC PICA United Kingdom
Service Centre for U.K., Northern and Eastern Europe, Southern Africa
7th Floor, Tricorn House,
Birmingham, B16 8TP England
www.oclcpica.org

OCLC PICA France
Service Centre for Southern Europe, Turkey and Israel
14, Place des Victoires
92600 Asnières sur Seine, France
www.oclcpica.org

OCLC PICA Germany
Service Centre for Germany, Austria and Switzerland
c/o Sisis Informationssysteme GmbH
Grünwalder Weg 28g
82041 Oberhaching, Germany
www.oclcpica.org